KIRTA

A Vor...

SHUBALANANDA SARASWATI
(AKA L.H. KOPP)

ISBN: 979-8-9861639-1-8

Cover and interior design by:
Editing by: Parvati Markus

Every effort has been made to obtain permissions for photographs or pieces quoted or adapted in this work. If any acknowledgements have been omitted, or any rights overlooked, it is unintentional. Please notify us of any omission and it will be rectified in future editions.

Dedication

Dedicated to Baba Harihar Ram-ji and the ancient Aghor lineage

Aghoranna Paro Mantro

Nasti Tatvam guro param

Table of Content

Sing the songs of celestial love, O Singer!
May the divine fountain of eternal grace and joy enter your soul.
May the Lord stay there forever!
*May you always feel the presence of the Lord within as it plucks
the strings of your soul with the celestial touch.*
*Bless us with a divine voice, and may we tune the harp strings of
our life to sing songs of love to you.*

--Rig Veda

Introduction

Sunshine is streaming in through the sliding glass doors that make up one wall of our living room. With the low, soon-to-be setting winter sun, the room is set aglow. Alisa, my wife, plays harmonium and sings Kirtan, spiritually trancing and magnifying the perfection of this slow timeless "now moment". In this moment, Shubalananda Saraswati aka Larry Kopp is our friend. He is my wife's harmonium and Kirtan teacher. He has honored her as a regular member of his Kirtan band, singing as responder. In this moment, I cannot but reflect on the impact my friend, Shubalananda, has had on our lives.

Shubal ends his programs with a song, "I am a lone pilgrim, far from home". I have been watching him travel across the eastern USA, like Johnny Appleseed, spreading the practice of "namasankirtan" and sharing the teachings of his masters for 20 years. He truly is the lone pilgrim of kirtan, mostly unknown by the public, but respected by all the kirtan musicians everywhere.

The true essence of Shubal's dharma, however, revolves around the participation of a variety of saints in his inner growth. As he tells his story, you can see how each teacher he encountered gave him something; detachment, unification, knowledge, and bhava, the "Ray Charles" like soul that makes his singing so unique. From all this guy has seen and done, Shubal has turned out as one of a kind.

I remember when he first began his weekly kirtan at Karuna Yoga in Northampton, and I watched as his schedule and his fame grew. Soon he was singing almost every night of the week in a different town. Karunamayi said "I hear the tears of god love in your voice", and he brought those tears to many who sang with him.

I especially loved the years Shubal played in Krishna Das' band. He lit up the stage with his solo on "Mainline Jesus".

7

His guitar would drive KD to extremes of passion. We all loved Krishna Das' sound when Shubal was the musical force.

Early in our acquaintance, when I was going through a very difficult time, Shubal responded with great sensitivity and wisdom. He touched my heart with his kind understanding words. In his direct, matter of fact voice, he shared a powerful mantra with me, with the instruction, "Repeat this mantra daily, many times a day."

I did not know at that time that this mantra was, "the powerful mantra of Goddess Chandi," and, "a chant for protection and to raise kundalini."   Here is The Navarna Mantra: "Aim Hrim Klim Chamundaye Vicce"

Many months later, Alisa and I had finished plans for "The Embodiment Sanctuary" our home healing practice. In order to share the joy, we asked Shubal to bring kirtan to our home. This was the first time we personally hosted kirtan, and we felt honored. The purity and power he evinced during his kirtan opened hearts and created a palpable spirit of unity. Wow! Wow!

It was powerful... Transcendent... Joyful... Ecstatic! He taught and directed us to focus all that emotion to the space between the in-breath and the out-breath. He shared the teaching of Sufi master, Hazrat Anayat Kahn, "Kirtan is God's great gift to the human race. Music is the only art that has no form. It has no meaning conceptually. It exists only in this moment and then is gone. Kirtan is just a vibration on the wind."

That is exactly how it felt, and that is why more and more people wanted to come and sing with Shubal. However, because he saw kirtan as his sadhana rather than a "career" he devoted himself to teaching the practice rather than self promotion. Shubal took to the road. He spent the next 20 years traveling throughout America, sharing his practice and opening venues for the teachers he describes in this book. The stories in Kirtan

Wallah all reflect the greatness and wisdom of the teachers he encountered in his journey.

Prior to his time with Ram Dass, Shubal was a top-notch blues guitarist. He led his own band for years. I remember a night about 15 years ago. There was a large outside nighttime gathering; there were bonfires, everybody was dancing. There was lots of good food and laughter. Later that night, I saw someone step onto the makeshift stage and lay down a blues riff over the party drone that felt like something between a punch to the gut and a "Thank you Jesus"!

Looking through the crowd, toward the stage I was surprised to see Shubal up there with a Les Paul guitar. Here was this older guy, wearing a hooded sweatshirt, playing such strong, artful, raunchy and exquisite blues guitar. We did not speak that night, but I never forgot. For me, this music of his was way beyond good, it was pure heart song - from the real place.

In his autobiographical account, Kirtan Wallah, A Vortex of Love, Shubal presents so much more than a chronological accounting of his major life events. In these pages he reveals his struggles to understand and make sense of an inner identity which often found itself in direct conflict with the circumstances of his life. "Here I was, this forty-year-old Jewish guy from Queens trying to be a seventy-year-old black man from Alabama."

Eventually the inspirational blues guitarist, the husband, the father, the salesperson and businessman found himself stuck, He felt a conflicting inconsistency between his "world" and the true longings of his heart. Inwardly he searched for a new and clear direction. He longed for a deep unification of heart and mind, a direction, within which, everything he was feeling would settle down and lead him to his true Dharma. Like Arjuna in The Bhagavad Gita who turns to Krishna, distraught and dejected with the imminent path laid out in front of him, Shubal was aware that something needed to change.

I recall the first line of a Baha'i prayer attributed to Abdul Baha. This prayer reminds us that we are all on a journey from self to Self. "Oh, God, make me a hollow reed, from which the pith of self have been blown so that I may become as a clear channel through which Thy Love may flow to others." Whether by Divine intervention, or by the ardor of incessant longing and struggle, Shubalananda Saraswati was quickly approaching a life changing, life clarifying experience.

Synchronistically, Shubal finds a book at work, "Miracle of Love" stories of Neem Karoli Baba, by Ram Dass. Then an unexpected gift arrives from his estranged father. A book written by his cousin: The Pickpocket and the Saint, based on the oral teachings of Neem Karoli Baba! I know that when the time is right, with or without conscious awareness, events will transpire to make clear and self evident the true meaning of life. Shubal's employer, Mirabai, dear friend of Ram Dass, instructs Shubal to pick up his phone and call Ram Dass. "He would like to meet you."

Dear reader, what transpires between Shubal and Ram Dass must be read in his own words. It is magical and full of emotion. It is like the classical Persian and Arabic poetic archetype of Layli, the Beloved, sought after by the tormented Soul seeking to be reunited with his true love. It was this forehead-to-forehead, heart-to-heart, soul-to-soul life altering audience with Ram Dass, which broke him free. It was the beginning of a profound self-acceptance and preparation for what was still to come.

Who is this man, graced by gurus, upagurus, and enlightened saints? Why has he chosen for himself the path of devotion, unwavering in his commitment to "God, Guru and Self?" How has he been able to muster the dedication and physical capacity to maintain over twenty years of weekly Kirtan all over the east coast. Shubal's guru tells him "It's time now to sit quietly and think of God"

A "Vortex of Love," is exactly what this man's life has been and still is about. Aptly named, a vortex references an energetic swirling of anything toward a central axis. My wife and I have found ourselves swept up into this Vortex of Love. One night, having dinner with a mutual friend, Shubal told the story of a great teacher who had reached the time to release his body. His disciples gathered around him to receive his last earthly blessings and instructions. Then one disciple asked, "Please share with us, through your wisdom, the shortest, most direct way to realize enlightenment?" The Master hesitated but a mere second, and answered, "enlightenment is easy, just don't compare".

I believe this book is part of the Holy Grail of Kirtan. On one hand, it is a personal historical account of one man's journey into the burgeoning maturity of East meets West. Shubal provides skillful and intuitive insight into many of the champions of early Kirtan that helped to raise the shakti, the transcendental power, and sublimity surrounding the poetry of chanting the names of God.

Knowing Shubal, I imagine that this undertaking was motivated by a heartfelt intention to create a permanent record of the sage wisdom with which he was entrusted. This book is important for present and future Kirtan Wallahs. The two included appendixes read like a devotional and inspired textbook for any serious student of Kirtan. I believe, much after Divinity has called Shubal back into herself, "A Vortex of Love" will remain a future gift to us all.

With much love and gratitude,

Mark Tanny

December 31, 2021

PROLOGUE

I was sitting in this bar in between sets, looking up at the stage at my Les Paul Deluxe guitar. It was just more synchronicity: the day after my great meeting with Ram Dass, my band was gigging and Mirabai was coming to hear me. They called this club the Speakeasy, which was ridiculous because you couldn't speak, you could only shout; although it was an easy place to lose your wallet or your girlfriend. My beautiful Les Paul had the spotlight. It was the cherry Sunburst model, my favorite guitar. That is unless I start thinking about the Gibson 335 or the SG, also very choice guitars. I have no patience with the Strat.

I was six years old when I insisted my parents give me a ukulele for my birthday. Those four little nylon strings felt so good under my fingers. There is something, as Ronnie Earl used to say, about "spanking the plank." There was Grandma Bea and the electric guitar, and then the Les Paul and the Fender 4 tens bassman, and I was a rockin' Jewish bluesman.

Here I was, this forty-year-old Jewish guy from Queens trying to be a seventy-year-old black man from Alabama. Ever since childhood, the draw of black music magnetized my brain, from Stephen Foster to Robert Johnson, from Charlie Patton to Charlie Mingus. After the birth of my brother, my mother had to stay in the hospital for six months. My family hired Sarah to come each morning from Harlem to take care of my brother and me. Her deep gospel voice resonated inside me and awakened something that has been my best friend all my life, whether you believe in karma or not.

Finishing my drink at the Speakeasy bar, I looked over at Bob, my bass player, gave him the nod, and we slowly made our way up to the bandstand.

12

E.J., our drummer, was Mirabai's partner. I worked for her at Illuminations, doing telephone sales for her gift company in Cambridge. She and I had an intertwined destiny. She had been to India, had a guru and a spiritual name, and a voluptuously loving disposition. I was drawn to her at a variety of chakras. I could not wait to see her, to share what had happened with Ram Dass after she introduced us. I was so intoxicated, the guys in the band thought I had gone crazy. I really wanted to play guitar for her that night—to express my thanks and love in a perfect slow blues guitar solo. Playing a slow blues solo on a Les Paul guitar is an inceptual experience. I continued to pump E.J. for information about Mirabai's whereabouts. Apparently, she was not coming.

There is a unity that occurs when four musicians each take one corner of the mandala (representation of the universe) and create a sand painting that touches the heart deeply, beyond any conceptual thought or material existence. Sometimes I think playing the blues is the doorway to the formless God. When you consider the expression of folks like Otis Rush, B.B. King, Muddy Waters, Otis Spann, and countless others, you can feel the transcendence of egoistic emotions and attachments. Ramana Maharishi once said, "Humans' natural state is happiness," and in a slow blues played by a master, joy shines through.

As usual, a strong surge of horripilation (the hairs on the body stand on end) ran up my body. I planted my feet firmly on the stage and felt my mind float up into the clouds, far away from my thoughts; I felt flowing through me the vortex of love that I was becoming. In that state of having no idea where the music is coming from, I felt us four musicians flowing into one sound. Ripples of energy moved through my body as I stomped my feet, shook my head, gritted my teeth, and twisted into some unknown Mississippi Delta mudra. Somehow a beautiful melody came out in a joyous voice. I could not have been happier.

I had spent my life split in the most unique way. With a wife and children at home, I needed a day job to pay the rent and put food on the table. However, my heart was focused only on music; I longed for the bandstand and the unity of four individual musicians merging into one. Every morning at 7 a.m. I put on my suit, got in my Peugeot, and drove off to be a salesman at Illuminations, Mirabai's gift company. I had always had a glib mouth. At 5:30 p.m., I took off my three-piece suit, put on my jeans and T-shirt, and drove to the blues club. I hid from my business friends that I played blues guitar, and I hid from my musician friends that I was a businessman.

The split was blatant, painful, poignant, and soon to be unified with the Zen slap of a divine hand. Synchronicity and grace, that is the only explanation. It was meant to be and the forces driving me were now beyond my thoughts and senses. I could let go of the pain, the grief, the illusive expectations, and begin.

But I was dragging a lot of baggage behind me.

Chapter 1

ENTER STAGE LEFT

God respects me when I work, but He loves me when I sing. --
Tagore

As I look through the picture book of my childhood from the time my father returned from the war until the time I left for college, there is not one photograph of me smiling. I grew up in Long Island being teased by my peers, who nicknamed me Dumbo. I was ashamed of my big ears. Finally, upon watching the movie as an adult, I realized that Dumbo was a great hero. Not only did he save his mother's life, but he could also fly!

We all have our dramas; we all suffer. Everyone's suffering is equal because, to each of us, our suffering is the worst in the universe. Scientists long ago discovered that memory is ninety percent false. In the mellow-drama of our psychological profiles, our childhood histories are nothing but a story, a poignant tragi-comedy based mostly upon fiction. Our minds manipulate reality and adjust our memory of past events in order to conform to a false self-image, one that we developed based upon our need for safety and love as children. Our entire psychology and our entire identity and sense of self are based upon these false memories. Everyone's story is an illusion.

The truth is that we are so much more than our psychology. It's time to look with amused forgiveness at the events that created the illusion of self, and remember we are not our story, we are not our body. We are not even our thoughts.

My earliest thoughts were of suffocation—the feeling of heavy wet wool on my face, a certain unique smell, and a gasping for air. I was "tucked in"—cool, starched, cotton sheets against my skin, the edge of the sheet entwined in my fingers, safe, secure. World War II was in full bloom in 1943. My father

Paul had been drafted. He and mom, Helene, awaited his debarkation in Brownsville, Texas. Paul's division was part of the Japanese invasion force gathering in the Philippines. Helene was seven months pregnant with me. A telegram arrived for Paul. Helene's brother, Howard, had been killed in a plane crash while training as a pilot. Paul was frightened that the news might cause a miscarriage, so he did not tell Helene right away. He said, "I've been given leave. Let's go back to New York and see the family."

Paul's parents, Eddie and Frieda, met them at the airport. On the drive home, Eddie spoke sadly, "Howard is dead. His plane crashed. He's gone." When my mother heard the news, something broke inside her. Later, under hypnosis, I went back to that very moment. I re-experienced my mother's incredible pain and grief. Her love for me turned to resentment, which I perceived. As a fetus I could not think in concepts, but I could feel the emotion and the programming began. In her grief, my mother no longer wanted me.

Early memories are not to be trusted as little ones live partly in the dream world, partly on higher planes. Was this a dream?

I am three years old, in bed sleeping. A noise wakes me up. I listen, the house is silent. I slip out of bed and walk down the hall into the living room. The lights are on throughout the house. I enter the room to find the TV is on, with the sound off. No one is home. The apartment is empty. Fear and distress build inside my heart. Where are my parents? My arms akimbo, tears flowing, spinning in a circle, a hole burning into me, I fall deeper and deeper into this empty fear, an undifferentiated distress. Finally, the door opens and mother and father return. They are angry and send me quickly back to bed. The die is cast.

The fear and distress followed me for years.

One year later, Mom gave birth to Jeffrey. As a teen, my mother had run in front of a car and almost destroyed her leg. The birthing experience reawakened the trauma and her leg became infected. She remained in the hospital while Jeff came home in the care of Sarah. At four years old my musical ear was already awake, and Sarah sang gospel, blues, and pop tunes to me. I sensed her sadness and anger, probably from leaving her own children alone after school to take care of these Jewish kids from Jackson Heights. Sarah was a great singer; she must've raised the roof beams in her gospel church. As she went around the house vacuuming, dusting, and singing, my lifelong love of blues and gospel blossomed in her care.

After six months, mom was coming home! Grandma and Grandpa were on hand, all of us in the living room waiting for mom. Grandma held little Jeff in her arms. Finally, the door opened and mom came into the apartment. Grandma put Jeff on the floor. Mom's eyes were fixed on the baby. She sat on the floor a few feet from the baby and smiled. At first, Jeff ignored her, but after a moment he turned, crawled over, and climbed onto her lap. I was watching. I felt so alone and scared. Assuming I am remembering correctly, this experience reinforced the initial illusion that my mother and I were two, based on my invitro experience of Uncle Howard's death. I based much of my behavior on the foundational experience that mother's love was not available to me.

At six years old, I discovered a ukulele at Aunt Ida's house. I put my fingers on the little frets and nylon strings and brushed my fingers up and down to make different sounds. So on my seventh birthday my parents gave me a ukulele . . . to their eternal dismay. I soon figured out that I could sing to the accompaniment of the uke. One of my happiest memories is from a summer day, walking behind Mom with my ukulele as she pushed my younger brother in his chariot, throwing my head back in ecstatic bliss, singing, "Old Black Joe." I was lost in

17

the music. I dedicated the first half of my life to learning to play guitar. At one time, I was hailed as the second-best blues guitarist in Boston. Playing the blues prepared me for what was to come.

We moved out of New York City to Long Island to live the American Dream of 1951—a little ranch house on a little block in the town of Baldwin. Mrs. Mendehall, my second grade teacher, spent a great deal of time teaching me to write with my right hand, even though I was a lefty. Everything always came out backwards, but an IQ test showed a remarkable future so they did not send me back to the first grade. I learned to use both hands, along with many useful defense mechanisms. I learned what true puppy love was with Carla Partenheimer. I loved Carla, but Carla loved Richie Carnivale, the typical class bully, who teased our friend Bruce's "feminine" style. Later it turned out Richie liked boys better than girls. Beginning with my mom, part of my karma was to experience unrequited love. Until I began to wake up, I repeated the experience of unrequited love many times.

Then the abuse began. Dad took out his frustrations on me with closed fists. He always got enraged at the family Sunday dinner, in front of grandparents, aunts, uncles, and cousins from Dad's side of the family. He'd jump up screaming, pull me from the table, fists punching into my face. One Sunday I put my arms up to protect my face, which was misinterpreted as an offensive move and the screaming escalated, the punching escalated. Grandma Kopp kept screaming at her son, "Paul! Paul!" I ran into my room, filled with shame. I was a victim of unsolicited violence from dad and disapproving enablement from mom.

At school, my clownish behavior, along with the taunting I received, resulted in my "spitefully shameless" personality. When I was a five-year-old in kindergarten, during naptime I lifted up the skirt of the girl next to me, curious as to what was underneath. The teacher caught me; my first detention was in kindergarten! I finally learned what was under a skirt when I looked up my third grade teacher's dress . . . underpants. When I was eleven, I drew a vagina on a hula girl dancing on a bulletin board outside my school classroom. I was kicked off the safety patrol for that one. One time I set off a fire alarm in school out of curiosity. Then there was the report on race relations my step-grandfather, Aime, helped me write. Aime Frappier (Grandma Bea's new husband) was from the South and deeply racist. He had me include several sentences about the superiority of the white race. The principal called my parents and dad hit the roof.

So there I was: a brilliant left-handed student forced to write with my right hand, forced to sit in the corner, forced to be the class clown, pretending I wasn't being beaten at home. And nobody knew.

I encountered my first musical icon, Harry Belafonte, at age eight. Grandma Bea bought me his first album along with a "mono" record player, all three speeds. I listened to "Day-o" and "The Jamaican Farewell" over and over again. That acoustic guitar, the folk melodies, the honesty in the lyrics and presentation—those songs drove deeply into me. I felt a resonance with the Deep South Black cultural experience; the soulful sound and truth of "real" music moved me.

One day I stole some change from my mother's purse. She found out and was so outraged that she took away my Roy Rogers' six guns. I ran into my room in tears and sullenly picked up my record player's arm and scratched a big X over and over again into my Harry Belafonte record with the old needle against the vinyl, repeatedly saying, "I hate her, I hate her!"

By the age of twelve I was done with the uke. It was my birthday, and I knew I was getting a guitar. My Grandpa Kopp, dad's father (the one who caught me masturbating and hugged me too hard when he said goodbye that day), had a friend who could get a deal. When I opened the case, I was shocked to discover it only had four strings; it was a tenor guitar. I began to crying inconsolably. My father and grandfather, totally exasperated, drove down to Jack Curran's music store in Baldwin and bought me the most beautiful $14 lime-green Stella guitar, all six strings present, action at about half an inch. I slept with that guitar. I sometimes still do. I took my Stella into my room, closed the door and, sitting on the dresser in my room with the guitar cradled into my near fetal position, I played a great D/A7 progression for "If I had a hammer." I got so lost in the playing and singing that when Grandma Kopp opened the door and peeked in, I returned from a "no-thought" feeling of ecstasy. I was aware of her mystified look as she quietly closed the door.

I had discovered the magic of music, but my dad's beatings continued, and my mom's lying. Mom could not tell the truth. She lied and lied to me and to everyone. With a passive-dependent personality disorder, she tried to create a world in which she was somebody. "Oh yes, my mink is in storage." When she said she loved her oldest son, she lied about that, too. It was so confusing. She would say to me, "If only you weren't so bad, if only you didn't goad your father, he wouldn't hit you." She was also a thief. She stole the gold ring her father, Grandpa Milton, left me. She cashed in the $10,000 insurance policy Grandma Bea had given me for my twenty-first birthday, and took bits and pieces of my trust fund from Milton until it was greatly diminished.

I learned my mom's lessons very well, and got lost in the free-floating world of the vertical split. Most of us are traumatized at some point in our lives. If the trauma of improper or insufficient loving from parents occurs while the ego is still forming during the first three years of life, a "vertical split" occurs in the sense of self, which manifests as self-doubt, low self-esteem, and self-deprecation. Those who are horizontally split are firmly entrenched in their egos, and have no doubts, no questions. They are successful in Caesar's world and do not worry about who they really are. It's like the vertically-split folks are sitting on the dock in the shadows, watching a yacht in the harbor with all the horizontal splitters dancing and drinking under bright colored lights. Ram Dass later told me the secret blessing: "You are split vertically. Therefore, you have access to the higher planes!" And on those planes the split can be healed.

Thank God for Grandma Bea, my mother's mother, who was also a total liar. Her son Howard had been killed in the war two months before I was born, but she transformed all her grief into love for me. They even named me Howard; I think she believed I was his reincarnation. Feeling her love was such a treasure! She lived in Florida with Aime and came for a visit each summer, bringing love into my life. When Grandma Bea visited, we would make a tent out of the bed sheets, create fantasy dramas, and have secrets together. The spark of her love kept me from losing my heart. And she was fascinated by spiritualism. She gave me a copy of Autobiography of a Yogi when I was eleven. I remember Yogananda's face on the cover, although I did not read it until years later. I still have a book she gave me, The Power of Believing, even though I now know that all beliefs, along with all opinions, fears, and negative subconscious thought forms, must go.

I developed my own personal roots. I organized a lip-synching cover blues band, Kopp's Kool Kats. We bought some closeout Chess records of Muddy Waters and Little Walter for a dollar each. On Friday nights, we put those records on my three-speed turntable and lip-synched the words to "I Just Want to Make Love to You," "Hoochie Coochie Man," and "Got My Mojo Working."

By the time I was fifteen I had crossed paths with Jean Shepherd, one of the unique personalities in the history of radio broadcasting. From 1961 through 1980, he had a weekly radio show on WOR New York where he told stories of his youth, played silly music on his nose flute or kazoo, and read the poetry of Robert W. Service and George Ade. He discussed literature, politics, and spiritual philosophy in a way that made my fifteen-year-old mind explode with new ideas and potentialities. You can still find Shepherd's podcasts. You might know of him from "A Christmas Story," the movie in which a boy's tongue gets attached to an ice-cold flagpole. That was just one of dozens of classic Shepherd stories.

Shepherd introduced me to Greenwich Village. I was a testosterone-fueled youth and Shepherd's description of the scene in the Village sounded so cool, so "bohemian."Shep told us which bookstores to visit, where to eat, which coffeehouses to haunt. My friends and I even developed a "Shepherd-style" of dressing. After a Sunday train ride into New York City from Long Island, we wandered into Village bookstores, where I learned of William Blake, William Faulkner, William Burroughs, and Jean Cocteau. Henry Miller opened the door to free sex, spirituality, and creativity. In Siddhartha, Hermann Hesse taught me about the Buddha, and about my own path in Demian and Steppenwolf. I could not stop reading. By the time I left for college, I had read most of the classics as well as a ton of trash. I started with the Hardy Boys and ended with Joyce, Kafka, and the Bhagavad Gita.

At the same time that I was immersing myself in Shepherd, the Village, and the beatniks, my ear for American roots music had grown. At fifteen, I was the leader of a Kingston Trio-like folk group called The Village Singers. Marvin, Peter, and I sang at the senior talent show in high school. When it was my turn to do a verse from a song we had made up about the teachers in school, I sang, "Mr. Gerardi teaches gym; we wish he would teach the rest of us," there was a roar of laughter so intense that something burned into my soul: my future as an entertainer.

The Kingston Trio introduced me to traditional American folk music. I studied Doc Boggs, Clarence Ashley, Bill Monroe, and others from the American White South. And from the Mississippi Delta, I studied Skip James, John Hurt, Son House, and the great Robert Johnson. I wore a black Robert Johnson mourning sweater for years. I worked all summer for a cigarette wholesaler to earn the $235 I needed to buy a Martin D28 guitar, and spent hours picking out their tunes on my new Martin.

On the weekends, my friends and I headed into New York City, Greenwich Village, where we would hang out at Gerdes Folk City and the Gaslight Cafe. They had open mics, and we would see Bob Dylan or Jim Kweskin or Dave Van Ronk there. Sometimes I got up to sing one of my teenage blues songs for the packed house. One night, after I sang a short set, Bob Dylan came up to me in a drunken haze and said, "Good blues, man!"

Finally, in 1962, I got away from my insane parents and moved into an equally insane environment at Michigan State University. Apparently, the Admissions Department had decided to admit a group of Jews from Long Island. They put us all on the same floor in the same dorm, and all of us quickly bonded together. However, they did mix in some Midwesterners. When we first met, my roommate, who was from a rural Michigan farm, asked, "Can I see your horns?" When I met the dormitory manager, he said, "So you are from Longgg Island?" That "buzz pronunciation" is often an indication of anti-Semitism, and I started to feel I was in the wrong place.

I found my way into the MSU folk music club and even onto the stage at a local coffee house. I developed a warm circle of friends, all of us playing instruments and singing traditional folk music. We organized the Glad Dog Jug Band; our star performer was a miniature white poodle. We actually got pretty famous and performed at the Ann Arbor Folk Festival. This was my second big fix. At the festival, one of the songs we played began with me doing a long solo guitar intro . . . in front of five thousand people. I clearly remember the burst of applause as my solo ended and the song began. Being a borderline personality, who experienced rejection from his own mother and father, finding myself accepted on a performance stage by a huge group of people touched a wound inside of me. While it did not heal the wound, it certainly did ease the pain.

On one extraordinary weekend in 1962, we drove from East Lansing down to Chicago for the Chicago Blues Festival. All the greats were there—Muddy Waters, Howlin' Wolf, Otis Rush, and many of the country players like Fred McDowell, Lightnin' Hopkins, Mississippi John Hurt, and Skip James. I was absolutely blown away when the 6'5," 300-pound Howlin' Wolf came out on stage on a tiny motorcycle. The Muddy Waters blues band, featuring Little Walter, played "Got My Mojo Working." I loved this music.

A hundred of us were sitting in the University of Chicago Commons strumming guitars when Mike Bloomfield came up to me. Mike Bloomfield! The star guitarist in the Paul Butterfield Blues Band in 1965 was possibly the "father" of white boys playing the blues. Even today his playing is considered among the best, despite the fact that he left his body quite a while ago. This moment, however, was way before the Butterfield Blues Band. We were all teenagers. Mike asked if he could borrow my guitar. I had no idea who he was, but I said sure. He stood before me, and while a friend of his played some rhythm, I watched Mike, spellbound. He had an amazing guitar style of string-bending blues melodies. I had never heard anything like it and I said to myself, "I want that." A few years later, at the Newport

Folk Festival, the Paul Butterfield Blues Band debuted their hard-rocking Southside Chicago Blues. When I heard Mike take a solo on his 1950s Les Paul guitar, I realized what I needed in order to "get that."

It was sophomore year at Michigan State when I met my initiator, Maura. Many of the friends I had made as a freshman lived communally in Lansing. Although I was required to live in supervised housing, I spent all my time with Maura, Larry, Helen, and the others who came and went from our Lansing hideaway. Maura was a little older than me, and whether it was because of childhood trauma or voracious appetite, she had a reputation that preceded her. On our first night together, Maura introduced me to smoking cannabis, and when I was floating, she asked if I was feeling "close." I had no idea what she meant until she reached behind her, pulled down a zipper, and her dress fell to the floor. I could not believe my eyes. I had been with Alice and with Janet, but I had never seen anything like naked Maura. Her body shone. She manifested the essence of the divine feminine. Her breasts stood out in perfect harmony, narrow waist tight with muscles, glistening pubic hair—a perfect physical beauty.

In the evenings that followed I was introduced to hippy life. Maura was expert in sexual matters and she put me into situations where anything and everything was okay. I believe that everyone's sexual proclivities are determined in part by their early experiences. Maura created a context for me where everything desired was okay; the only rule was love. Maura taught me how to use sex and love spiritually to reach great heights of pleasure and to merge the "two into one." Although Maura was young, she was on a spiritual quest. She brought much Eastern thought, meditation, and the spiritual power of the "two into one" into our relationship.

She was so promiscuous, though, that I could not make a real commitment to her. One night as we were making love she

25

said, "I love you." I felt this churning conflict and could not answer her. I did love her, but I needed a monogamous commitment, which she could not offer. The next morning she apologized to me for saying those words, and I accepted it. In life there are so many "should have's," but I truly wish I had told her I loved her, too. We left East Lansing together after a summer of love and returned to New York. Maura moved into a spiritual commune in New York City and I moved in with the NYC contingent of my Michigan State community. Maura and I were born on the same day. It was on our mutual birthday that we said our goodbyes, clutching each other's bodies for the last time.

I rented an apartment on East 6th street. My friends and I gathered in the evenings and Dick Siegel, Willie and I played Beatles songs or old folk songs on our guitars and sang. Dick and I decided to create a band. Big things were happening musically, like the Velvet Underground and Janis Joplin, and we wanted in. Grandma Bea bought me my first electric guitar for one hundred dollars—a Gretsch, but it worked. We played a few gigs in New York City during the summer.

Then I met Martine. A Midwesterner, she attended Michigan State and lived in our community on 6th Street in the East Village. An exceptionally beautiful woman, Martine was tall, dark-haired, and her body was filled with luscious curves, as was her psychology. We had an excellent time together. As our love grew, I began to realize I was going to marry this woman and she would bear my first child. We had so many great adventures together, with psychedelic drugs, each other's bodies, and the power of being young, free adults loose in the big city. New York was heading into winter. Martine and I had some friends living in Los Angeles, and it was hippy time in California. We were anxious to check it out. We pooled our funds and purchased a 1958 Nash Rambler with broken trunnions (the car bounced like we were driving on a trampoline), loaded it full of guitars and my cat, Govinda, and headed toward the Pacific Ocean.

I had been reading Henry Miller's Air-Conditioned Nightmare, in which he described a cross-country trip from New York to L.A. As he drove through America's wasteland, he read The Life of Ramakrishna by Romain Rolland. I identified very strongly with the great spiritual teacher, Henry Miller. When it was time for me to prepare for my "on the road" experience, I went to Weiser's Bookstore in the Village and bought a copy of The Life of Ramakrishna. During the trip, I read the story.

Paramahamsa Ramakrishna (1836-1886) was an uneducated child, living a simple life in rural India. One afternoon when he was seven years old, a black thundercloud floated in the sky and two white cranes flew across the cloud. This vision put him into his first trance. I was touched by the simplicity and the profound insight his life demonstrated. I did not realize that this book was going to impact my life in the most incredibly dramatic way twenty years later.

L.A. was a hippie wonderland—everyone smoking pot, enjoying free love and psychedelic visions. I got a job in the Free Press Bookstore, the center of activities in Hollywood. The psychedelic music scene was in full swing, as was the revitalization of the blues greats from the Fifties—Muddy Waters, Wolf, Son House, Lonnie Johnson, Skip James, and many other artists were performing the blues again. I soaked it up.

I had not yet figured out that because Sarah sang such beautiful music to me, and my mother seemed to prefer my brother, I had identified more with Sarah's culture than my own. This Jewish boy from New York was now pretending to be a black, alcoholic, blues thug from Chicago. It never really worked for me. Over the years my style became more and more personal until today I play the "sadhu's blues" (a sadhu is an

Indian mendicant holy man). It has evolved to become as real as it will ever be. Finally, I have found the old man's voice I was looking for when I was twenty. Instead of trying to be a black man from Alabama, I am now trying to be a brown man from Bangalore. The split never really goes away, it just transforms, until it finally unites when one reaches the higher planes.

When Martine became pregnant, we had a rousing, musical, orgiastic wedding in the shadow of the Hollywood Hills and headed back east to bring our new child into the world. We spent the pregnancy in a draft resistors' commune in Western Maryland, where we were constantly in danger. One of the fellows from the commune insisted on going down to the local bus station and handing out leaflets against the Vietnam War. The kids at the bus station did not like hippies and more than once came out to our house and threw rocks through the windows. All in all, it was great fun. None of us, though, were going to support the military/industrial war in Southeast Asia. We all found ways to stay home and fight to stop the war. Some of my friends brought their weight down below minimum standards, others gave ambiguous sexual preferences, others used drug addiction, some went to Canada. I decided not to go to Viet Nam, so when I was called, I gave the draft board a disqualifying lie and got a 4F status.

When my daughter Rachel was born, we left the commune and moved to upstate New York, not far from the city. I formed a blues band that played at the resorts in the Borscht Belt of the Catskills, a perfect environment for black music from the '50s. I had a great collaboration with John Nuzzo, an excellent harp player in the style of Little Walter. John later went on to become John Leslie, a famous porn star from the San Fernando Valley.

Then came a breakup with Martine, a hookup with Marg, another pregnancy, and the birth of Otis, my son. It all happened so quickly. I needed to be loved so badly, I clung to every opportunity. Otis was a joy to the world, radiating peacefulness. I know some babies come out crying and complaining, but Otis was peace all the way. Marg worked full time and I stayed home for the first year of Otis' life. I learned to be a house dad, doing dishes, diapers, dinner, then drugs and debauchery. Marg was a wonderful, sexy partner, and the first few years were filled with love and joy. Otis was surrounded by love.

However, my daughter, Rachel, felt deserted by her dad. I remember the moment I sat her on my lap and told her I was moving. The tears literally squirted from her eyes, and the pain in my heart was profound. As I drove away, I saw her standing in the doorway, crying. This was the saddest, most painful moment of my life. I loved her so dearly. It was not until years later, when Rachel was injured, that we spent hours together and healed her feelings of desertion. We have found our way to a loving relationship.

I continued to play in blues bands, turning many of the bars in Boston into my turf. I met a fellow named Ronnie Horvath, who was anxious to learn how to play blues guitar. We started a band together and I taught him much of what I knew. One night, after a gig, I was sleeping on Ronnie's couch when I heard him in the next room, practicing. He was playing a slide guitar tune in the style of Robert Nighthawk, and he was good. I thought, "The student has surpassed the teacher." Ronnie shortened his name to Ronnie Earl and went on to play with some of the top bands, like the Allman Brothers, The Thunderbirds, Roomful of Blues, and others. He's made many recordings under his own name, "Ronnie Earl and the Broadcasters." I am proud to say Ronnie has gone on to become the greatest living blues guitarist. He was a respectful student and is a wonderful friend and musical genius.

At the ripe old age of thirty-nine, I was living a life of complete desperation. During the day I was the telephone salesperson at Illuminations, and at night I would put on my jeans and play at the blues club. I was having trouble in my relationship. Marg seemed cold to me and I became convinced that she was sleeping around. My relationship with Martine and Rachel had deteriorated. I hated the idea of passing the terrible undifferentiated distress that kept me wandering in the borderland of my life on to my new son. I truly felt he would be better off if I were dead.

At this point, my father invited us all down to Florida for a week's visit. I took with me my skill at making French fries.

Shubalananda plays the blues

Chapter 2

RAM DASS

A night of heartfelt music can save the world. Sing on!
Ram Dass

Left to right: Krishna Das, Janaki, Ram Dass, John Cabot Zinn, Bernie Glassman, and Shubal

I am a connoisseur and master chef when it comes to French fries. I had learned the secret from Julia Child, and every time my family got together, the pronouncement was: "Larry will make French fries." Otis was now two years old and I had not yet introduced him to his grandparents. With trepidation, right after my fortieth birthday, I took my son and wife down to my parents' condo at the beach in Key Biscayne, Florida. It's always difficult around my parents. My father's sarcasm and my mother's lip-smacking disapproval made me worry about what Marg would think, what Otis would experience, and what trauma they would reawaken in me.

For dinner, I made my specialty potatoes and served them up hot in a big dish. The plate moved around the table until it was my turn to serve myself. As I would do at my own home, I reached out for the fries with my hand and took a handful. I had forgotten that bad manners were a punishable crime in my family. Dad jumped up from the table and pulled back his fist in anger to hit me just as he used to do in my teenage years in front of *his* family. Now he was doing it in front of *my* family. I freaked out, thinking, "This is my lineage—liars, thieves, and bullies—and this is all I have to offer this new son of mine. I might as well kill myself; it would be a gift to my young son."

I ran back to Boston and leaped into therapy for the first time in my life. My therapist was a sweet woman, with a last name of Paradise. I'm sure that during our time together, I blew Eleanor's mind as well as my own. Neither of us foresaw the transformation that was about to occur. I had no expectations from this therapy other than the idea that having someone to talk to could mitigate my inclination towards suicide. I had been using a variety of substances to ease my pain and was anxious to free myself from these behaviors. Ellie suggested I consider meditation as a way to clear all the muck out of my mind and body, and I immediately thought of Mirabai Bush.

Mirabai owned Illuminations, the small gift company in Cambridge where I worked as a telephone salesperson during the day. We all knew that she and her now ex-husband John (aka Krishna) had been hippies in the '60s, had gone to India, and then founded their business on the rainbow sticker that swept America in the '70s. They started out selling their rainbows out of the back of a VW van and the ubiquitous stickers ended up in thousands of stores and on the back windshields of untold numbers of cars. Wandering around in the basement of the company building, I could see the mandala calendars, spiritually-themed stickers, and books the company sold earlier in its history. In particular, there was a book called Miracle Of Love, written by a famous hippy guy from the '60s, Richard Alpert, aka Ram Dass. He was the fellow who, along with Tim

Leary, introduced LSD to America. I knew he had gone to India and become a yogi. I had listened to a few of his lectures in the '60s on WBAI, Paul Gorman's "Lunch Pail" show.

I first started working at Illuminations around Christmas time, a year before the Florida visit. We celebrated the holiday at work by choosing a Secret Santa—you put your name in a hat and got a gift for whoever's name you pulled out. The first year I pulled out Mirabai's name. I knew she had been to India and I had something in my possession that I had carried around for twenty years—the copy of the Life of Ramakrishna by Romain Rolland I had bought for my road trip to L.A. As we drove through America's purple McD's majesty, amber waves of greed, I read of this little man who went into a trance that he described as "....houses, doors, temples and everything else vanished altogether; as if there was nothing anywhere! And what I saw was an infinite shoreless sea of light; a sea that was consciousness."

Mysterious India sounded so exotic and romantic to me, so very different from everything I detested about my parents and the "straight" society in America in the '60s. India and Hinduism filled me with the implication that I was more than my experiences and thoughts.

Ramakrishna was one of India's greatest saints; some called him an avatar. He became a priest at the Dakshineshwar Kali Temple in a suburb of Kolkata (then Calcutta). After years of pleading with the murti (statue) of the fierce goddess Kali to grant him a vision of her, he became desperate. He decided he would rather end his incarnation than to live without seeing her face. He had reached for a sword to end his life when the Mother intervened, took him in her arms, and dried his tears with her sari. He slipped into a deep trance. Afterwards, Ramakrishna practiced each of the world religions, one at a time. In Hinduism, he studied yantra (mystical diagrams), tantra (spiritual practices), and mantra (repeated word or phrase). He continued his studies into the mystical components of Islam, Christianity, and Buddhism. In each of his studies he quickly reached the truth and saw the face of divinity as defined within each tradition.

His final enlightenment came when the tantric saint, Totapuri, arrived at Ramakrishna's temple. Again and again, he tried to teach Ramakrishna the truth of the formless God, but every time Ramakrishna merged into his samadhi (absorption in higher consciousness), he saw the face of Kali. Finally, Totapuri picked up a piece of glass, pushed it into Ramakrishna's forehead between his eyes, and said, "Now concentrate, concentrate!" Again, Ramakrishna merged into his samadhi. In his own words, this time when the face of Kali appeared to him: "I drew the sword of discrimination and I sliced Kali in two, and I merged into the formless God."

One of the most beautiful books ever written, The Gospel of Sri Ramakrishna, tells about the last five years of his life. It was written by a devotee who identified himself only as "M." It's like reading the gospels of Jesus, yet Ramakrishna lived only a hundred and fifty years ago and we know these stories to be true. I liked the idea of being the kind of person who carried around a book like The Life of Ramakrishna. It was good for my self-image, so I held onto this book for twenty years. When it was Secret Santa time at Illuminations, I wrapped it up and anonymously gave it to Mirabai for Christmas.

The next year passed quickly. As my son grew; my relationship with Marg deteriorated. The split between my art, my psychology, and my family continually undermined my happiness. When it came time for the next year's Secret Santa, from a basket with sixty names in it, I coincidently again pulled out Mirabai's name.

A few weeks earlier I had begun reading Miracle of Love , stories about Neem Karoli Baba (Maharajji, as the Westerners call him), a book I found in the basement at Illuminations. I was very much enjoying the mood the book created, the apparent love the author had for his teacher, and the miraculous stories; it all seemed so magical. When I read the last chapter about Neem Karoli Baba's mahasamadhi (when a realized being leaves his body consciously and with intent), I felt moved and sad, like at the end of a good novel. I was so sorry I had missed him. I put the book down and came out of my room for dinner with my wife and my son. I sat down and looked over at my boy, Otis. Suddenly, I was completely overcome with love for him. Waves of laughing and crying at the same time washed over me, and I looked at him tenderly with tears in my eyes. Marg looked across at me with wonderment in her eyes. She said, "What's wrong with you?" I thought, "Is there something wrong?" That thought brought me back into my body with a shudder. I turned to my mashed potatoes.

Christmas was approaching. This time, for Mirabai's Secret Santa gift, I wrote the story of my attachment to The Life of Ramakrishna, the trip to California and Henry Miller, how I carried the book around for years, finding Miracle Of Love and Maharajji, seeing the miracle of my son at the table, giving her the book last year, and the feeling of the waves against the shore. She was moved by my gift, but told me she had lost The Life of Ramakrishna the day of the party last year and had not seen it since.

These complex events were only the beginning. I had a relative, a famous therapist named Sheldon Kopp, the son of my grandfather's brother, who grew up with my father in the Bronx. He had become kind of a guru in the D.C. area. His books were national bestsellers, such as If You Meet the Buddha on the Road, Kill Him! His series of books explained his insights into the mind, using examples from his childhood. When Sheldon described my father, he revealed that even in childhood, my father had a mean streak—the kind of kid who would stick out his foot on the sidewalk to trip girls as they walked by. My father saw himself as a failure and Sheldon as a success. As Buddha said, "You are what you eat."

Near Christmas, I received a gift in the mail from my father, an extremely unusual occurrence. It was a copy of Sheldon Kopp's newest book The Pickpocket and the Saint, based on the oral teachings of Neem Karoli Baba! I was shocked to overload. This had to be more than a coincidence! I felt like I was being drawn in like a moth to the flame. I read Sheldon's book and found myself in it. He basically nailed all my games, even the "spiteful shamelessness" and the vertical split. Finding my psychology described so accurately in a book allowed me, for the first time, to differentiate myself from my psychology. I felt like a man with a rather unique psychology rather than a deformed human being.

I showed Sheldon's book to Mirabai, told her of the amazing synchronicity of getting the book, how it was partly about Maharajji, partly exactly about me, and how my therapist suggested that I learn how to meditate. All that to lead up to the question: "Would you be willing to teach me?"

"Well, I could," said Mirabai. "But I know someone who might do a better job. I'm having dinner with him tonight; I'll ask him if he would like to meet you." She was smiling.

The next day Mirabai said that she had talked to Ram Dass and he would like to meet me. It turned out that Mirabai had been with Ram Dass in India at Neem Karoli Baba's ashram, and they were best of friends. She gave me his number and said to call him right now. I had read Miracle of Love, and I had been around for Be Here Now and "Turn On, Tune In, Drop Out." As a matter of fact, I had dropped out several times. But Miracle of Love left me a little intimidated about meeting Ram Dass—this guy was the real thing. I dialed his number. The voice coming through the phone sounded so powerful, and the vibration went directly into me. We spoke briefly and made a plan to meet the next day. My heart was pounding.

That January evening we celebrated Marg's birthday. About eight of us went downtown for a birthday dinner. I sat silently watching a man at the next table light up a cigar and fill everyone's food with his vile smoke. I listened to people gossiping at our table. A cacophony of sights, smells, and sounds all floated before me like a miraculous show. I was sitting in a silent crossroads. The next day's meeting with Ram Dass could potentially be the most important moment in my life. I sat at the table thinking, "Look around and see how this feels. This is now and tomorrow it may all be different."

A friend lent me his car to drive down to the South Shore where Ram Dass was living. I felt calm, centered, and ready to meet this magnificent man. As I pulled up to his house, I was amused to see the name "Dass" on the mailbox. He greeted me at the door and invited me into his basement apartment. As I looked around, I felt quite at home. His room was like a hippy den with pictures of Hanuman on the wall and incense burning. We introduced ourselves and he offered me a cup of tea, which I refused, thinking it is best to fast. We sat down facing each other in overstuffed chairs in the living room.

Ram Dass began to stare at me. His sanpaku eyes are large and riveting, filled with light, filled with love. At first I was uncomfortable. On one level I wanted to impress this man, and on another level I wanted to be exactly myself with no pretenses. When I averted my eyes, he gave me an immediate response. "No, no," he said. "Maintain eye contact with me. There is much going on here beyond the words." So we began. We sat and stared at each other without speaking. Time slipped by. In his eyes I saw real honest caring love, something I had not ever seen from my parents.

I thought, "This guy sitting here, he doesn't even know me, but he's looking at me with so much love. This guy is loving me up. I am excellent at reading phonies, and this guy seems to be real. How can this be?" Tears began roll down my face, old tears of the sadness and ache of eons. As I stared across at Ram Dass, I saw tears running down his cheeks. Suddenly all this grief and sadness seemed so poignant and I began to laugh. With complete empathy, Ram Dass laughed also. The energy kept shifting from cold and sharp and angular to soft and present, always right here. At least an hour passed in this silent exchange of love. Then, when I felt so intimate and loving with this stranger, he said, "Tell me your story."

I blurted out, "I was an abused child." All the tears—all the suffering of this little child at the hands of brutal unloving parents—came pouring out, and I said what it was like to be me. He heard my mellow-drama and spoke a sentence that absolutely shocked me: "You are split vertically; therefore you have access to the higher planes." He knew the work of Sheldon Kopp! The vertical split is one of Sheldon's metaphors. Later on I found out Ram Dass and Sheldon were great friends.

After he heard my tale of woe, Ram Dass told me a few stories of his time in India with Neem Karoli Baba. In retrospect I realize the stories were meant for me, and they were specifically designed to shift my low self-esteem into a more neutral zone. "Maharajji was getting ready to send me back to America," Ram Dass said. "Maharajji called me over and said, 'Go back to America, and teach. Tell the truth and love everyone.' Knowing myself, I was perplexed. I said, 'Well, the truth is I don't love everyone, and I do not feel pure enough to teach.' Maharajji stood in front of me and looked me up and down, from my head down to my feet. Then he walked behind me and again looked from head to foot. He came back in front and stared straight into my eyes. He said, 'I don't see any impurities.'"

The story struck home so deeply in my heart. The reason I wanted to meet him was to examine my impurities. I understood the principle of the pickpocket who only sees pockets. So much of what we see is based on projection. The entire universe, through our eyes, is colored by the qualities of our ego, our persona, mirror, mask, shadow. When those who are devoid of these qualities view the universe, all they see is loving oneness. When a seeker is seen by a seer, a brief vision of oneness is sometimes shared.

As we talked, Ram Dass began punctuating our conversation with two questions: "What are you thinking?" and "What are you feeling?" These reflect the classical Buddhist state of concentration with mindfulness. The mind is sharply tuned to one-pointedness, while noting all the experiences entering through the five senses without judgment. He was introducing me to Buddhist nirvana (a state of enlightenment).

Then he asked me what was in my past, a secret, something I had never told anyone, something with shame attached. As I looked through my mind, many thoughts and experiences came to the surface. I was wondering, "Is this like the priest's confessional?" I remembered how my parents began shaming me when I first discovered masturbation around six years old. The shaming had gone so deep, although I knew that almost every sentient being in the universe masturbates, that I hid this secret even from my wife. And so, with a sudden rush of breath, I finally admitted to another person, "Yes, there is a secret. I masturbate!" I expected to feel shame as I revealed my dark secrets; after all, I desired to impress Ram Dass with what a cool person I was. Instead, I felt so relieved! The weight of shame had been lifted from me and I began to take the first steps toward self-love.

Then Ram Dass asked me what, of all my characteristics, I would like to give up the most. I said, "I tell lies. I want to be truthful." My mother, her mother before her, and back into prehistoric Hungary all come from a lineage of liars. Even as a small child I observed my mother lying about everything. If a leaf was green, she would say it was red. She was obsessed, a passive-dependent personality, and she simply could not tell the truth. I so much wanted to be the last link in the chain of lies, but for some reason I had the same obsession. When I was younger I would say, "Oh, yes, I had a Mercedes. Oh, yes, I've been to Antarctica."

Ram Dass seemed to understand this completely. He said, "I will help. When you feel the impulse to lie, just offer it, send it up, send it to me, send it to Maharajji. I will help."

He continued to punctuate our conversation with questions, bringing me into the present moment: What are you thinking? Where is your mind? What are you feeling? What is coming in through your senses? Witness it. He was gradually training my mind to be in this moment with mindfulness, slowly bringing me closer for a quick glimpse through his eyes. One of the essentials I discovered during those hours was that enlightenment is simply being in the moment with mindfulness.

After an hour of talk, he signaled me over to the floor, where he spread out one of Maharajji's blankets. I could literally feel the radiation from this blanket that had been worn by the great holy man. My mind was swirling with love and presence. I lay face down on Maharajji's blanket and began to relax every muscle. He started his massage with my legs, almost Rolfing them 180°. I surrendered to the pain and continued to relax my body. He began to move up over my hips onto my spine. Apparently he was searching for something because when he found these two spots in the middle of my spine, he began to press with great pressure. Tears and snot and spit covered my cheeks. Ram Dass, with his hands, rubbed my face and made the mess even worse. He smiled. "Sometimes it's good to be messy."

This mystic massage over, he asked me to stand up. "What are you thinking now?"

"*I love you.*" From deep in my heart I felt the powerful stirring.

"What are you feeling now?"

"So much love for you." The stirring began to expand, and I felt overwhelmed.

"What are you thinking now?"

"I just *love* you, I *love* you." I had only that one thought.

"What are you feeling now?"

"My knees are trembling."

"GO THERE NOW with your mind!" Ram Dass appeared to be very interested in the trembling of my knees. As I began to focus, he said, "Now try and move that tremble up." I found that I could cause the shaking to move up my body if I visualized it in my mind. He said, "What are you feeling now?" The shaking reached my abdomen. "What are you thinking now?"

At this point, I loved this man so much. I felt so seen, so accepted. Even after revealing my darkest secrets, this man was seeing deeper. It felt like he was loving me as I was—my first taste of unconditional love. He spoke, "Come over and sit again."

When I sat down, the trembling did not cease. At this point the visualization was around my heart center. With my mind, I continued to move the shaking up until it reached my lower jaw. My teeth chattered like the teeth in Harpo Marx's pocket. As it moved higher, I felt a warmth burning behind my eyes. It moved still higher, reached the top of my head, and exploded out through my skull into the vast blue sky, filling the whole of my awareness. My thoughts and ego mind floated by on the peripheral corner of my consciousness, like a small dark raincloud in a clear blue sky.

Now is this vast silence. My heart slows way down and my breath stops and I hear the silence of God's music. It is like I am the fireworks, shooting out over the clear Coney Island nightin orgasm beyond orgasm, on fire in the peace of silence.

He asked me again, "What are you thinking?"

I looked over at him and what I saw amazed me; it shook the foundation of my ego's security. I saw Ram Dass' form, but I also saw that he and I had merged. He and I were one! I said softly and lovingly, "Ram Dass, we're the same person." The whole of creation had become one vast consciousness. The trees outside the window and walls, the whole of my reality merged into one. I saw that all of us sentient beings are simply neurons in the brain of God, which sent me into fits of deep deep laughter; this *shakti* (divine energy) laughter went beyond any past experience. It felt so good to really laugh. The simple answer to all our questions, to all our ceaseless searching, is always right *here*, a mere glance away. It was right here all the time, but I hadn't known how to look for it.

He said, "What are you feeling?"

At peace. For the first time, I understood what it felt like not to have any tension in my stomach, not to have the slightest expectation of anything, and for the mind to be completely focused on the present. I felt good! This is who we really are, this good good feeling. I was so happy. I laughed and laughed.

He asked, "What are you thinking?"

I saw the perfection of the universe. This moment is just right, no more, no less. The universe is a harmony, a cacophonic harmony of boiling life, fear-love-life; this harmony is a unison of perfection, balanced perfectly on the edge. There is a seed in every loss. I could finally forgive mom and dad because, without them, THIS could not have happened. I experienced a clarity to everything. All the while, I was hearing amazing music, silent flute music. There was hardly a breath, hardly a heartbeat.

Suddenly Ram Dass' face began to change and he became my grandfather, then a doctor who once operated on my twenty-five-year-old body, and then a Native American, then a black man with an Afro. Face after face—Tibetan, Chinese, Jewish, Indian—until finally it settled. I squinted, but could not make out who it was. I twisted my neck around and squinted again, and suddenly it struck me like a brick—MAHARAJJI!

"Maharajji, O Maharajji, it's YOU!" Maharajji just smiled.

Without any thought in my mind, with nothing in my heart but a wave of love, I saw that Ram Dass had disappeared. His body was gone and had been replaced with the form of his guru, Neem Karoli Baba. I was sitting in the presence of Neem Karoli Baba eleven years after he left his body! As clearly as any experience I have ever had in the physical realm, as concretely as any log I have chopped or any brick I have laid, Neem Karoli Baba sat across from me in the living room, staring into my eyes. I basked in the blazing heat of the love radiating across the room, and stared into the eyes of my Beloved.

I said his name, over and over. But then I misspoke his name . . . Oh, MahaRIji."

Maharajji said "What?"

I was shocked, horrified. Suddenly my self-conscious little mind fell into full embarrassment about mispronouncing his name. In the movies, you see someone pull the cork out of a magic lamp, the smoke rises and becomes a genie. Now imagine that film reversed. I felt myself falling down, down, down, back into the bottle of my ego, my personality, mirror, mask, shadow. I could feel the constriction, the self-consciousness come upon me like a slap in the face. I had mispronounced the guru's name, *Oh Oh Oh*, and now he thinks badly of me . . .Ram Dass (he was Ram Dass again) just smiled, with this very interested look on his face. As I floated back down, I felt my "small self" returning, but so much had changed. My head was pounding, a headache seemed to coat the inside of my skull, but my heart felt so light, so consecrated with this new sense of self and purpose. My experience did not compute with my rational mind. I was confused. I asked Ram Dass "Is this real, or am I crazy?"

He said, "No, it is not real and yes, you are crazy." Then he gave me the most personal look of love. I felt like I had fallen in love. This man gives so much, and I was filled with love. He spoke, "You know, Ram Dass loves everyone just the same, but I really love you, Larry." At that moment the door burst open, one of the Das brothers returning. Ram Dass and I had been at it for over four hours. There seemed to be no time, but it was time to go. I was mostly out of my body, but wherever I was, I was loving Ram Dass, loving this man who had just shown me who I really was and how to become that all the time. As I was beginning to think about highways, and my head was hurting, he hugged me in his bear-like way. I turned to go and then stopped at the door. He came over and we hugged again.

The mid-January air punctuated the clarity of the physical plane. I stopped at the rocky coastline and walked down the beach to that changing, wavering line between the ocean and the sand. I raised my arms toward the sky. The cold ocean wind blew in my hair. I heard the waves touching the beach and smelled the ocean filled with moldering decay and seething life.

I was reliving the eleventh chapter of the *Bhagavad Gita*, in which Arjuna asks Krishna, "Please, show me your real form." Krishna speaks, "Beware, I am death!" And then he gives Arjuna the vision of a huge conflagration. On one side stood Arjuna's family—his friends, his grandfather, his guru, everyone that Arjuna knew—all falling into the flames. On the other side of the fire, bubbling up from the flames, were babies, babies, babies.

I got home and Marg said, "Well, how was it?"

I answered, "I met my father and he made me whole. I saw the face of God."

Chapter3

MORE RAM DASS

Love is the song of the soul singing to God. –Paramahansa
Yogananda

Ram Dass and Shubal in a bear hug

Lines intersect, paths cross, the electric bolt of energy ignites, the world is saved, and a cold heart learns to love. A small nothing in the face of mankind, but it is who we are; if we are to grow into our next incarnation, we must become who we are most dramatically.

A few days after meeting with Ram Dass, I had an impulse to go down to the basement at Illuminations, where I had picked up that copy of *Miracle of Love* and discovered a miracle of love. I was searching for something, not knowing what. I looked in cabinets, inside desk drawers. Finally, I pulled opened a drawer underneath one of the work spaces and found the dusty and unopened copy of *The Life of Ramakrishna* by Romain Rolland. As I held the book in my hands . . .

I imagined *we are sitting in the cremation grounds on the banks of the Ganges, just outside the city of Varanasi. It is midnight and the Indian full moon fills the skies. The only sounds are the crackling of burning logs and bones, and the howling*

46

jackals pacing back and forth outside the fire's light. There is a chill in the air, the acrid smell of the fire, and the "India" smell of incense, cooking spices, farts, body odor, garlic, smoke, urine, and the intangible essence of India. We are watching a burning log, keeping warm, remembering that life is fragile. The harmonium begins, finger cymbals clink together, the tabla beats the rhythm as we start to sing, Sitaram Sitaram Sitaram. *The essential "Ramness" of the atmosphere of India, the echoes of the ancient times blend with the spirit and the form, with the essence and the shadow. We are one with Sitaram, there on the banks of the holy river.*

A week later, Mirabai invited me to a company party. All the employees of Illuminations were there, along with their current spouses. John (Krishna), the co-owner of the company, introduced me to his new partner. The woman had such a strange look in her eyes as we shook hands that I felt myself slipping in and out of this plane of awareness into a mysterious magical place where everything is just as it is. This strange woman came up behind me and whispered in my ear, "There ARE natural laws in the universe." Immediately my knees started shaking. I felt that energy again moving up my spine. My entire body twisted and turned with the surge of energy. I closed my eyes and felt stars radiating from the center of my head. Some guys from the shipping room were sitting on the couch watching me. I could feel their amusement at the way I was moving, so I turned slowly to look at them. When I met their eyes, they ceased laughing. I did not know what they were seeing, but their eyes were bulging out of their heads and their mouths were hanging open. It must've been the light of the Maharajji shining through me.

At the end of the party I caught a ride home with a young Indian fellow, Ravi Khanna, who had been traveling with Maharajji the day that Maharajji chose to leave his body. I felt this man's shakti, I felt the shakti of the great teacher, and I fell back into the seat with bliss running through my body.

The next morning, I got up early to go to work. My normal trek was about two miles down Mass Avenue, across the bridge, and then up the Cambridge side of the Charles River, almost to Harvard Square to get to Illuminations. This morning, though, my sense was to take the Mass Avenue bus to Central Square and walk over that way. As I stepped onto the bus, I was dazzled by beams of light shining out of the eyes of all the passengers. Even the bus itself seemed luminescent; everything was transforming into light. Tears filled my eyes as I saw God in all the passengers' eyes.

My second meeting with Ram Dass was poignant. I arrived with *prasad*, an offering to the holy man of a loaf of bread baked by Marg and a bowl of fruit chosen by me. We talked, we looked, we did all we could, but I was so busy looking for the shake, looking for the shakti to move, that it never happened. After a while we sat across from each other in the living room. We talked about my personal life and about Maharajji. I turned my face and fixed my eyes on Ram Dass' beautiful foot. He caught my fascination and lifted his foot and put it down on my lap. I immediately began to massage his feet in the classical Hindu way. I looked across at him. "Ram Dass, are you my guru?"

Ram Dass smiled, "I don't know much about the guru game, but I will play." I became aware in that moment that Ram Dass and his guru Neem Karoli Baba had catalyzed my beginning, my awakening experience.

At one point, Ram Dass and I meditated facing each other, sitting cross-legged, knees touching. I felt myself trying to move higher and higher; finally I looked at Ram Dass and said, "What should I be eating?" He sighed a deep sigh. We stood up and it was time to go.

Earlier in the visit I had given him a Tibetan *mala* (a string of prayer beads) and asked him to bless it. He put it away with some of his precious Maharajji icons and, as I was leaving, he pulled it out and threw it across the room to me. I reached my hand out and felt the mala wrap around my wrist. I received one of his wonderful hugs and we shared a loving goodbye. As I was leaving, he came to the door and said, "Thank Marg for the bread." I got in the car and drove home, filled with the new knowledge that shakti never comes when you expect it; for shakti to move, you must be immersed in your "be here now."

When I got home, Marg and I sat down together on the couch. She asked, "So what happened?"

"Ram Dass thanks you for the bread."

When I said that, I had a vision of the great man, Ram Dass, coming to the door to send a simple message to Marg, the loving kindness that so filled his being, the perfection of his character so refined that he would not let such a simple thing pass without notice. As I thought these thoughts and felt this wonderful love for this magic man, again, right there on the couch, the energy soared, my knees and my teeth chattered, and I was filled with this awe-ful laughter, this deep laugh at the amazing synchronistic perfection of everything, and I began to cry at the beauty—art beyond art beyond art, this beautiful dream of perfection filled with the miracle of a loving heart.

Energy soars, heart expands, the tears and the laughter are the same, all is really love. Love is all there really is, and we keep this between us until we dissolve.

Ram Dass and I talked shorthand on the phone. He would say a few words, I would get it; I would start to speak, he would get it. Our conversations were like jazz musicians riffing to each other. We talked of our lives becoming prayers, and the best way to love. Sometimes we would be silent together on the phone, feeling the purity of our love mingling in this most intimate fashion. One of the great truths he taught me in those days was that there are many relationships deeper, more intimate, than the sexual. The bond between the teacher and the student is the greatest of all.

I asked him, "Baba, what is your job? What does it say on your passport?"

He replied, "My job is to turn your frown into a smile."

I wrote to Baba Hari Dass; he had been with Maharajji in India and was now a teacher for the Western *satsang* (spiritual community) at Mt. Madonna Institute in California. I told him I had seen the face of God and was filled with bliss and love. He wrote back, "How nice that you have attained peace. Now you must retain peace!"

One afternoon, as I sat down to meditate, I silently said to Maharajji, "If you are such a great guru, give me one-pointedness." I began to meditate. After a few minutes I was distracted by a small image of Maharajji in the corner of my inner vision. He said, "Give to me and I'll give to you." I understood. Those words have become the theme of my life. The phrase shows up in many of my songs. "O Lord, you set me free . . . I give to you, you give to me."

Then came the dream, just weeks after first meeting Ram Dass. It is said that when you dream of Maharajji, it is given from HIS will. I believe he sent me this dream:

I was lost in the North End of Boston. My therapist Ellie was there and we were driving in her car, trying to get our bearings. We saw Jay, my other therapist, and picked him up. He also did not know where we were. I jumped from the car and found my way to someone's front door. The house was filled with women in various stages of undress, and they were all calling to me. I thought, "No, I've got to figure out where I am." I crawled out the window into the backyard, through a fence and into Leverett Circle, under the expressway. Sitting in front of an old bodega was a fat Italian man in a sleeveless t-shirt. He looked up at me and pointed across the Charles River at the Bunker Hill Monument, but the tower had transformed. It had become pink and had little minarets sticking out of it. When I saw the monument, I became oriented, saw where I was and knew how to find my way home.

In retrospect, I can see that the dream was Maharajji's message, showing me my life. The little sleeveless man was Maharajji. I was lost but he showed me the way home. It's not that he took me home, but he pointed the way. He showed me the beginning of my *sadhana* (spiritual practices), the beginning of the quest for my real self.

Ram Dass instructed me to study hatha yoga (physical postures) and Vipassana meditation. In order to immerse myself in Vipassana meditation, I scheduled a retreat at the Insight Meditation Society (IMS) Retreat Center in Barre, Massachusetts. Vipassana meditation works like this—you get up early, go sit on your cushion, focus on your breath with mindfulness (being aware without judgment of all the information coming in through your senses) for forty-five minutes. Then you get up and slowly perform walking meditation (as you walk, you think "lifting, moving, placing.") Then back to the cushion for another forty-five minutes. There are short breaks for breakfast and lunch, no dinner.

I had committed to a five-day retreat. At the end of the first day I felt so much frustration that I made plans to send the message home for my partner to call IMS and tell them I had an emergency and had to return home immediately. With a great amount of inner discipline, I refrained from sending that message. I was determined to find a way through. I immersed myself in the practice, each day quieting down, less struggle, streamlining thoughts . . . until the last day of the retreat.

It was a beautiful spring day, so instead of going for the morning meditation, I went for a walk outside on the path that extends out from the Center in the form of a lariat. You walk the short part of the "rope" as you leave the center, then enter the forest to walk the large loop, returning on the initial path back to the center. As I circumambulated, I realized that this hike was a metaphor for the life I was enjoying. We all start in the center, and then we wander through a world of illusion, projection, and fear, ultimately coming back to the center. I heard a mourning dove calling, *"Who, who, who* are you?" I came to a small meadow and lay down flat on my back, staring up at the white clouds floating through the pale blue sky. My heart soared back to the place where the universe is alive with one consciousness. On the periphery of my vision, a small black rain cloud floated over my head and dropped a light sprinkling of sweet water on my body.

I needed to share the wonderful insight I had received with Larry Rosenberg, the Vipassana teacher who was conducting the retreat. I began walking back towards the center on the narrow path. As I turned the corner, there was Larry walking towards me. I said, "Larry, did you know I wanted to speak with you? "

He said, "Normally, at this time of day, I take a nap. But today I felt the impulse to take a short walk. Don't get me wrong, I don't believe in miracles. But come, let's walk and talk."

I told him of my insight with Ram Dass, of the bird flying around the Vipassana center questioning everyone's sense of self. I told him of the small rain cloud and how my heart was expanding. I asked him how to reconcile this new sense of self that was evolving in me. There was this large Self in me that understood through experience the oneness of the universe, but I also felt the small self in me that was filled with petty attachments, desires, and unhealthy behaviors. I asked Larry, "How can these two selves become one?"

Larry said, "You remind me of a good friend of mine, Mel Bucholtz. He's a therapist in Cambridge who has resolved the struggle that you are experiencing."

This completely astounded me. When I was a freshman at Michigan State University, I had a friend named Mel Bucholtz who was a few years older than me. When he was studying psychology in graduate school, we would sit together and have long discussions about Eastern philosophy, relationships, and God. I remember one conversation when Mel said, "I feel so much more comfortable in the East than here."

I said, "Yes, I like New York City much better also." Of course, Mel had something in mind a little bit further east than New York. It turned out that Mel was a good friend of Larry's. The synchronicity implicit in this coincidence led me to Mel's door a few months later. He facilitated the end of my relationship with Marg and eased me into bachelor life.

I began studying Vipassana meditation with Larry, and very quickly began having out-of-body experiences. Long sessions of watching my breath were coupled with the warm fuzziness of "no-thought." I began spending Sunday afternoons with a young Tibetan *tulku* (a reincarnation of a lama who has recently left his body). He used to say, "When Buddha became enlightenment." It took me days to understand he was commenting on the state of enlightenment. A "person" does not become enlightened, but disintegrates into the oneness of enlightenment. He also used to say, "Bring only your questions here; leave what you know at home." He told me that one day I would become a teacher. These days I teach *kirtan* (call-and-response chanting).

Sometimes, when I called Ram Dass, he would tell me of his adventures. This was around the time of his Burma retreat with U Pandita, the foremost master of Vipassana. During his retreat, Ram Dass meditated for eighteen hours a day. At first his mind was focused on his plans, until finally he saw his thoughts floating by on the very periphery of his consciousness. This reminded me of my own experience sitting with Ram Dass. The teacher, U Pandita, asked Ram Dass to note whether he awoke on an in-breath or an out-breath. Can you imagine that level of mindfulness? This insight of one's consciousness floating on the periphery of one's awareness is also consistent with a story Krishna Das told me about his early Maharajji experience. I infer that Maharajji uses this epiphany with many of his students.

After the fourth week of the retreat, Ram Dass' father called him; his stepmother had cancer and he needed to come home. U Pandita said, "Don't go. If you stay, you will become Buddha, you will become enlightened." But Ram Dass could not rest with his stepmother suffering, so he caught the next flight home. Perhaps this delayed his enlightenment, or perhaps it was the perfect karmic act for him and his final awakening.

Months later, Ram Dass asked me to organize a lecture in Cambridge for him. I searched around town for a hall and finally settled on one of the lecture rooms at Harvard. I was happy to facilitate Ram Dass' return to Harvard after they had fired him. The event came off flawlessly. During the lunch break, I went out to my car for a sandwich and a snooze. I felt my love for Ram Dass grow in my heart, until I wrote it down as a poem for him. It was spring and there was a light rain in the air, and the smell of the buds and flowers was intoxicating. As I walked back to the lecture hall, my way was blocked by a car door swinging open. It was Ram Dass. As he stepped out of his car, he took my hand in his and we began to walk towards the building. I took out my poem and I read it to him:

Seeing your face, O beloved
Cleft of stone and saffron,
Chisel your love
With mallet of strength
With edge of bravery.
Doubt not, my beloved,
You are straight as the arrow,
Firmly rooted in the earth,
Ringlets in the sun and clouds,
Sweetly embracing arms
Reaching to God as Michelangelo's secret message.
O beloved,
We are the same person.

He listened to my poem, and we stopped for a silent moment in the rain (the raindrops fell like tears on my page), and he said, "You ARE a *bhakta.*" It warmed my heart greatly to hear him say these words: a bhakta is a true lover of God. I loved Ram Dass so much in that moment. Then we walked into the lecture hall, his hand still in mine. He let go to walk to the front of the hall, then turned and gave me a look, a smile, and a wave. Michelangelo's secret message, written on the ceiling of the Sistine chapel with God reaching out to Adam, giving life to Adam by pointing his one extended finger at him and saying, "Adam, we're all one; we're the same person."

At the end of his lecture, Ram Dass asked all five hundred of us to chant OM together. I let loose my big voice OM, which may have been louder than others. He stopped us. He said, "I did not say chant a blues OM. Just chant OM." And we tried again. This time I held back a little, but it was such a funny, loving, and intimate exchange in front of everyone.

I collected many of Ram Dass' lecture tapes. His stories, sense of humor, insight, and translations of esoteric concepts of *yoga* all drew me closer to him. At the end of one of his lectures, I heard an *ektar*, a one-stringed instrument, part drum, and a deep baritone singing *Jayanti Mangala Kali* (victorious, auspicious, black and terrifying, adorned with skulls).These words sounded like magic. The sound went through me, opened my heart, and started a thought. Music, playing my Les Paul in the nightclubs, had been my life. Somehow, that place and that music did not have a deep home in me anymore.

Music was my life, and then I heard Krishna Das, ektar and all, singing the verses from the *Chandi Path* (the stories of the Divine Mother). I now sing those same verses in honor of Maharajji, Ram Dass, and Krishna Das, and the whole Das *mishbucha* (Yiddish for family) at the beginning of every kirtan. I was so deeply moved by his sound. A few years later I heard Krishna Das' album "Pilgrim Heart" and saw a golden door open. I heard the beauty of the album and knew that I, too, would be leading kirtan. I had found a clear way of unifying my music and spirit. I had found my *dharma* (one's duty in life), my reason for being.

The last time Ram Dass and I were able to spend a few hours alone together, he had sprained his back. He was lying on his bed while I massaged his back and shoulders, easing some of the pain he felt. Then we sat staring at each other for a while. He began to speak, "Larry, the way you are now—calm, centered, strong, confident, humble, loving, alert, so beautiful—this is who you are. Remember this." Before I could speak, he added, "Now talk to me about God."

I did not have to think about what to say. As I massaged his feet I said, "Your request reminds me of my walk to work a few weeks ago. I was listening to one of your lectures on my Walkman, when suddenly I felt this powerful wind fill the trees and wrap itself around me. All the hairs on my body stood on end and I realized that this force was Ram."

When it was time to go, we stood at his front door embracing. He's a very tall man. He leaned over and kissed me on the lips. I received the kiss with all the love in my heart and I will never forget the power of our intimate love.

Although Ram Dass primarily teaches kindergarten, he is not a nursemaid. I must take responsibility for the fact that in the three years that I was close to Ram Dass, I did not develop some of the practices to the degree that Ram Dass suggested. I knew I was not doing the work. One day we were at a retreat. After his discourse, I went over to him and said, "Ram Dass, can I call you?"

He said, "These days when the phone rings, sometimes I answer and sometimes I don't. You can try. But you should know this: I am only a man, and there is only so much I can do." I understood. He was passing me on to the next classroom. He had done all he could for me and now I needed the intensive care unit.

I was silent on the drive home from this visit, angry because I loved him so much and wanted to hang out with him, sad because he had obviously cut me loose, and scared because I felt abandoned and lonely, like when I was little. Within weeks, however, the flow continued—first with Sathya Sai Baba, then Karunamayi, and then Shree Maa, Harihar Ramji, and all the others. Although I did not have contact with Ram Dass on the physical plane for many years after this, not a day passed when I did not think of him and send him my love.

Every year, there is a party celebrating Maharajji's mahasamadhi (Neem Karoli Baba left his body on September 11, 1973) near my home in western Massachusetts. The party is called the NKB Bhandara. A *bhandara* is an event where the guru's devotees cook a giant meal and feed as many people as they can. Neem Karoli Baba was often asked, "How does one become enlightened?" His answer always was, "Feed people!" After he left his body, in celebration of his life, every year his devotees cook a huge meal and feed as many people as wander into the farmhouse. I try to attend each year. I get there early and sit alone in the temple. I sing *Sri Ram Jai Ram*, slow and deep, and, by his grace, he comes and gives me the thrill of horripilation, and I remember. Maharajji's presence is always so tangible at the bhandara.

When I arrived at the bhandara one year, I looked around the grounds. I saw a wheelchair surrounded by a group of people and I knew it was Ram Dass. We had not spoken for ten years, and we had both obviously been through much—a paralyzing stroke for him, a busy time for me with my gurus and my anger. It is said that the sadhu's greatest *siddhi* (power) is the cessation of anger.

I had heard that his memory was impaired. As the crowd lessened, I knelt in front of Ram Dass and we stared into each other's eyes again. I could see that he did not recognize me, but I remained silent. Then, like a light turning on in his face, he suddenly knew me again. He reached up with his hand and pulled my forehead right against his. He pressed our third eyes together in another embrace and, with tears, I whispered, "Baba, Baba, remember. We're the same person, we're the same person."

He asked me, "So, who is your *sadguru* (true guru)?" I had been thinking about this for years. Was it Neem Karoli Baba, or Shree Maa, or Bhagwan Ram, or who? When he asked, though, the answer came to me ringing clear. I said, "Baba, it is you in our next lives." Our eyes remained locked until it was time for me to move on.

Later that night, at kirtan, he was sitting right across from me and the other musicians. Krishna Das was singing. I was playing my guitar very hard and staring at Ram Dass, and he was staring at me. When it was time for him to leave, he backed his wheelchair out of the room and backed up down the hallway so that all I could see of him was his dark outline. He reached his hand into the air and saluted. I bowed my head. There never was a love like Ram Dass and there will never be another like Ram Dass. I know that he was there for me in the beginning, and I know he will also be there at the end. After all, he and I are the same person.

Ram Dass

Chapter 4

SATHYA SAI BABA

What, then, is the essence of kirtan? Its essential purpose is to earn the love of God. Combining one's voice, tune, feeling and rhythm, immersing oneself in the singing, harmonizing the feeling with devotion and love, the sacred words of the song should be an outpouring of love towards God. That alone is devotional singing. --Sathya Sai Baba

Satya Sai Baba holding lingam

One morning, as I was sitting at my desk at Illuminations, just two weeks after my last Ram Dass retreat when he cut me loose, the phone rang. I had moved up inside the company and now they called me the National Accounts Manager. Basically, this meant I had my own office, where I spent my time on the phone calling the big gift distributors and making sales. Illuminations had become a fairly large "corporate" company. When the phone rang, it was always answered by the receptionist at the front desk. But on this day, I watched the light flash on the phone and on impulse I picked up the call.

Marisa Rahm, from Sunrise Point, Arkansas, had found one of our mandala calendars from the early hippy days of Illuminations, when Mirabai and Krishna sold rainbow decals and calendars out of their garage. She was curious about what kind of company published such a thing. She lived with her husband, Seral, and three children on top of Sunrise Point, a mountain in the Ozarks. Seral built the home himself and they pretty much lived off the land. They were devotees of the Afro-haired desert sadhu, Sathya Sai Baba.

Sathya Sai Baba began his guru days as a child. When he was nine years old, he threw down a bunch of lotus flowers and they spelled out "Sai Baba " on the ground. Shirdi Sai Baba was one of India's great nineteenth-century gurus. There are many stories of his miraculous activities and his brilliant teachings. He used to insist on receiving *dakshina* (donations) from the devotees who came to see him. He said, "Give me ten rupees." Then he took those rupees and threw them into the fire. When the devotee protested, he reached into the fire and pulled out the rupees unburned.

Sathya Sai Baba told his students that he was a reincarnation of Shirdi Sai Baba, the second of three incarnations of this enlightened soul. The third Sai Baba was yet to come. There is a theological paradox contained within this theory of Sai Baba's. Many of the great teachings say that once *nirvikalpa samadhi* (full enlightenment) is attained, there are no more rebirths. The Buddhists, however, do suggest the possibility of a *bodhisattva*, someone who has reached nirvana but reincarnates again out of compassion to relieve beings of suffering.

From my days in the blues world, I knew that after the success of Muddy Waters and Howlin' Wolf, Chicago was filled with bands like Little Muddy Waters or Howlin' Wolf Junior. To some extent, I was a bit skeptical of this reincarnation story. When dealing with gurus, however, it is not a bad idea to suspend disbelief in order to get an inside look at what is going on. The next summer, I loaded my Peugeot, put my son in the shotgun seat, turned right at Tennessee, and went to visit Marisa and Seral Rahm in Sunrise Point, Arkansas. We spent a week on top of their mountain, sleeping in our tents and enjoying the incredible sunrises. We did some recording in the studio they had built in their mountaintop ashram, and heard many stories about Sathya Sai Baba and his miracles. Apparently, he could wave his hand and materialize a mala or a finger ring or diamond earrings. He would give these materialized products away to the devotees sitting around him.

One day, while we were driving on the mountain dirt roads, I went over a tree limb and hit a rock so hard that the entire car shook. We got out to look underneath, but everything seemed fine so we drove on. A week later it was time to drive home. Again we loaded the car and prepared for our thirty-hour drive from Arkansas to Boston— a nonstop odyssey of highway, Holiday Inns, and fast food. I had placed a picture of Sathya Sai Baba on my dashboard in front of the steering wheel so that the image was reflected onto the windshield in front of me. We arrived home in front of my apartment in Boston around 10 a.m. As we were unloading, I noticed a small puddle of oil underneath my car.

When we finally settled in, I sat talking with the woman who had been staying at my apartment while I was gone. She said, "Last night I dreamt that you were coming back, and I thought I might see you this morning. But the strangest thing, in the dream you were traveling with your son, but seated next to you was this strange-looking black man with an Afro." I was dumbfounded. I took out the picture I had been carrying and showed it to her. She said, "Yes, that's the guy."

The next morning I took my car over to the mechanic to see about the oil leak. He looked under the car and said, "You have a hole in your oil pan the size of a silver dollar."

I said, "Well, that's interesting. I know that I hit a rock during my vacation in Arkansas, but I drove all the way from Arkansas to Boston and the oil light didn't indicate a problem. I didn't notice any leaking."

He said, "There's no way you could've driven 1500 miles with a hole that size in your oil pan. Your engine would have seized."

I suspended disbelief.

Marisa and Seral came east to sing at the annual New England Sai Baba retreat. They had written and recorded many songs dedicated to Sathya Sai Baba, and they traveled around to regional retreats performing their music and selling cassette tapes. They invited me to bring my guitar and join the band. At that time there were millions of Sathya Sai Baba devotees around the world. His birthday was more celebrated than Christmas in New Zealand. The New England regional retreat had well over a thousand people in attendance, including several hundred from the Boston community. As always happens when my guitar is out, we totally rocked the house. People were standing on their chairs shouting and clapping.

I received an incredible introduction to the Boston Sathya Sai Baba community, which was to be my home for the next seven years. They were a group of about two hundred Indian families, part of the Indian Diaspora, desperate to hold onto the old values of home. They practiced the old ways, and singing *bhajan* was a major part of their spiritual practice. Bhajan is similar to kirtan, yet more complex. The phrases are longer and more complicated; the melodies adhered to the complex *rag* (music scale) and *taal* (rhythmic pattern) of Indian classical music. Bhajans are hymns, songs to God. I was totally drawn to learn this practice, but I had no idea how to pronounce Sanskrit, nor did I understand the music. They were singing call-and-response mantras so quickly that, at first, it sounded to me like nonsense syllables. This was way before Krishna Das' first album came out, long before "kirtan" was a familiar word in the west.

As kirtan is to meditation, bhajan is to prayer. So, while my heart was completely connected to my love for the Divine Mother (partially a result of the very improper loving I received from my Earth Mother), I began attending the regular Sunday afternoon bhajan sessions of the Boston Sathya Sai Baba Center. I watched them sing their bhajans and picked out the melodies on my guitar, and sang with as much intensity as I could. The chorus usually was sung by over a hundred people, and the leaders were often untrained. All the Indian devotees of Sai considered it a privilege to lead a bhajan during one of these sessions. Therefore, many people came forward to lead who had no musical ability. The bhajans could be musically chaotic, with unpredictable key changes and confusion. I was never sure whether a scale was unknown to me or the singer was just off key. But I kept my ears open and my fingers busy. There were only five or six Westerners in the entire community. Soon I was able to comprehend what was happening musically. I created a special tuning for my guitar that adhered to the drone of classical Hindu instruments. Within a few months, I was singing in Sanskrit and beginning to understand the meaning of these bhajans. I was using my power guitar to support the singers and the other musicians.

There was a series of cassette tapes from the Mt. Madonna community, where Baba Hari Dass (once Ram Dass' teacher at Maharajji's ashram) lived. The music on the cassettes included the Hanuman Chalisa, various kirtans, and a bhajan called *Manasa bhajare*, which starts with (in translation): "O mind, worship the Lotus Feet of your God and Supreme Teacher. That will take you safely across the ocean of life and death."

I was beginning to discover how to combine music with my spiritual practice, and I worked hard to learn the bhajan. When the moment arrived for me to lead my first bhajan at the Sai center, I sang *Manasa bhajare* because it was the only one I knew. What I did not know was that it was the first bhajan that Sathya Sai Baba had ever taught. It is said that he composed it. I realized I had stepped into quite a bit of synchronicity. The Sai Baba family was very pleased to hear me sing their anthem as my first choice. Afterwards the leader of the group came up to me and said, "Now we have a new excellent bhajan singer."

However, as my skills developed, my Chuck Berry/Muddy Waters roots started to show through the classical model of bhajan. The Indians in this community, clinging tightly to their old traditions, were not pleased with my "go for the jugular" style of singing. Many times I observed them putting their fingers in their children's ears when I led a bhajan. They called my singing style "Hard Rock Bhajan." However, they did love me and my guitar style, and many of the centers around New England vied for my attendance at their special programs. Since then, I have discovered that most Indians completely understand my kirtan style, especially the gurus.

Mr. Ravindrin was the seventy-five-year-old, white-haired father of my friend, Sundar. Mr. Ravindrin lived at Sai's ashram, *Prasanti Nilayam* (Abode of Peace), in India. When Mr. Ravindrin was forty years old, he worked for the Indian railroad. His then nine-year-old son, Sundar, found a photograph of Sai Baba on the sidewalk. The boy was sure this was a picture of a great soul. He took the picture home and began to sit in front of it, thinking of God. Very shortly thereafter, his father became ill. Mr. Ravindrin was diagnosed with throat cancer, got fired from his job, and was sitting at home waiting to die. Sundar said, "Father, we must go meet this holy man." Mr. Ravindrin was an atheist; he disliked sadhus and holy men very much. He was, however, frightened by his illness, so eventually Sundar convinced him to visit Sathya Sai Baba.

When Mr. Ravindrin arrived at the ashram, he was in a crowd of more than a thousand people. Sai Baba pushed through the crowd up to Mr. Ravindrin. Sai touched him on the forehead, and said, "I cancel the cancer." Through the touch, Mr. Ravindrin was awakened. He was convinced he was healed. He returned home and began to meditate. Eventually, in order for him to return to work, he had to see a doctor. The doctor was astounded to discover the cancer gone. It is also true that, after Sai Baba's touch, Mr. Ravindrin developed the most powerful bhajan singing voice. Prior to the touch, he never sang. His devotion grew and finally he moved to the ashram. Every morning at 4 a.m., he and a few other sadhus would sing verses from the *Bhagavad Gita*, filling the ashram with the most heavenly music.

Mr. Ravindrin took over the responsibilities of the carpool at the ashram. One day, he had a terrible toothache. (When I met him, he had no teeth, but that did not mitigate the power of his singing voice.) He knew that the next day he had to drive to Bangalore to pick up some auto parts, so he sat in front of his meditation table and prayed, "Sai Baba, you must help. You must make this toothache stop hurting if you expect me to drive to Bangalore tomorrow." Immediately upon completing this prayer, there was a knock at his door. He found a small man standing in front of him, who said, "Sai Baba says, 'Give me the keys!'" Sai Baba did not let Mr. Ravindrin drive again for two years.

While visiting Sundar in Boston, Mr. Ravindrin took me under his tutelage and grilled me on pronunciation, melody, and, most importantly, *bhava* (emotional and spiritual energy,

Ray Charles-like soul). We spent many hours singing in unison in order to perfect my melody and pronunciation. When it comes to mantras, pronunciation is key. Mispronouncing mantras renders them useless. Mr. Ravindrin's last words to me were, "It is *madtha pidtha*, Larry, not *mata pita*.

One day, all us Westerners were riding in a car to the South Shore of Boston for a bhajan session. We had been asked to take an older Indian woman, Mani Bashyam, with us. She sat quietly in the back of the car while we talked about Sai Baba and bhajan. None of us had any idea who Mani Bashyam was. Slowly, though, we got to know her. She was born a Brahmin in the same village as Sai Baba. They were the same age, and they grew up together as friends. She told us many stories of how this saint behaved in his youth and teenage years.

One story concerned a day when around seven children were making sand castles in the desert sand. One of the boys said, "I am hungry. I wish I had some sweets." Sai Baba reached deep into the sand, and when he withdrew his hand he held a silver plate filled with candies, no sand. This story was related to us by Mani, who I am sure would never lie or exaggerate, so I believe this really happened.

Mani had been trained to sing and play harmonium from the time she was two years old. When she sang, tears ran down her cheeks, and we were also moved to shed big bhakti tears. For the year that she spent in Boston, I spent as much time as I could around Mani, listening to her sing and tell stories. I would accompany her on my guitar. She once said, "You know, Larry, I can't think of anything that I want. I seem to have no desires." As the Indians got to know her better, they occupied more of her time. However, I assumed the responsibility of being her driver, so whenever there was a bhajan session somewhere, I picked up Mani and she told me stories as we traveled.

We finally found out, through research in an old Telegu storybook about Sathya Sai, that Mani had written the words and music to the *vibhuti* (sacred ash) song that is sung at all the Sai Centers across the world; she was actually famous. Mani Bashyam worked with my singing voice and my pronunciation. She taught me that power and humility are not mutually exclusive, and that a stone can be your guru. (She meant that the guru is a perfect mirror, reflecting back to you your own divinity.) She taught me how to sing from my love center.

At a certain point a terrible story came out of India. The news reported that four young men had attacked Sai Baba's ashram, broken into his private living quarters, murdered his cook, and attempted to murder him. They were stopped by the ashram police and quickly taken outside the ashram gates and shot. We could not understand how this could happen in the home of an enlightened saint. Surely, if Sai Baba was able to materialize a necklace, cure cancer, couldn't he stop a horrible event like this? As we all mused about this terrible gossip, a message came from the ashram. Sai Baba instructed all devotees to stop discussing the events at the ashram and to behave as if nothing has happened. This seemed extremely strange to me, even cult-like. What could've been the boys' motive? Why were the boys murdered? Why were we silenced?

Shortly after that, a miracle occurred in my life. My parents sent me three thousand dollars, the result of a small inheritance. I put eight hundred dollars into my Peugeot, and the rest into a round-trip plane ticket to India. I wanted to see for myself what India looked like, I wanted to kiss the ground of the homeland, and I wanted to spend time at Sai Baba's ashram to get a feeling for what he was really like.

A few weeks before I left, my friend Patty told me a story about a group of boys, including her son, who had gone to Sai Baba's ashram. One by one, the boys went into Sai Baba's office to receive a private interview. One of the boys came screaming out of the room claiming that Sai Baba had touched him inappropriately. The boy was inconsolable, and the trip to India was cut short. The adult leader of this group of boys conducted an "investigation" and found that Sai Baba had done nothing inappropriate and that this must have been the result of a strong imagination. I suspended any judgment until I could see for myself.

I purchased my plane tickets, got my shots, bought all the equipment I would need, and shaved my head to prevent head lice. Now I was ready for India. My friends gathered around in support of my journey. I received gifts from many of the Sai devotees; they had great expectations that I would receive much blessing and transformation. I was looking forward to my trip with great anticipation. I wrote a song called "Soon I will see You," and dreamed of India. Just three days before I was to board my plane, I stopped at a traffic light in the rain and a drunk driver careened around the corner and smashed into the back of my Peugeot, destroying it. He backed up, sped away, and left me standing in the rain. I limped my car home and sat deliberating my choice: I could cash in my ticket to India and repair my car (no collision insurance), or I could tow my car to the junkyard and go to India. It really was no decision at all.

The mystery began as soon as the plane floated over Mumbai, the lights of the city looking more like open fires than street lights. As I left the terminal, the physical sense of India hit me—the odors, the smoke, the people—and the very life of it knocked me to my knees. It felt like awakening from a dream. I went from the International Airport to the Domestic Airport several miles away, at 2 a.m. India time. It was the middle of the night, but Mumbai looked like New York City at rush hour. People filled the streets, vendors, families setting up house on the sidewalk, buildings made up of flattened tin cans. I saw men huddled in the darkness around burning auto tires, trying to keep warm. I saw the Sai Baba Hotel, which looked very dangerous to me—dark, dirty, broken down.

Arriving at the domestic airport, I discovered it was mostly empty, the shops closed, people sleeping on benches. I found a good place to rest, as I had a five-hour wait before my plane left for Bangalore. Suddenly, three intimidating Indian policemen approached me. In India, the police wear military-like uniforms and carry big rifles. The first policeman came up to me, "Passport and ticket, please." He was not smiling. I was more than a little paranoid. I was not happy about giving my precious papers to this strange, menacing soldier. I held one side of the ticket and passport and he held the other. He verified I was an American and I was going to Bangalore, and for the first time he looked at me. He saw the mala around my neck and suddenly his face transformed. He said, in this very friendly tone, "Oh, Sai Baba! I myself have becoming a devotee of the first Sai, Shirdi Sai. Come sir, sit over here. I will watch out for you, keep an eye on you, and I'll wake you in time for your flight." However, he forgot to wake me for my flight and I was lucky to make it on time.

The plane trip into Bangalore (a dog trotting across the runway delayed our flight) was smooth, and the cab ride to Prasanti Nilayam ($15 US for the ninety-mile drive) was exhilarating. At first I was thinking, "This cabbie could drive me to a back street in Bangalore, kill me, and steal my money and passport." But even though he was somewhat amused by this "western yogi," the driver was respectful. He called me Tukaram Maharaj, after a famous Indian saint.

We stopped along the way for a cup of *chai* (black tea with spices). I saw the barista take a filthy fingerprint-laden glass, dip it into a bucket of brown, brackish water, pick up a cloth that smelled like it was soaked in poop, and dry the glass. Then he filled it with a brown liquid he called chai and handed me the cup. I sauntered behind the taxi and discreetly poured it into the dust.

At this point, an ancient decrepit woman came up to the taxi with a little four-year-old girl, begging money in the traditional Indian way. As anyone who has been to India knows, the Indian way to beg is silently, persistently, achingly, sufferingly, to reach out palms facing the sky, uttering a pathetic, "Uh,uh,uh." Here was this old Indian lady begging from me and, at same time, teaching her great-grandchild the family craft. This is an aspect of the Indian caste system, which determines one's lifework at birth. I imagine the begging tradition in this family went back eons. One interesting Indian homily is, "May my hands always be like this (speaker assumes the traditional Indian prayer posture, with palms together pointing toward the chin), and never like this (hands out, empty palms pointing toward the sky)."

Finally we arrived at the town of Puttaparthi. The ashram, *Prasanti Nilayam*, rose out of the desert like some magnificent wedding cake, all pastels, towers, statues (a sixty-foot-high Hanuman) and thousands of visitors from all over the world, all colors, all sizes and shapes. I was in heaven.

Here are some excerpts from the journal I kept of my India experience:

Getting *darshan* (sight of a holy person)

There's a lottery here to see how close you can get to Sai Baba. The room holds 20,000 people. Sai comes out and walks around a little and then goes back, twice a day. People begin arriving outside the gate in long lines at 4 a.m. Everyone angles for their "lucky row" in hopes of getting a low lottery number and getting a chance to speak with Sai Baba—you get up near the front, Sai comes over your way, you ask for an interview, and the prize is being granted a private interview. All over the ashram, you can hear voices calling after him, "Interview, Swami? Interview?" Sai's response is "Go for the innerview." Just before the gates open, a tall Indian in a turban comes out, gives a long speech in Telugu (every word in Telugu seems to end with goo), draws numbers out of a hat, and when your row number is called, you get to go into the mandir (Hindu temple). Since the shootings, however, in order to enter the mandir you must pass through a metal detector. Could Sai Baba not dematerialize weapons?

I arrive, I sit, days pass—third row, sixth row, tenth row. Finally, the morning arrives when I am sitting right up front, and I begin to develop this pain in my belly. It gets worse and worse until I can no longer bear the pain. A small man sitting behind me asks me what is wrong. I tell him my stomach is burning like fire. He reaches into his wallet and takes out this tiny piece of paper, folded the way Americans fold their cocaine. But this is not a drug in the normal sense; it is vibhuti, sacred ash from Sai Baba himself. (Many gurus give this ash as a gift. It has no material value, it is just ashes, but it is instilled with the guru's shakti and therefore has great value. Sai claimed to materialize vibhuti ash, but a friend once saw little round pellets of ash between his fingers before this "materialization.") He takes out a little vibhuti, puts it on my forehead, then reaches around me and begins rubbing my belly. Immediately, the pain disappears and I fall into a deep meditative state. Finally, I hear the little man say, in this most delightful song-like voice, "Swami coming, Swami coming." Sai comes down the aisle, but stops before he reaches us and turns back the other way.

One night, I am thinking I need some direct sign from Sai. If he is going to help me grow to the next step, I need him to come over to me in the next darshan, I need him to come right up to me, take this letter I am writing to him, and bless me. Then I will know . . . marry the woman? change my lifestyle? make my move?

So the next morning at 4 a.m. my lottery number puts me in the fourth row, and I figure, no hope, I will never get close enough for him to bless me. Then I see Baskar sitting almost in *front of me in the first row. (There are 15,000 people in the room today, and I am sitting next to this guy who I met yesterday in the chai shop, too much coincidence.) He says, "Larry, come and take my spot."*

I say "No no, Baskar. This is all about love. You got the first row, you keep the spot." At this point, the fellow sitting in front of me in the third row jumps up and runs out into the middle of the aisle and sits down. He is descended upon by the seva dals (guru police) and dragged off, and I take his spot in the third row. Then the one in front of me in the second row apparently gets a major call of nature, because he jumps up and runs out of the room, so there I am now in the second row. Baskar is laughing at all this, and all the others sitting in the front row have also been watching and listening. Then, just as Sai enters the room, they turn around and say, "Hey, there's room up front," and they all push to the sides and make a spot for me in the front row. Now I am sitting next to Baskar. This is all just too much (or, as Ram Dass would say, "just enough").

Sai turns the corner. He's walking down the other side of the aisle and I am thinking, well, no contact today. He passes us by, walks about 25 feet down the other side of the aisle, then stops, turns, and comes directly over to me and Baskar. He says to Baskar, "When you finish school, come and work in my hospital." How did Sai know he was a medical student? Then he turns to me. I am dumfounded at these proceedings, so I sit there speechless. He reaches down and takes the letter out of my hands (he takes the letters, and the mythology is that he grants the requests). He lifts up his robe for me to touch his feet (a custom of great respect, rarely given). He places his hand on my head and blesses me. The next thing I remember is that everyone has left the room and I am sitting alone on the stone cold floor.

73

The living conditions

The food deal here at the ashram is very interesting. There is a Western-style kitchen where for about 25 cents you can have a three-course meal with a lassi. It is Indianized Western food, which makes the mashed potatoes "interesting" and the vegetables "different." The commercial shops in the bazaar around the ashram advertise "pizza" and "hamburgers," but both are quite unlike anything I have ever seen before. I feel very much at home here in the Western kitchen. There is a sign on the wall, "Before you speak, ask: Is it the truth? Is it kind? Does it improve upon the silence?"

The Indian kitchen is quite a different story, filled with unknown dishes of various colors, the only consistency is the fiery hot spices. The one time I ate there, I experienced burn blisters on my lips from the chilies. Can anyone explain why the hottest food on the planet is called chili? The Indian kitchen is an adventure of flavors, pains, and diarrhea—authentic South Indian food!

Illness last night, began with a non-smoker's cough. Took my malaria pill at 9 and woke up at 3 with a dizzy fever and a cough that tastes like blood. Not sure if it's something in the pill or in my lungs, but I am sick sick sick. My right leg is hurting so I walk with a limp, my left foot is not healing (the sandal wore it raw) and I have mosquito bites everywhere. My right hand is swollen. Bought some cough medicine and it smells and tastes terrible!

Sometimes India feels like 5,000 dirty men, sneezing, coughing, farting, and talking in a hot thick cloud of red dust, incense, garlic, mosquitoes, farts and BO. The bazaar here is amazing. Thirty rupees to the dollar and a rupee is worth a dollar. Pictures of Sai Baba, Sai Baba incense, bhajans blaring out tinnily over cheap speakers hung up over the bazaar from all the stucco kiosks that sell cassette tapes for around $1 each, vendors selling powders of all colors to be mixed with water and used as *cosmetics, a fellow sitting in the mud making sandals, and every now and then a giant yak-like creature comes barreling down the street and you better get out of the way.*

You can get a shave for ten cents and it's always with a "new" blade. (With a new blade, there is no chance of acquiring AIDS). You can buy all kinds of clothing, shawls of the finest cotton and silk, have suits made (Indian style); you can get anything you want at Sai Baba's bazaar, and it's all at ten cents on the dollar. I am accumulating things so quickly—a beautiful silk shirt, a bag full of new malas, a ton of incense, a statue of Hanuman, and many jewels and treasures for my woman friend. I have more than 50 cassette tapes of bhajans. I have to buy a new suitcase.

One of my shed mates decided to buy a bag of candy and hand it out to the village kids. I joined him. As we entered one of the back streets in the little village, he opened the bag and began handing out candy. More and more kids kept coming from everywhere, from out of the windows, the doorways. I was so surprised to see the children becoming violent. Soon we were buried in a sea of five-year-old's all fighting for a piece of candy. As I extricated myself, I looked back and it seemed like an angry ant hill, all these children, all this noise.

The days are winding down, five to go and I wish it were 50. This morning I got a front row seat, and Sai came down the row on my side all the way up to the soul next to me. Then he turned without a glance and went to the other side. He flipped me a piece of candy, however. Darshan in the afternoon was quick and quite painless, but at one point he turned around and gave me the strangest look. I don't have any idea what he was saying, but I felt a chill up my spine, and my eyes shut.

Then, in the chai shop for a cold drink, these five young Indian men, Baskar and his friends—only Baskar speaks English—come in and sit down all around me. They buy me some chapatis (Indian bread) *and we talk about Sai and the USA. When*

I told them I sold my electric guitar to help finance the trip, they warmed up considerably. They thought this was a wonderful thing to do. They invited me to go with them to the outskirts of the city to do some service at Sai Baba's farm, where they were planting coconut trees. A field, mountains in the background, an old sadhu sitting in the dirt, Sai's milk cows mooing at us—the real India, the sounds and smells, the visions of eternal peace, love, one human family, one thought, one love. They gave me a papaya and sent me on my way.

Leaving India

There was no leaving India—the cab that didn't show up to take me to the airport; the other one that did have all the Western sadhus in it. There was the sweet/sour buttermilk that eased my cramps (the papaya gave me dysentery), the expensive cotton shirt from the store in the "5-star hotel," Bombay airport at 1 a.m., the mosquitoes, the four-hour wait for the plane to leave, sitting all together Indian style. There was the woman of amazing beauty, a veil over her face, who got me the buttermilk. She seemed quite ordinary until she draped the veil over her hair and suddenly her face changed; I think she was a secret goddess. Then the terminal in Amsterdam. After the 10-hour flight from Bombay, I spent $25 to rent a shower stall, and for the first time in two months I washed my body with hot water.

After a few hours under the shower, I dressed in clean clothes and walked into the terminal. I was hoping to have a wonderful cup of Dutch coffee and a croissant. As I entered the giant terminal, I was confronted with the 30-foot-tall billboard of a naked woman holding a can of coffee, complete frontal nudity. I realized with a shock that I had not had a sexual thought in weeks! Probably the first time I had taken such a break since I was six years old.

Then I am back in Boston. Waiting for the dogs to inspect my bags, seeing the face of my lover in the crowd, stepping from

76

the airport into the bitter cold February weather, driving past McDonald's, the Stop & Shop, the neat, trimmed yards, and the powerful materialist wealth machine of the American lifestyle. I thought of The Air-Conditioned Nightmare *by Henry Miller, and the sweet, small, saint of Dakshineshwar and the waves of bliss that washed him clean.*

Actually, I never left India, and I am still sitting in Ramakrishna's room, laughing uproariously at some little joke, listening to the words, like jewels, which awaken the heart, singing with old friends (we've done this together for so many lives) . . . God singing God's names to God, Brahma's hand moves, time is of the essence, we turn towards home.

There were many stories abounding about Sai Baba's miraculous doings. One story had a Westerner having a heart attack at Sai's ashram. The fellow apparently died at the hospital. His wife put a picture of Sai on his chest, and three hours later the man came back to life. This was reported across the world as a Sai Baba miracle. Later, however, it was investigated by an impartial group, and it was found out the dead man never was really dead, probably just asleep.

Another story had a young Australian boy getting a private interview with Sai. During the interview, Sai, through his spiritual power, intuited that the boy's mother was very sick back in Australia. Sai turned one wall of his office into a Star Trek transporter and sent the boy back to Australia right through the wall. This story swept through the American community as proof of Sai's god-like power. Again, though, it was determined that this really never happened.

Then there was the story that Sathya Sai Baba had announced the end of the Kali Yuga and the beginning of the Prema Yuga. (In Indian history, time is divided into *yugas*, exceedingly long periods of time. There are four yugas, each one holding a grosser consciousness than the previous. Krita, Treta,

Dwarpa, and Kali. We are currently in the Kali Yuga, the most materialistic period of time. Sai's Prema Yuga, the Age of Love, sounded like something Satya Sai Baba made up). Oftentimes, word came down from on high about world changes, or new general community rules. When we heard that the Kali Yuga was over and we were entering a period of divine love, there were celebrations throughout the satsang. Many of the local Boston community were saying how different they felt; they could sense the change, the beginning of the epoch of love. Shortly after the celebrations wound down, it was announced that Sai Baba never said it; it was a rumor spread by unknown persons at the ashram.

While I was at the ashram, a story spread like wildfire about a young boy in North India who became ill and died. The mother sat on her porch grieving with the boy's corpse lying before her. A Sai Baba devotee happened along the road and he had with him a picture of Sai Baba coughing up a silver Shiva *lingam* (an egg-shaped stone said to represent Lord Shiva, see the photo at the top of this chapter). He placed it on the dead boy's chest and the boy came back to life. The specific picture was available at the ashram store, and I had a great time standing in a long line waiting to buy my three copies of this picture. Since all 20,000 of us staying at the ashram wanted that picture, it was rationed. I went back the next day to buy three more, and the sales fellow remembered me and said, "You bought yesterday, no pictures today." I did bring those three pictures home, had them copied, and gave one to everyone in my Boston community, just in case one of us dropped dead.

Back home, I continued my Sunday afternoon meetings with the Sai Baba community. We also met three or four times during the week for extended bhajan programs and delicious meals. I continued learning bhajan, and having my Boston "little India" experience. Every Wednesday night, the Westerners would get together for informal conversation; we'd sing a little, drink tea, and have satsang.

A few years later the scandal broke at Sai Baba's ashram that could not be denied. First there was the shooting in Sai Baba's personal quarters at the ashram. When the full story came out, we heard that four of the graduates of Sai Baba's elementary school had attacked Sai Baba's home with the goal of murdering him. Their statement was that Sai was sexually abusing the students, and they were on a mission to stop this behavior. The stories were all over the Internet. Boys who were living at the Sai Baba elementary school were complaining that Sai Baba was abusing them. Some of the stories were so compelling it was hard to discredit them. Finally, the truth came to me in the form of a first-hand story from someone I loved. Alaya, the young son of Marisa and Seral from Sunrise Point, was interviewed in a local Arkansas newspaper. When I read the story, I was horrified. I knew this boy to be absolutely truthful. Below is a paraphrase of his newspaper interview.

"Every year, my parents, my sisters, and I would travel to India and receive very special treatment from Sai Baba. My father had a personal relationship with Sai since he was a young teenager. My parents taught us that Sai Baba was God, the father, as Jesus was God, the son. We would go to India, my parents would get private interviews, and Sai would sometimes be alone with me in the interview room. One year, as my parents were packing for the annual visit, I said I would not go to India. My parents were concerned. They asked why. They knew I had been receiving such special treatment from Sai Baba—private interviews, affectionate hugs, and special opportunities at the ashram. Finally I had to tell them. Sai Baba had been touching me in a bad way. He wanted to put his fingers in bad places."

This really hit home to me. Although I was already moving on from the Sai center and the related gossip, I had not completely broken with Sathya Sai Baba. But I knew this boy, and I knew that these rumors were irrefutably true, so I had to take this as a lesson that, as Shree Maa says, "As long as you are in a body, you have more to learn." Many gurus become intoxicated with money, power, and/or sex. The karma they create is immeasurable. The higher you evolve, the greater your fall. Sathya Sai Baba told all his devotees that he would live until ninety-six, and shortly after his death, the third avatar, Prema Sai Baba, would be born. However, Sai Baba died a little bit earlier than his forecast (he was eighty-four), and so far, there is no appearance of the third incarnation. While I understand that it is not for me to judge, my sense is that when Sai was young, he did have some spiritual attainment, but as he got older, he appeared to have slipped.

The Sai community gave me the great gifts of satsang and bhajan. I am so grateful, and thankful, and, in spite of all, I give thanks to Sathya Sai Baba, who presided over my teachings. As has been said, however, "Open heart, open eyes."

Chapter 5

MATA AMRITANANDA MAYI

Darling Children, to gain concentration in this spiritually dark age, bhajan (kirtan) is better than meditation. By loud singing, other distracting sounds will be overcome and concentration will be achieved. If kirtan is sung with one-pointedness, such songs will benefit the singer, the listener, and also Mother Nature. Such songs will awaken the listener's mind in due course. Kirtan is a spiritual discipline aimed at concentrating the mind on one's Beloved Deity. Through that one-pointedness, one can merge in the Divine Being and experience the Bliss of One's True Self. By letting the mind expand in the sound of divine chanting, each one can enjoy the peace born of one's inherent divinity. --Mata Amritanandamayi

Mata Amritanandamayi

Mata Amritanandamayi is a world teacher of the highest degree who has dedicated her life to God. She was born into a small family in Kerala, South India. From early on her leanings were towards God, and she offered teachings and healings to the local villagers. Her parents were told of this, but they discounted the stories and subjected *Ammaji* (beloved spiritual mother) to significant abuse, both physical and mental. She was forced to

81

do all the cleaning in the house, and was occasionally beaten for not meeting appropriate standards. Because the villagers were bringing stories to her parents, Ammaji's father eventually spoke to her, "If you are a saintly person, perform for us a miracle."

Ammaji said, "Miracles are not good. My job is uplifting the downtrodden, not making miracles. But in order to make all realize what is happening in this body, just once, I will offer a miracle. Everyone gather here tomorrow morning."

The next day all the villagers gathered outside Ammaji's home. Her parents and the rest of her family were there, ever so skeptical. Ammaji said, "Please take this big copper bowl down to the river and bring me a bucket full of water." A few boys went off with the bowl down to the river and came back with it full to the brim. Now Ammaji asked, "Please take this bowl into the kitchen and cover it with a cloth." It was done as she asked. Ammaji said, "Now bring the bowl outside and give everyone a cup full of the contents."

As the cover was removed, everyone was amazed to see a wonderful Indian pudding filling the bowl. Ammaji's parents were shocked. Ammaji's mother began spooning out cupsful to the villagers. Although there were more than five hundred villagers receiving the Mother's prasad, the bowl never became empty and everyone got a cup full of the holy food. Her parents were convinced, but they continued to abuse her anyway until it was finally time for Ammaji to start out on her own.

Ammaji began coming to the United States toward the end of the twentieth century. When she first came to Boston, there were only a few devotees. The early darshans were so intimate. The programs were in an old Greek Orthodox temple, and hundreds of us would pack in. Her program began with kirtan. She is the greatest *kirtan walli* (female kirtan leader), singing all the traditional kirtans and composing many new ones. Her band is composed of the best musicians in India. At 3 a.m. when they sing Shiva kirtans, the energy is so intense all the *chakras* (energy centers in the body) are stimulated.

During her third visit, several of the most amazing events took place. The temple filled early. As we walked in the front door, we encountered a large Indian-style bazaar. There was food cooking, stalls selling bangles and flowers, and tables with dozens of *murtis* (statues of deities) for sale. Soon the room was filled with about two thousand people. It was one of those events where you run into the friends you only see once a year from all the different communities, the different satsangs, the different yoga centers. The spiritual community of Boston was there. When the room was full, we all stood and chanted Ammaji's mantra as she came in the room. She walked through the crowd, occasionally stopping to bless someone with a tap on the top of the head. I felt an implosion like fireworks as she stroked my crown chakra.

She climbed the dais, sat in meditation, and the room grew silent. Ammaji has the ability to expand her aura to tremendous proportions. I felt a warm purple glow begin to surround me as I sat in her aura. Soon all I saw was her sweet face; the rest of the material world had been lost in a sea of purple. Then she began to sing and her voice filled the room as she sang the lead part on a Krishna kirtan. All two thousand of us sang the response. The energy spun like a tornado higher and higher until Ammaji threw her head back and almost shouted in a laughing voice, "Ma!Ma! MA!" I could not believe the power and the joy that arose within me as my senses received the amazing power of her shakti, through her voice, through her aura, through her love.

Then Ammaji gave a short discourse, translated by one of her swamis. The words were simple. She talked about the power of love, the need for sadhana and the need for a spiritual teacher to lead you down the dangerous path of awakening and enlightenment. After her discourse, all of the *seva dals* began bustling around the room preparing for Ammaji's hugging darshan. Somehow all of us pushed and squeezed into a long processional line that began at Ammaji's feet and ended way back at the doorway to the hall. I was with my friends, Chris and Claire, in about the middle of the line. It was quite a wonderful feeling to be surrounded by so many conscious people, all working to live loving lives, sharing the love of an enlightened teacher, and all of us loving each other real good.

Ammaji began giving her hugs, each of us getting a few seconds sitting in her lap, receiving her kisses, and listening to the sweet mantra, "Ma, Ma, Ma," which she whispered in each ear. My friend Chris was a devout devotee of Sathya Sai Baba. Chris had been to India many times and had become very close to Sai. Soon it was time for Chris to receive a loving hug. As he inched his way towards her on his knees, she reached out her arms and took him close against her. She stroked his forehead, and whispered in his ear, "Sai Baba, Sai Baba, Sai Baba."

Chris thought, "How on earth did she know that?" Then he thought, "Of course, the greatest saints have access to the *Akashic Records.*" The Akashic Records is a plane of consciousness where everything that has ever happened, is happening, or will happen is "written" in a metaphoric "book." Some with awakened *kundalini* energy (the spiritual energy that sits at the base of the spine) have the ability to put their consciousness into this plane and see the future, the past, and the present.

As Ammaji was giving darshan, the kirtan band was rocking out with different lead singers. Everyone poured their hearts out as they sang, facing the Divine Mother, offering her their love in the form of bhakti, of music. At one point, I heard a familiar voice leading the kirtan—Bhagavan Das. I had never met him but I was very familiar with his music. He was the fellow who introduced Ram Dass to Neem Karoli Baba. He traveled all over India with his ektar—the instrument was used as a drone before the harmonium was invented—and everywhere he went the doors would open up for him and his beautiful singing voice. He reminded me of Murshid Sam, an American Sufi who sang his *wazifas* (Islamic mantras) so beautifully that wherever he went in the Middle East he was welcomed. Little did I know that my destiny also included this gift.

Bhagavan Das' kirtan was one of the very best. I moved in close and sang with him for an hour. When he was finished, I went over to him and gave him an almost blushing "*Namaste*. . . me . . . Ram Dass . . . kirtan . . ." (*Namaste* is a greeting, meaning "I honor the aspect of you that is one with God.") He hugged me and all I remember is that he was soaked in sweat and then so was I. This seems to have been an omen. Although I played in his band for a while after that, things happened and he could no longer come to Northampton, so we never got very close. Bhagavan Das did, however, give me a very important lesson in leading kirtan. Once, when I was playing guitar in his band, I asked him, "How do you want to be accompanied? Shall I play chords, or shall I play the melody, or do you want me to just drone?"

He looked me up and down and said, "I don't care what you play, just keep it simple because I don't want anyone listening to you!" In other words, kirtan is not about fancy musicianship; it is about meditation.

It was now my friend Claire's turn for darshan with Amma. As she crawled up into Ammaji's arms, as requested, she handed her glasses to one of the attendants and surrendered herself to Ammaji. As usual, Ammaji stroked her forehead, whispered secrets into her ears, and installed a small taste of her amazing shakti into Claire's heart. After the hug, Claire turned to the attendant to get her glasses back. When she put them on, she said to the attendant, "These are not my glasses."

85

The attendant said, "Yes, yes, those are the glasses you handed me."

Claire took the glasses off, looked at them, put them back on again, took them off, and exclaimed, "My God, I can see perfectly without them!"

The attendant laughed. "Oh, that happens all the time." It took a few days for her vision to return to its usual abnormal state.

Then it was my turn to get a hug. Sometimes there are pivotal moments in one's life, wherein an experience, a thought, or flash of light can change everything. These moments occur frequently in the presence of a great saint. Ammaji gave me one of my most precious possessions, an insight that changed my total perspective and gave me a clue to finding the truth. When I moved towards her, she grabbed the back of my head and pushed my face right down between her legs. She held me there for almost a minute against her *yoni* (vagina). There were no thoughts in my head. After a time, I felt her lift me, bend her head towards me, kiss my cheek, and whisper in my ear, "Ma, Ma, Ma." As I moved back, her eyes were fixed on mine, mine were fixed on her. I said, "Ammaji, may I ask a question?" Her attendant nodded yes and I asked, "How can I overcome my addictive behaviors?"

She gave me a reply that expressed the entire spiritual path in one sentence. Ammaji said, "Your addictions are like combs for a bald head."

What a funny way to say it! I realized I had been scratching a wound on my soul that no longer existed. The wound had healed long ago, yet my vestigial behavior continued to be a manifestation of this wound, this negative subconscious thought form, that I had installed in my head in childhood. Then, in her incredible profundity, she spoke the truth: "The medicine for your illness lies in the space between your thoughts!"

That is the key. The first goal of all yogic practice is to quiet the thinking mind. We sit and watch our breath, or chant the mantra, or watch the candle flame, all with the goal of first developing "one-thought mind." Then, when we can focus our minds on one thought for more than ten seconds, we begin to perceive the quiet truth of the space between the thoughts. Those words, the recognition that my happiness and freedom lay in the space between my thoughts, moved me into a totally new direction. I decided that *japa*, the repetition of God's names—whether using a mala in silent repetition or singing the names at the top of my lungs with a group of like-minded sadhus—was a way to access the beautiful silence that truly does exist. I found that within the silence is the voice of God.

We receive information from our chakras—the energy centers that are actually sensory perception organs on the higher planes of consciousness. Each chakra is activated by the kundalini as it rises in the spine, giving us a closer perception of reality. There is no question that we, with our five senses, perceive only a fraction of what's really out there, and the chakras fill in the blanks. The information is fed to our brains in the space between our thoughts, so we must quiet our thoughts to perceive it.

Adyashanti, a great Zen teacher, once said, "When I was young I was shocked to discover that my parents actually believed their thoughts!" Thoughts are simply electric impulses running through the brain, some useful, some detrimental. The most effective way of avoiding destructive behaviors and circular negative thought forms spinning through the brain is to recognize that our thoughts are, for the most part, not who we are and are not useful for receiving love and bliss.

Great sages have the ability to express everything concisely and perfectly. There is a Zen patriarch's poem that says: "The great way is easy for those with no preferences." No preferences! So simple and yet so difficult. I once asked

Cambodia's great saint, Maha Goshananda, who lived near me in Western Massachusetts until he left his body, "How does one become enlightened?"

This man, the head of the Cambodian Buddhist community, the Dalai Lama of Cambodian Buddhism, answered, "Enlightenment is easy, just don't compare!" Again, how simple; that's all, just don't compare. I am so busy comparing my left hand to my right hand I can only imagine living in a world where everything is equal and there is no need for comparison because all is one.

Later that night, during the hugging, the Boston satsang led kirtan. The group could sing but they did not have a musician, so they asked me to play guitar. Around 2 a.m. we were shuffled onto the stage near Ammaji while she gave darshan to the thousands in line in front of her. The stage gave me a perspective on the event. Sitting behind her, I saw a sea of people in this long line, all waiting for the hug, all connected in the rhythm of love vibrations emanating from this great Divine Mother. I watched the faces on each one as they surrendered to her arms, awash in her sea of love. Each approached her with a clear personality, and each, as they entered her, lost all appearance of self. I saw nothing but smiles of bliss and heard only sighs of love. This was so similar to standing behind Ram Dass after one of his lectures.

Our group began to sing a kirtan half-heartedly. Some nervousness and plain lack of ability left them a little adrift. I did my best to support on guitar, offering them the melody lines, keeping a strong rhythm, but things quickly went downhill. After they finished the third kirtan, they clearly had run out of songs, so they turned to me and asked if I could lead a kirtan. I had finished writing an English bhajan for Ammaji, "Flowers in the Stream." Without even thinking, I began to sing my new bhajan. The sound man began turning up my mike until the whole room was filled with my voice. *"Amma, we're all flowers floating in the stream, each one the same, O holy Bhavani, endless are your names."* My eyes were closed in my usual kirtan trance, but afterwards a friend told me what happened. Ammaji stopped giving darshan and turned around to watch me sing. She kept her eyes on me for the whole five minutes while I sang. When I finished, I found a quiet corner to sit and enjoy my inner experience.

In this moment, singing with all my heart and soul to the Divine Mother, I found my dharma, I found my path, the doorway, the answer to all my ceaseless searching: *I can sing God's names!*

Hazrat Anayat Khan, the founder of the Sufi Order of the West, taught that music is a doorway to the formless God. It is simply vibration on the wind, the only art form that has no material substance. Painters have their canvas, authors have their books, dancers use their bodies, but music is simply a vibration on the wind. It has no physical form, no meaning. Music simply occurs; the listener infers no conceptual definitions or meanings (of course, with some exceptions). Yet this inceptual art form provides deep emotional experiences, transcendental epiphanies, and spiritual awakenings. Finally, music exists only in our *be here now*, entering our eardrums in the present and then it is gone, a kind of vibrational Tibetan sand painting. So it exists only in the present. Due to this wonderful lesson from Ammaji, and the musical teaching of the great Sufi saint, Hazrat Anayat Khan, I realized that music and the names of God were my doorway.

Later, after everyone had gotten their hug, Ammaji picked up a giant bucket of pudding and walked through the hall giving everyone a big handful of brown glop. When she came over to me, she put the glop in my right hand and turned away. Then she turned back as if recognizing me, and gave me another big glop in my left hand. I ran into the corner and stuffed myself on the great pudding prasad of the Divine Mother. This was one of the most amazing evenings of my life.

I joined the local Mata Amritananda satsang. We met every Sunday, sang some kirtan, had tea, and talked together. Sometimes we did *seva* (service) in the community. This was during the very early stage of my development as a kirtan leader, but they occasionally would let me lead. Mainly I played guitar and sang in the chorus (as all learners should do for a long time). I absorbed the feelings of the melodies and the names of God. These names and forms have always been hypnotic to me. I fit right in. Ammaji gave me a great gift. She has her ways, and she has her work, and she has moved thousands towards the light. Her greatness is exemplified by the transformation of her hometown, Kerala. She has gifted the community with education, water, housing, and protection. She is the most well-known and beloved teacher who visits the USA from India. However, it is said that your guru must hold your eyes and know your name, so my search continued.

Again and again, I honor her and I touch her feet.

Chapter 6

SRI KARUNAMAYI

I, by the light of soul, realize that the beauty of the heavens and the grandeur of the earth are the echo of your magic flute. –Sharif

Karunamayi with Shubal

One day during the time when I was still part of the Boston area Sai Baba community, we received a phone call from a friend in New York City who asked us to host Karunamayi ("mother of compassion"), a spiritual teacher from Andhra Pradesh, India. We were happy to do this, and set up an organization called the Boston Satsang with the purpose of hosting various spiritual teachers and gurus in the Boston area. All of us Sai Baba friends went about renting a hall, advertising the program, and finding a place for her to stay. As we began this work, word got back to the Sai community that I was working for another guru, which is against the rules of the organization. They asked me about it, and I felt so bad. It felt like mistrust, and seemed like a very silly rule. Without getting into psychological details, I withdrew from the community, stopped the Sunday sessions, and turned my attention to the hosting of Karunamayi.

Karunamayi was born to Brahmin parents in Penusila, South India. From an early age, she showed an above average interest in religion and would go into a meditative trance quite often. Her mother, although a religious person herself, insisted that Amma, as she is affectionately called, finish her education before focusing on her spiritual life. Amma worked hard in school and graduated college near the top of her class. As soon as she was finished with school, she left of her village and for ten years she lived alone in the jungle, meditating. She wandered through the forest; the local villagers left food out for her. During this time of *tapas* (austerities), Amma performed sadhana in many forms.

Amma told us an amazing story concerning her kirtan practice. Every morning she woke in the small hut the villagers had built for her, washed in the local stream, heated some chai, had a small breakfast, and then began her walk among the trees and flowers. She sang *Sitaram* or *Sri Ram Jai Ram,* and the birds gathered around her. After a few months, the parrots and macaws began to sing the kirtan in response to Amma. Her chorus was now in place and she spent her years of sadhana singing kirtan with the birds.

While she was in the forest, a fire broke out in her village. She ran home to find much of the housing destroyed and many of the villagers suffering with severe burns. Amma spent weeks in the village, burying the dead, nursing the wounded, and offering solace to the survivors. The nearest hospital was such a great distance away that none of the wounded received any medical care. Amma was so moved by the experience that she committed herself to raising the funds to build a hospital near her village that would serve the citizens for free.

After Amma's time in the jungle, she created a small ashram in Bangalore and, together with her cousin, a fellow we came to know as Swamiji, started offering darshan to the community. Some Western devotees who were friends of mine wandered into her ashram, where they sat with her for many evenings discussing America and various ways that Amma could serve there. These trustworthy Westerners were true yogis who had been traveling in India for many years, and they were immersed in their practice. They were there to advise Amma in the beginning, and it was not long after this that Amma decided to come to America and begin to teach.

Amma allied with friends, devotees of Shiva Bala Yogi, and together they set up a nonprofit and began planning a national tour. Her first stop was New York City. It's interesting how many of the people who gather around gurus, the great souls, are many times possessive and behave in unusual ways. It sometimes seems like the area close to enlightenment is an Intensive Care Unit (ICU). There are many stories of this. Sri Ramakrishna's cousin used to stand outside the gates of the ashram and pretend to be Ramakrishna, giving darshan to the unsuspecting visitors and even collecting money from them. The people who gathered around Swami Nityananda built a wall around him and would not allow any of his old friends to see him. The New York folks around Amma were actually from Texas, and even though they followed a different guru's teachings, they very much loved Amma. They helped considerably in getting her started in the U.S.

All of this led up to the day when we got a call from Smriti, one of Amma's helpers, who asked if we could put up this meditation teacher for a week while she gave some public discourses. At this point we had no idea who Amma was, but we quickly agreed. I had done programs for Ram Dass and had a good idea of how to do this. We began by renting a small Iyengar yoga studio. Then we pooled our money to put an ad in the local spiritual newspaper and crossed our fingers. We knew the protocols for hosting a spiritual teacher, so we began cleaning house from top to bottom. We prepared *sattvic* (pure) food—no garlic, no onions, no mushrooms, and no hot spices. We thought we were ready.

We gathered on a clear Spring morning, anticipating Amma's arrival. Waiting in the yard, I played and sang until a Lincoln town car pulled up in front of the house. Karunamayi had arrived. As she stepped out of the car, I had never beheld such a powerful radiance of Mother love before. Her dark face, with jewels in her nose, ears, and hair, and her bright red sari made her look exactly like a Hindu painting of the goddess Durga. None of us had ever seen anyone like her. She was shining like a *jyoti*, the flame of enlightenment. Her face held the purest look of love I have ever seen, and in that first glance, I fell in love. Tears dripped from the outside corners of my eyes and when I turned to Chris, he was crying, too.

We all pressed into the meditation room. She sat in a chair and we gathered at her feet. She kept looking at me, then pointed at me and said "Sing!" How did she know I devoted my life to music? This was the first example of Amma reading our thoughts. I sang *Kali Durga Namoh Namah* like never before. Later on, she said, "You have the tears of God love in your voice." The tears of God love filled my eyes.

We put on several small programs in the local yoga center. We had very fine turnouts, and she spoke with amazing insight and love. I got to sing bhajan after bhajan for her. I reached into my Sai Baba song bag and sang for her at a level that she did not expect. When I sang *shlokas* (poetic forms in Sanskrit) from the Chandi Path, she looked at me with amazement. She asked, "Where did you ever learn that?"

Near the end of her visit to Boston, she called each of us in for a private darshan. Her room was filled with the smoke of incense, so it felt like we were floating on a cloud. She was sitting cross-legged in an overstuffed chair and beckoned me to sit at her feet. I basked in the radiance of the love in her eyes. She looked at me as if I was her lover, but it was much more than romance—it was the awareness that she and I are one! She did not say much. She told me a little of my past lives, a little of my karmic relationship to those around me, a little of my destiny, and she stroked my forehead and dried my tears. As I sat at her feet, I was captivated by her looks and sounds of love. I felt completely seen.

I was wearing the little Hanuman medal given to me by one of Maharajji's devotees, and I asked Amma, "May I have spiritual name?" Somehow, Larry did not seem spiritual enough for me any longer. She smiled and said ,"You are Maruti, one of the names of Hanuman." The name always felt a little tarnished to me because I had telegraphed the name with my medal.

I had been thinking earlier in the day that I wanted her to bless the mala that I got from Sai Baba's ashram. I had been carrying it around in my pocket waiting for the right moment. In that meeting, I had the fleeting thought of asking her to bless it. She immediately said, "What have you got there?" She twirled her hand around in the air and suddenly in her hand was a mala of *rudraksha* beads (the seeds of an evergreen tree), symbolizing Shiva's tears. (It is true that her hand went out of my field of vision for an instant.) She placed the mala around my neck and said, "I have materialized a mala for you." It is still one of my most prized possessions. Whether it was a trick or not, I make the assumption that it is a symbol of our bond. I love that mala, and I love her.

Later that summer, Karunamayi facilitated the most exceptional healing experience for me. She was giving darshan at a private

95

home in New York for all the folks who had hosted her during her American tour. The house was packed, with over a hundred people stuffed into a living room. A *takhat* (wooden platform) had been erected for Amma to sit on. She had on a bright red sari and was seated there in lotus position, meditating. As the musician, I sat next to her on the floor. As soon as everyone settled down, Amma thanked us all for the work we had done. She talked a little about the meditation practices she was teaching, we sang a little, and then it was time for darshan. Karunamayi stood up and stepped in front of her takhat. Everyone in the room assembled in a long line. One by one, each of us came up to receive a blessing, ask a question, bow down, and even touch her feet. I was very near the front of the line. I was able to bow to Amma, tell her how much I loved her, and receive a small dot of *kumkum* (red powder) on my third eye.

After receiving this blessing, I moved to the side and watched while others approached Amma. Soon I climbed onto the takhat behind Amma and began to meditate. Her back was to me as she gave blessings to each person in line. Five or ten minutes later, I opened my eyes and saw them bring out a large basket of fruit for prasad—a hundred little hard red unripe plums. Prasad is blessed food; instilled with the shakti of the guru. Neem Karoli Baba used to throw fruit at his devotees. Sathya Sai Baba used to throw candy into the crowd. Down in the corner of the basket, I saw two peaches. They were especially ripe, stems and leaves still on them. I could almost smell them. I love fruit more than any other food. "Too bad," I thought. "I went up for darshan too soon to get prasad." I was disappointed, because I knew a little about the secrets of blessed food. But my attention kept being drawn back to those two peaches, drawing me away from my concentration. They seemed to be calling my name. I forced myself to let the peaches go and began to meditate, eyes closed.

Again, I was distracted and opened my eyes. One by one, people were coming up to Amma for blessing. I watched as a young woman bowed down. Her shirt fell open and I found myself looking in! Here I was, standing behind a manifestation of the Divine Feminine and where was my mind? I was very unhappy with this aspect of myself. I made a loud silent prayer. "Amma, please take these sexual thoughts away and refocus me on the divine. I no longer want to be the kind of person who looks at women so objectively and disrespectfully." At this point, I fell into a deep meditation and lost all body consciousness.

When I opened my eyes, the darshan was over. Amma was walking out the door on the far side of the still-packed room. She suddenly turned around. She began to push her way through the throng, apparently with some goal in mind. I watched as she came closer and closer, until she was standing directly in front of me. She stared into my eyes, and withdrew from her sari *those two peaches*! She put them in my hands and I could not believe it. I burst into tears. Not only had she read my mind, but I could feel something had changed inside of me. As I looked at Amma, her beautiful face and form so much like the goddess Durga herself, I felt a new kind of love, something that had been missing throughout my childhood, throughout my many relationships, even throughout my spiritual searching. I felt the essence of pure mother/son love. I said, "Amma, you know what is in my mind." She said "Of course, *nana* (little child in Telegu)." The tears poured from my eyes.

I remembered a teaching story of Shirdi Sai Baba. One day he gave two oranges to one of his Western students. He told the student to go sit by the Ganges to eat them. The student sat by the river and peeled the first orange. He had started to eat it when a beggar came up to him and asked for the other orange. The student said, "My guru told me to eat both of these oranges

97

and it is great karma to disobey one's guru. Therefore, I cannot give one to you."

At this point, the beggar said, "Sir, I want you to know that I have not eaten for three days and, if you do not give me the orange, I surely will die of starvation. What is the greater karma, to disobey your guru or to allow me to die?"

The student, realizing his dilemma, spoke to the beggar. He said, "You are right. I cannot allow you to die, so here is the orange." The beggar wandered off with the orange.

The student finished his first orange and returned to the ashram. As he walked to the gate, he saw Shirdi Sai waiting for him with arms folded, tapping his foot. Baba asked, "Did you eat those oranges?"

The student replied, "I ate the first orange, but the beggar was starving and I gave the second orange to him."

Babaji spoke with great anger, "Go back to America. Never say my name again. Never think of me again. You and I are done for the rest of this incarnation. Go!"

The student sadly returned to America. Now he had nothing. He had lost his guru, he was impoverished, and alone in what now felt like a strange country. However, three weeks later he bought a winning lottery ticket and became a millionaire. The point of the story is that the student was being tested. He was given two oranges: one was the orange of material wealth; the other was the orange of spiritual wealth. He ate the one with material wealth and gave the orange of spiritual wealth away. So the beggar became enlightened and the student got rich. (Perhaps the beggar was Shirdi Sai in disguise.)

Remembering the story, I took those two peaches from Amma out of the room and ate them both with great relish. I wish I had saved the pits and grown trees, but alas, the pits are gone. I recognized that it was time to let go of boyish activities.

Old subconscious thought forms, however, never die; they lose their hold by surrounding them with new healthy subconscious thought forms. With Amma's help, I became gradually less identified with the sexuality of the second chakra, and when I find myself objectifying the opposite sex, I remember the mantra, "O Mother, your forms are so beautiful." The great saint Ramakrishna was sent a prostitute as a test; he was found at her feet crying this same wonderful mantra.

At the airport, Amma and I sat alone on a bench while everyone else was busy with luggage and tickets. Her deep eyes looked across at me with that look of passionate love that was so new to me. I felt washed clean in this shower of clarity, truth, and love. She gave me a deep look of love, sighed deeply and said, "Ahhh, attachment."

I felt so much love for her that my heart beat fast. I also sighed, "Yes, Amma, but good attachment."

Suddenly she looked so serious and said, "No . . . permanent attachment." So I learned there are three types of attachment: good, bad, and permanent. The permanent attachment is the attachment of the small self to universal love and awareness—the only attachment worth its salt.

Amma's great gifts also came in the form of relief from suffering. At one point I developed this strange feeling in my chest, like my heart was beating irregularly. I would get dizzy when it happened. Finally, one day at work it got so bad I drove to the emergency room, where they found that my blood pressure was way too high and my heart was beating irregularly. My arteries looked clear, so they sent me home with some medicine that made me even sicker. My partner at the time was in London to attend an Amma retreat and she told Amma of my plight. Amma took a small packet of vibhuti, pressed it between her hands, recited a mysterious mantra, and told my partner to "give it to him in water, a little every day, and he will be fine."

When I picked my partner up at the airport, she told me this story. I demanded the vibhuti right away. As I put the powder on my lips, the feeling in my chest began to dissipate; by the end of the day, I was feeling perfectly normal again. Future checkups found my blood pressure where it had always been, low normal, and found my heartbeat regular as James Brown's drummer.

A quick story about vibhuti: A couple, people I know well and trust, went to India to visit Sai Baba's ashram. They were invited into the private interview room and given a few gifts. The next day they left the ashram to travel in North India and the fellow contracted typhoid fever. The hospital seemed negative about his recovery. The woman sat outside his room meditating. She was interrupted by an Indian woman who said, "Do you remember me?" My friend responded negatively. The woman said, "Yes yes, I was inside Sai Baba's interview room with you. He gave me this package of vibhuti and told me to give it to you. He said not to do it that day, but to wait till the next time I saw you. My husband works at the hospital and I'm bringing him his lunch. Here is your vibhuti." My friend applied it to the lips of her sick friend and he immediately began to respond. Within three hours they both walked out of the hospital.

The next summer, Amma came back. This time she was accompanied by her swami and two older devotees. Our experience from the previous year allowed us to find a much larger venue. The mailing list and better publicity attracted a turnout of over three hundred people. On this visit, she initiated people into the Saraswati mantra. I wanted to activate this mantra inside me, so I asked Amma for this initiation, which took place with her alone in her room. She closed my eyes, opened my mouth, and with a stick of *tulsi* (holy basil) dipped in honey, she wrote the mantra on my tongue. Amma contains many of the qualities of the goddess Saraswati—the aspect of God that is the essence of knowledge, music, and the arts. The mantra—*Aim Srim Hrim Saraswati Devyai Namaha*—evokes the unifying force of music and creates the connection between the left and right brain, the intellect and the inceptual emotional mind.

After receiving the mantra, I went home that night with a female member of our community who needed a place to stay. My plan was to put her on a couch in the living room and deny any temptation. The initiation had left me with an inner glow that needed to be tenderly nurtured. Amma was planning an early morning meditation the next day that we all wanted to attend. By the time I finally got my housemate settled on the couch and crawled into bed, it was well past midnight. Sometime toward dawn, I was brought back to consciousness by my housemate, standing next to my bed, asking, "Can I join you?"

After being celibate for several months, here was a very beautiful woman crawling into my bed and asking me to make love with her. I could bury my face between this woman's breasts, or I could get out of bed and go to Amma's 6 a.m. meditation. Somewhere inside of me, I knew that Amma was testing me. I jumped out of bed, took one last look at the voluptuous body spread out on the bed in front of me, and took a cold shower. Later, when Amma came into the room to begin the meditation, she gave me a very long, loving look.

The second gift was a private interview. Amma sat alone in our meditation room and one by one folks were allowed to come in and sit with her for a few minutes, ask questions, receive blessings, and be in her presence. During this visit, she had been working very hard and was very tired. Swami was asking each of us to take only a few minutes with Amma and move quickly along. Of course, given the opportunity to sit with this beautiful enlightened saint, no one was going to cut their visit short. So all morning the private interviews went on and on. Finally everyone had received their interview and it was time for Amma to go upstairs and have lunch. There were just three of us left in the room. As we stood by the entrance, Amma came out of the room and started to go up the stairs to take rest. She stopped on the stairs and reached down to a table that held a bowl filled with strawberries that we had been giving out as prasad. She inserted one of those delicious strawberries into each of our mouths—the taste was so sweet—then told us a story:

"Once there was a great devotee of Jesus. He loved Jesus so much that at the end of his life God sent an angel to grant him a wish. When the angel appeared and told the old man of the boon God was granting him, the old man smiled. He looked the angel in the eyes and said, 'Please grant me compassion, because from compassion comes all else.'"

At that moment the door burst open. A woman entered with her hair awry, her purse hanging open, and a look of total distress on her face. She blustered into the room and spoke. "I know I am late. I could not find a place to park. There was great traffic. I got lost. I know I've missed my interview. I am so upset." Even though Amma had not had a break in six hours, was exhausted from her travel, and was probably hungry, she came back down the stairs, took the woman by the arm, and went into the meditation room. She sat with the woman for twenty minutes, came back out, smiled at us, and went upstairs for rest. We were stunned. In some way, she must have felt the presence of that woman long before she reached the house and was waiting on the stairs for the woman to arrive. She used it as a teaching moment for all of us. Then, with the greatness only a saint can achieve, she demonstrated the teaching through her own behavior.

The next year we put on a program at the Montessori school in Cambridge. This was a really big venue and we were expecting hundreds of people. Amma had a desire to stay with an Indian family during this visit. Our friend Prithi agreed to host Amma and her entourage for the three days of programs.

On the morning of the first darshan, Amma was driven to the venue by Prithi. When the car arrived at the school and we opened the back door for Amma, we discovered that her feet were buried in red kumkum powder. Amma often demonstrated the ability to transform energy into matter. It was never totally clear to me whether she was actually demonstrating a spiritual power or whether she had developed excellent magical techniques. One of the ways Amma demonstrated this spiritual power was to have kumkum or vibhuti form at her feet until her feet became buried in the magical powder. In this case, Amma had manifested the red powder and there was about a pound of this stuff surrounding her feet. We all felt that a holy event had occurred, and I asked the Swamiji for some of the powder to share with the Boston community. The owner of the car, Prithi, claimed it was her car and she wanted all of it. I observed her selfishness and let it go.

After the event, Chris and I drove Amma home. Suddenly the car became filled with a perfume-like smell and Amma began to laugh. I turned around to the backseat and discovered her feet were covered in vibhuti. Amma was laughing and laughing, and she said, "Larry didn't get any red powder this morning, but all of this vibhuti is for him." After Amma stepped out of her sandals and went into her room, Chris carefully removed the sandals and the powder intact. He built a small Lucite case, put the "relic" inside along with a photo of Amma in the powder. It sits prominently in my *puja* (altar) space.

Another amazing vibhuti event occurred during one of our afternoon meditation sessions with Amma. There were about seventy-five of us in the room meditating with her in silence when the room suddenly filled with the scent of incense. Some of us opened our eyes to see that her feet had become buried in vibhuti. I am a rational human being and I know that in the West we went out into the universe to discover the nature of reality, while in the East they went inward and discovered universal principles that we, in the West, are still unaware of. All of us there believed a miracle had occurred. Some burst into tears, some burst into laughter, some sat silently in meditation. It was as if a mass hypnosis took over the room. The energy grew in intensity and soon everyone was crying. Amma walked around the room, drying our tears with her sari, which became soaked in the tears of her devotees. Whether this was a miracle or a magic trick was irrelevant. It was a profoundly heart-expanding experience.

At this same retreat, after our 2 p.m. meditation, Amma asked me to sing kirtan. I was definitely in the mood, so I ran for my guitar. I chose to sing the bhajan "Amba Parameshwari," knowing that the kirtan ended with a call-and-response of *Amma, Amma, Amma, Amma*, moving from the root chord to the four chord back and forth. This chord change (the opposite of the "amen" chord progression) is dynamically heart-opening. If you are Jewish, you remember the *Shema Yisroel Adonai Elohenu*, that "nai" syllable explodes your heart. It's the four change. As we sang to Amma back and forth, the energy in the room rose and rose. It felt like a southern Baptist church with everyone singing out *Amma*, with her sitting right there listening. When the kirtan ended, some folks gasped, others burst into spontaneous laughter or clapping.

I thought, "I am the world's greatest kirtan wallah."

As soon as this thought went through me, I saw Amma whispering to her assistant, who then came directly over to me. She bent over and whispered in my ear, "Amma says, 'when you sing to the Divine Mother, you sing *softly* and *sweetly*.'" I was exposed, caught, dismembered, and forgiven all in a quick moment. I never forgot this lesson.

The second night at the Montessori school brought me a major teaching. We had a wonderful turnout and the program went well. Amma sang, I got to sing a little, her discourse was beautiful, and the darshan line was filled with light. At the end of the program, Amma chanted OM with us. Suddenly, out of the unity, I heard someone chanting a harmony OM with an operatic voice, very loud and slightly off pitch. My musician's ears burned. When the OMs finished, not yet having exorcized my anger at my mother, I went over to this woman and said, "You know, that was just ego. The right thing to do was to sing OM in unison with the rest of us. Many of us know that you sing with an operatic voice, but that was ego. Please don't do that again."

The woman became extremely upset at my anger and went right over to Amma. I watched them talking to each other and pointing at me from across the room. When I was in India, I had purchased a bit of clothing for special moments, in particular a beautifully embroidered silk shirt that I was proudly wearing as I stood next to the platform from which Amma had spoken. One of the candles at the edge of the platform touched my shirt sleeve and up it went in flames. I was able to put the fire out without being burned, but the message was clear.

The next morning was private interview time. I knew I was in trouble. I was the leader of the community and I had allowed my anger to override my compassion. I had not learned Amma's lesson. I was the guardian at the door of the room when the interviews began. My opera-singing friend was the first to arrive, and she glared at me as she entered the room. I knew my goose was cooked. She spent twenty minutes with Amma, and when she came out she looked at me with an angry and hurt expression. The next person for an interview was my partner, who was also familiar with my anger. More than anything her intention was to help me heal. She spent twenty minutes with Amma, and when she came out she turned to me with a poignant look. She clicked her lips at me with a *tich tich* sound that made me feel like a small bad child.

At the end of the day, it was my turn in the interview room. I was expecting Amma to blast me for showing anger when I was leading her community event. I knew I was wrong and I was ready for the punishment. The room smelled of incense. Her eyes locked on mine as soon as I entered the door. It was like staring into the eyes of my most intimate lover, eyes of complete love, acceptance, and understanding. (I remembered Neem Karoli Baba telling Ram Dass that he could see no impurities.) I sat in front of her on the floor while she sat cross-legged in the chair and looked down on me. For several minutes we stared at each other. She looked at me with so much love, then spoke words that were so unexpected, so profound, so healing, so astounding, that I could barely contain myself: *"I see how your Earth mother has hurt you. Let ME be your mother."*

Tears began to flow, my heart pounded, my body shook, and I was lost in love.

I had been understood.

She touched my face with her hand and began to dry my tears with the edge of her sari. She stroked my forehead and brushed my hair back from my face, touching me with so much love, the way I'd always wanted my mother to touch me. Again, Karunamayi had created the environment where something inside me shifted. I saw that while mother love, in many human lives, is sourced from the Earth lineage mother, the truth is that mother love radiates from every bit of matter and energy in all of Her universes. More specifically, the source of mother love is found in the unconditional awareness of one's guru.

I had been seen.

Then her face became stern and she pointed her finger at me. "Now remember, when you represent *me*, you do it with love! Now go and chant the Mrytyunjaya mantra a thousand times a day and I will see you next year."

I thought, "Good grief, that will take me forever, but let's see if I can do it."

Here is the mantra (which comes from the Rig Veda) that she asked me to chant:

oṃ tryámbakaṃ yajāmahe sughandhíṃ puṣṭivardhánam
urvārukam iva bandhánān mṛtyor mukṣīya māmṛtāt

"We worship the three-eyed one, Shiva, absorbed in bliss, full of fragrance, the source of all nourishment. As a fruit, when it ripens, separates easily from the vine, please release us from the bondage and sufferings of the mind and let us experience our eternal blissful nature."

I began to chant the mantra. At first it took me about six hours to chant it a thousand times. I took my mala and a cup with ten small stones in it. Each time I circled the mala, I would take a stone out of the cup. When the cup was empty, I was finished for the day. I worked hard all year. I missed some days, but most days I was able to complete a thousand mantras. Eventually I could chant the thousand mantras in only two-and-a-half hours.

Then it was next year and Amma was back. When I was first alone with Amma, I honored her. Then I said, "Well, I did it."

"Did what?" she said.

"I chanted the mantras."

"What mantras?"

"You remember, last year you asked me to chant the mantra a thousand times a day and I worked hard and I did it!"

"I did? You did?" And she turned and walked away.

Again, she had stunned me. I knew that a saint could meet someone, and then see them after twenty years and remember their name and their whole story; a saint has total recall. How could Amma not remember? Then suddenly it struck me. *I was so forgiven that she did not even remember what happened.* Again my heart flew at the greatness of this woman, the power of her love and insight.

Sometimes I found myself alone in a room with her. She asked me to sing again and again, and my heart opened wide during those meetings. Once I asked her if I could sing some of the songs I had written to her, and we staged an impromptu concert that had us all in tears. At one point I said, "This song is in country-and-western style."

She interrupted me, "These songs are beyond style." Then she told us to get into a recording studio and make an album of these songs, which we immediately did. She released it on her label. *Saranagati* (surrender) was an inspiration from Karunamayi, who brought about the creation of, well, everything, in one sense. She said, "Watch me dancing on the planets." And in a more personal sense, she brought out the soul in me.

I am filled with the remembrance of Amma's wonderful gifts: permanent attachment, a voice filled with the tears of God love, the peaches, the manifested mala, the Mrityunjaya mantra, and the amazing love she radiated. It was all wonderful. She read my thoughts and dried my tears. She opened my mind to see women as goddesses, and said, "Let ME be your mother."

There is so much irony in the playing out of karma. While there is truth to the chain of events that caused Amma to decide not to come back to Boston, it filled us with sadness. I understood that, in a sense, it was my responsibility. Chris had put a wrong address in an ad, I had chanted the wrong mantra as she entered the Hall, sales and donations were off. Amma's entourage seemed focused on raising money, and they were condescending to the local communities as they traveled. Amma's swami was so upset he decided not to return. Here in Boston, we loved Amma so much and this felt like a divorce. Karunamayi and Swamiji left Boston days early in kind of a huff, and I drove back to my home alone. Even today, I think of Amma often. I sit in front of her sandals and mala and feel waves of her love.

I knew that Shree Maa was coming to my home the next day. The synchronicity of Amma leaving and Maa arriving only one day apart did not escape me.

Chapter 7
SHREE MAA & SWAMI SATYANANDA SARASWATI

Singing is a very high sadhana. --Shree Maa

Shree Maa and Shubal

I met Shree Maa and her swami during the first of their three cross-country tours. Their ashram, Devi Mandir, was in the mountains behind the vineyards of Napa, California. Maa and Swami Satyananda Saraswati traveled together in a small RV. When they came to the Boston area, my partner and I drove down to a small church on the South Shore of Massachusetts to check out this Mother. We arrived late, near the end of kirtan. As I approached the chapel, I heard this unearthly voice singing *Sri Ram Jai Ram*. It was so innocent, so delicate—the voice seemed to come from another world.

When I entered the room, I saw a black-skinned, eighty-pound woman, her eyes pointing in opposite directions, wearing a cotton sari and no jewelry, sitting in what seemed to be a trance and singing to her most intimate beloved. Swami Satyananda told us that Shree Maa was an incarnation of Chandi, the original Divine Mother, another name for Durga. I could clearly see that something was going on inside this woman.

The next night she offered darshan in the home of her host. It was surprising to be sitting around in the living room and have Shree Maa walk in and sit down in a chair like a regular person. We had been taught to treat Karunamayi like a queen, so I was not used to the style of this simple saint. I was able to sit and listen to her amazing kirtan. I listened and watched her Western-style band, which included a mandolin, several guitars, and different types of drums. I thought, "I would really fit in with this band."

Near the end of kirtan, one of the guitarists came over to me and said, "I hear you play guitar. Go get it." I ran out to my car, where I always keep my guitar (just in case), got out my Martin and made it back into the living room as she was finishing her kirtan. Maa looked over at me and said, "Let's do one more." So for the first time I got to accompany Shree Maa as she sang kirtan. Later in the evening, I bought a cassette tape of Maa's music, which later proved to be extremely useful.

The next year, I got a phone call from Agastya, one of Shree Maa's disciples, who asked if I could host Shree Maa in New England. She was planning a national tour for the summer and wanted to come to Boston. Remembering that I had done programs for Ram Dass as well as Karunamayi, he knew I could handle the job. Ironically, when the plans were finalized, we realized that Shree Maa would be arriving one or two days after Karunamayi left Boston. It was going to be an interesting summer.

On the day after Karunamayi departed, I drove hundreds of miles to Ananda Ashram in New York to pick up Shree Maa and her entourage. I drove down the New York State Thruway through the most incredible thunderstorms and onto the campus of Ananda Ashram. I had the sense that something important was about to happen. The ashram was completely deserted. I wandered for an hour looking for Shree Maa, to no avail. After a while I ran into a long-haired hippie who was traveling with Shree Maa. He told me that the bass player in Shree Maa's band had contracted Lyme disease and was in the hospital on antibiotics. Shree Maa would not leave Ananda Ashram without him, so the entire Boston program was now in jeopardy. I had to return to Wendell alone, and we spent a worrisome twenty-four hours wondering whether Shree Maa and her sadhus would ever arrive.

Early the next morning, the day before the first program, Swami Satyananda called to say they were on their way. I live on a mountaintop, about a mile in on a dirt road, filled with ruts, potholes, and often flooded in various places, so I went to meet Shree Maa at the beginning of the dirt road. I watched as two RVs, eight cars, and a truck drove down our dirt road and onto our steep driveway. The car doors began to open and at least a dozen sadhus and children piled out. We gathered around Maa's RV, and followed her through the garden and across the yard into our meditation room. The sadhus all came in with their mandolins, guitars, banjos, and tablas and immediately we began to sing kirtan. The energy in the room was so high that my head was buzzing. I played with all the vigor I could muster on my guitar and, when the first song was over, I had broken three strings. Swami Satyananda said, "I love a guitar player who, when the kirtan is over, has no strings left." This photo was taken at that moment, and you can see the joy in my face.

Shubal singing to Shree Maa

We offered the usual Hindu ceremony and washed Maa's feet. I remember her saying, in a delightful tinkling voice, "Oh, this is so cold!" We put the water we used to wash Maa's feet in the pitcher and placed it on the table. As we were sitting around Maa and enjoying the wonderful peaceful atmosphere emanating from her, my friend Scott noticed the pitcher on the table. It was a hot summer day, so he drank the entire pitcher. Later, he told me that this was the most delicious water he could remember. Interestingly enough, Scott is now Sadananda Saraswati, one of Maa's devotees.

After the kirtan, Maa retreated to the RV to take rest. I stood at the door of the RV with my partner. Maa turned to me and asked, "Do you want to marry this woman?"

From somewhere deep inside of me, not really having anything to do with free will, I answered, "No, I want to marry you, Maa!"As I spoke, I was shocked, knowing my partner would be very unhappy with this answer. Somehow Maa disguised my answer, though, because my partner swore she never heard me say that, even though I was standing right next to her.

The week that Maa spent with us in Wendell was one of the most amazing weeks of my life. Her sadhus sat around my living room speaking softly of spiritual moments with Shree Maa. We would spontaneously break out into kirtan and sing for hours. People from all over New England came to meet Maa. Our house bustled with energy—people cooking, singing, meditating, chanting the Chandi Path, laughter, tears, great joy—all totally in the moment, all immersed in our "be here now."

Shree Maa is a *tantrika* (one who practices the path of tantra).Many say she is the reincarnation of Sharada Devi, the saint/wife of Paramahamsa Ramakrishna. Others say she is a manifestation of Chandi Maa. As a child, she received initiation from Aghor Baba, a wandering sadhu in the sect of Dattatreya, an avatar of Lord Shiva. Her main sadhana is to chant the Chandi Path, the seven-hundred-verse poem detailing the exploits of the goddess Chandi in her battles with the demons. She lives on the side of a mountain on the periphery of Napa, California. Her ashram is locked; unless you are invited, you cannot get in. She no longer travels, she takes few new students, and is surrounded by mystery—the mystery of *nirvikalpa samadhi* (a meditative state of total absorption and bliss). She and Swamiji regularly practice the *homa*, the fire ritual. Swami Satyananda sits at the head of the fire pit, leading the chant. At the end of each of the Chandi Path's seven-hundred verses, we chant

Swaha! and throw the rice containing our projected negative qualities into the fire. Swaha! tells the deities that you have completed that mantra. It literally means, "I am one with God."

The Chandi Path is an ancient system of mantra worship of the Divine Mother. It contains three stories about the exploits of Chandi, the fiercest form of the goddess Durga that represents the power of shakti, the divine feminine force of the universe.

The three tales are prefaced by the story of Surrat and Samadhi. King Surrat ruled his subjects as if they were his own children. Through politics, he is deprived of his sovereignty. One night he leaves his kingdom on horseback under the pretext of hunting. As he wanders through the forest, he comes upon an ashram. Before he can enter, he meets a man and asks him, "Who are you?"

The man says, "I am a merchant named Samadhi. My children and my wife have stolen my business and deprived me of my wealth. I have come wandering in the forest, grief stricken."

Surrat and Samadhi enter the ashram together and approach Medhas, an enlightened saint. They say, "We have lost everything, yet we are completely attached to all that we have lost. How can we escape the suffering of this attachment?"

The sage replies, "From hearing the stories of the Divine Mother, from immersing oneself in Her consciousness, one gains final liberation. She is the supreme knowledge, the cause of final liberation, and She is the cause of the bondage of transmigration, and sovereign over all the lords." The businessmen and the king ask to hear the stories and the great seven-hundred-verse poem begins.

The first story: Before the beginning of time, a great snake lies coiled and sleeping. Also sleeping on the snake is a giant blue-skinned god named Vishnu (or Narayana), with four arms. A lotus flower grows from the dirt in Vishnu's navel. Seated in the flower is the god Brahma. As the flower opens, Brahma begins to move his hand, which sets in motion a vibration that creates the entire universe. The sound of this vibration is OM.

But right at that moment, two demons appear from the dirt in Vishnu's ear and begin to move towards the flower, intending to prevent the creation of the universe. Brahma, sensing what is about to happen, calls to Chandi with the most beautiful poetry, asking her to come and awaken Vishnu so he can destroy these demons. She quickly agrees. Chandi wakes up Vishnu and he battles the demons for days. They are equal in battle, each inflicting and sustaining wounds, until they pause. The demons, intoxicated with their exceeding power, brag to Vishnu, "You fight very well. Ask a boon from us."

Vishnu, clearly sensing his opportunity, replies, "The only boon I require from you is that you allow me to slay you both right now. What need is there for any other boon?"

The demons say, "All right Vishnu, but you may only slay us at the spot where the earth is not flooded with water."

"So be it!" Vishnu grabs the demons, takes them onto his lap, and very quickly severs their heads with his discus. And that's the end of the first story in the Chandi Path.

The second story: There is a battle between all the gods and all the demons. The king of the demons is The Great Buffalo, a shape-shifter demon who chooses to portray himself as a buffalo. The demons win the war quickly and overtake heaven, exiling all the gods to Earth. The gods all get together and go to Brahma, Vishnu, and Shiva—the Lords of Creation, Preservation, and Destruction. The gods say that since their collective group is not strong enough to defeat the demons, would each of the triumvirate shine a beam of light from each of their third eyes? Brahma, Vishnu, and Shiva do so, and the three beams combine into one single beam, which creates Chandi, the original divine mother. Then, each of the Gods gives Chandi one of their weapons and she becomes all powerful. Chandi goes into battle and destroys the demons, one by one, with her bloody sword. Finally she faces the Great Buffalo, pins him to the ground with her foot, and cuts off his head. The demons are defeated.

The third story: In which Chandi is called into battle with the great demons, *Shumba* (self-conceit) and *Nishumba* (self-deprecation). Again, all the demons, led by Shumba and Nishumba, win a battle with the gods and expel them from heaven. Chandi is sitting in the center of the universe, radiating her intense light everywhere. One of Shumba's emissaries sees her great beauty, and when he returns he tells Shumba he's found the most beautiful woman in the universe, so beautiful surely Self-Conceit must have her as his wife. Shumba sends his emissary back to relay a message to Chandi: "Madam, today is your lucky day. The most powerful leader in the entire universe, Shumba, has agreed to take you as his wife. Please come with me, the wedding is being arranged."

Mother responds, "How wonderful! I would love to marry Shumba. Unfortunately, when I was a young child, I made a vow that I could only marry the man who could defeat me in battle. So please go back to Shumba and tell him to do battle with me. I am only a woman. Surely, he will defeat me, and we can be married."

So the trap is set. Shumba and Nishumba send their various generals. They are all quickly destroyed. Finally, they send *Raktabija* (the seed of desire), a demon with a very special power—every drop of blood he sheds in battle creates a brand-new Raktabija. Up against Chandi he goes. Each time she wounds him and he sheds a drop of blood, a new Raktabija springs up. Soon there are tens of thousands of Raktabijas in battle with Chandi Maa.

At this point, Chandi stretches her mouth open wide, and from deep inside there comes a dark crone—black, wrinkled skin, bloodshot eyes, withered breasts, red tongue hanging from her mouth, wearing a necklace of skulls and holding a severed head in her right hand. Kali emerges from Chandi's mouth. Kali opens her own mouth wide and begins to swallow the Raktabijas whole. One by one she takes the Raktabijas in her mouth, chews them up and swallows them down until they are all destroyed. No one can defeat the Divine Mother.

Finally, Shumba and Nishumba enter the battlefield. They are aware that Maa has destroyed their entire army. First Nishumba confronts Maa, who removes his head with her scimitar. Then the great one himself, Shumba/Self-Conceit, draws his sword. Quickly, *Mataji* (respected mother) cuts him in two with a smile, and quiet returns to the universe. The gods sing a beautiful song to the Mother, *Narayani Namostute* (O Goddess, may my surrender ever deepen). The story ends and the sadhu, the businessman, and the king sing a poetic song and make devotional offerings. The Divine Mother is pleased. She offers each of them a boon.

In the Chandi Path, all the demons' Sanskrit names, as translated into English, are negative subconscious thought forms, undermining emotions, or ego-associated behaviors (e.g., Shumba and Nishumba translate as self-conceit and self-deprecation). The basic metaphor of the Chandi Path is that we are all gods and goddesses. You reside in your heavenly abode until the demons—these negative thought forms and ego behaviors— come and attack you. You have the power to resist and overcome these demons by focusing your thoughts into one pure thought—that of Chandi Maa, the Mother who lives within you as your true nature. The power of that one thought overcomes the demons and allows you to transcend psychology and join in the free play of the universe.

There is so much about the Chandi Path I do not know. There are secret mantras built into the poem that cause various reactions on the physical plane. There is a variety of *pranayama* (breathing practices) that can be used during the chanting of this poem; each breathing pattern establishes a different perception of reality. The expert chanters of the Chandi Path can chant the entire poem aloud in just an hour (it takes me six hours). They can chant it forwards, backwards, and in a variety of excerpted ways, each having a different impact on consciousness. Some chant it nine times a day for 1008 days at a time. The poem is a protectress, a bloody metaphor, a warrior queen, a political polemic, and a physical exercise—a map of the route to enlightenment.

Here are a few verses from the end of the story, told through Swami Satyananda Saraswati's translation of the Chandi Path:

After hearing the story, the king and the wise businessman set forth to practice disciplined meditation. With the object of obtaining the complete intuitive vision of the mother, they stayed on the sand bank of the river . . . They gave the offering sprinkled in blood taken from their own bodies. Thus they propitiated Her for three years with concentrated minds, whereupon the sustainer of the world was extremely pleased, and She Who Tears Apart Thoughts (Chandi) spoke to them in a perceivable form. The goddess said: "O King, and you businessman, delight to your family: you have attained to extreme bliss, and I am completely satisfied. I shall give to you whatever you pray for."

Then the king chose an imperishable kingdom, which will remain with him even in another life, and also the return of his own kingdom, which was forcibly taken from him by his mighty enemies.

Then, the wise businessman, whose mind was filled with indifference for worldly objects, asked for that knowledge which removes the attachments of egotism and possession.

The goddess said, "O King, within a few days your kingdom will be returned to you. And after having slain your enemies, you will remain there firm and unshaken. And after your death, you shall take birth from the God of universal light. The manifestation of wisdom, he who belongs to all colors, tribes, and castes, will be the name by which you will be known on earth.

O best of businessmen, I grant you the blessing which you desire of me. I bestow upon you the fullest attainment, and you will remain in the highest wisdom by which you will attain liberation . . .

The goddess then vanished, having been praised with devotion.

Having obtained the blessing from the goddess, the best of warriors, he will take his birth from the light of wisdom, and will become the manifestation of wisdom, he who belongs to all colors, tribes, and castes.

Klim Om

At the end of the summer, Shree Maa and Swamiji held a retreat at Devi Mandir for all of us who had hosted her tour. My partner and I packed up and headed across the country to Napa, California, bringing our tent and a growing love for this strange woman and her very strange swami. Devi Mandir is about twenty-five miles outside of the city of Napa, in the foothills surrounding grape country. You drive for miles into the wild country, not seeing a business, a home, or even a farm. Finally you arrive at the base of a hill that looks more Japanese than American. Getting to the temple takes you up through the trees, with a noisy brook following the path. The ashram is gated, closed to all except invited guests on special occasions. We parked at the bottom and made our way up the winding path, taking notice of the flowers, little statues, and special markings on the trees.

We crossed a little bridge and came upon peacocks in the trees and on the ground, calling to each other. At the top of the path, standing in front of a temple (a converted motorcycle garage), stood Shree Maa. She came up to me and grabbed my nose, saying, "Arunachala!" (Shiva's mountain). She shook my head back-and-forth. It's true my Jewish nose stands out formidably on my face, but I could not think of a greater blessing than to have the Divine Mother grab me by my third eye and shake my head. I knelt and touched her feet for the first time.

My partner, however, was having problems. She would not sleep with the rest of us in tents (she needed her own room in someone's home), and she demanded special time and treatment from me and everyone else at the ashram, especially Shree Maa and Swamiji. It got so extreme that at one point Swami Satyananda took me aside and said, "This Shakti does not inspire you. Leave this Shakti. I will find you one that does inspire you."

After we had all settled, we began our regular sadhana: up at 5:30 a.m., *arti* (a song in praise of the guru, offering the light back to its source), meditation till 7 a.m., breakfast, chanting, chores, and satsang. That afternoon, after singing kirtan in the temple, Shree Maa said to me, "I don't like the name Karunamayi gave you, Maruti. That is the name of a cheap car. I will find you a new name."

The next morning after breakfast, Swami Satyananda said to me, "Your name is Shubala." Shree Maa interrupted him, and said, "Shubalananda!" I felt like a child at Christmas. I was so happy. Shubala is one of Shiva's thousand and eight names. *Shu* means excellent, and *bala* means strength. Maa created a powerful double teaching with this, because bala also means "sing." And *ananda* means bliss. So my name meant The Bliss of the Excellent Strength of the Consciousness of Infinite Goodness. Or it means Excellent Song of Shiva. Spiritual names are given as a goal for the soul. They are not where you are at; they are where you are going. The name that Shree Maa gave me was an excellent challenge. Years later, Ma Chetan Jyoti wanted to shorten my name to Shubh. Apparently, this means *pure* in Hindi. I have a long way to go on that one, too. Shree Maa also told me, "If you could be the way you are when you lead kirtan all the time, you would be fine!" And, "Your job is to sing to the Divine Mother."

The next day I met Maa and Swamiji and they took me for a walk on the hillside. We stopped in a small clearing in front of a five foot-tall Shiva lingam, decorated as if for a festival. Maa looked right at me and asked, "What do you want?" In the atmosphere of a great saint, your mind naturally quiets down. As soon as you begin to climb up the hill to the Devi Mandir, you gradually feel an atmosphere of peace descending. Basking in the love and the concentration of Shree Maa, I looked inside and could not find anything that I wanted. My heart felt so full, my mind so empty, I could only smile as if looking at my teenage love. Then from somewhere inside of me, a request came forward, "Maa, I want you to sing through me."

She turned to Swamiji, "What did he say?"

Swamiji said, "He wants you to sing through him."

She looked back at me, "Okay."

The retreat ended with a private interview with Shree Maa and Swami Satyananda. They were so wonderful and loving towards us in that last morning. Maa told me my job was to sing to the Divine Mother and she gave me a special song to learn. My partner asked Maa, "May I have a name?" Maa smiled and said in a tone which implied the obvious, "You are Durga!" When Shree Maa had first met her, however, Maa said, "Too much I-me-mine." We were the last ones to leave. I was filled to overflowing.

As we were leaving, Swami Satyananda asked me for my copy of the Chandi Path. When he was at our house, he had written in the book, "To Maruti, may she bless you always with her love." Now he wrote my new, beautiful spiritual name "Shubalananda" over the name Maruti. I was standing next to him, so filled with love. I kept repeating, "My love, my love, my love." When he handed me back my book, I looked at what he had written. "To Shubalananda, may she bless you always with her love." He followed it with, "To Shubalananda, who has excellent strength. That's you!" He signed it, "My love, Swamiji."

What a strange man! I have no doubt that Swamiji, through his very intense sadhana for many years and his innate genius (he speaks over twenty languages), has developed the *siddhi* (spiritual power) of reading thoughts. Shree Maa clearly also has this siddhi. She tells us that, in deep concentration, she looks at you and sees all the thoughts you have had over the past three weeks as images in your aura. Many times when she looks at me, she looks like she is tasting bitter herbs and turns away.

Eventually, we left the ashram and headed into San Francisco and Fisherman's Wharf, where we broke our light fast with a fish dinner and caught our plane home at dawn the next day. Reintegration took a while.

Shortly after returning from this retreat, I got a phone call from Eileen, owner of Karuna Yoga in Northampton, saying, "I heard you were a great bhajan singer. I am opening a new studio called Karuna (compassion) Yoga in Northampton and I'd like to start a regular kirtan there. Would you be willing to set up a weekly practice?" That began what has become a full-time sadhana for me. It grew until I was out six nights a week, all over the East coast, little Johnny mantra seed, teaching folks this beautiful life practice. I became the kirtan wallah whose guru sings through him. Nowadays, whenever I feel sick or exhausted, I go inside and say, "I can't do it tonight. Shree Maa, you have to do it for me."

Chapter 8

TRAVELS WITH SHREE MAA

Kirtan is not verbal. It is from the heart. To merge into the heart is kirtan. --Ramana Maharshi

The next March I returned alone to Devi Mandir to celebrate Navaratri with Shree Maa and Swamiji. Navaratri is the nine-day celebration of the Divine Mother. When I arrived, I set up my camping gear at my assigned spot at the bottom of the hill, next to a stream, surrounded by the beautiful garden forest of the Devi Mandir. We fasted and chanted the Chandi Path every morning over the homa fire pit. We spent the day in silence, meditating, doing seva around the ashram and basking in the pleasure of the community of sadhus all working together, sharing their love of God. Every night we gathered in the temple and, after arati, Shree Maa's band rehearsed. We were getting ready for the next summer's tour, when Shree Maa planned to return to many of the cities she had visited the previous summer.

One night I was thinking that, since I would not be traveling with the band, their rehearsal might be more effective if I did not join in with my guitar. They were working on a song that was in 4/4 time, but it had one measure of 5/4 time in the middle of the song. After a few failed tries, they asked me to get out my guitar. The next time they played through the song, my guitar supported the action. Maa looked over at Mitra, the bandleader, and asked, "What was the difference? Why did it work this time?"

Mitra looked over at me and said, "Shubal!"

That night, right before dawn, the ashram cat wandered into my tent and sat on my chest, waking me up. He sniffed at my sterno-heated espresso maker, then sat for a moment in front of my makeshift puja and began to purr and knead the ground. Later, Swamiji told me this cat does his japa in this way. I felt honored to have the cat's darshan.

Another night, after we finished rehearsing in the temple, I could tell the band was sounding very tight; we were all well-practiced in Maa's unique songs and singing style. I had written a song, called "In Her Room," about the peace that she radiated. The sadhus were quietly sitting around when I spoke, "Maa, can I sing a song I have written for you?" On one level, I wanted to sing a love song to my beloved; on another level, there was an element of ego involved. I still wanted to be special. Maa very kindly gave me permission and I began to sing. However, the skin of an almond I had been eating was stuck in my throat. The harder I tried to sing, the croakier it got, until I could barely get the words out. The satsang was laughing. They knew that Shree Maa was giving me a lesson.

Near the end of my retreat I wanted some private time with Swamiji to discuss sadhana and life in general. On the day I was leaving, he said he would meet with me. The day dragged on as I watched him meet with other people and I wondered why he was ignoring me. Finally, he asked me to step into his office, a small trailer filled with about fifteen computer screens, papers, all kinds of stuff everywhere. We sat on the floor and I asked him, "Swamiji, how am I doing?"

He said, "Don't you know? Did you have a good time while you were here socializing with the sadhus?" Then he abruptly ended our interview. I realized I had missed an opportunity by not delving deep enough into my sadhana while I was there. Part of me, still caught in wanting the approval and love from others, felt I had disappointed Swamiji. The vibe that I got from Swamiji was always confusing. I never knew whether he found me good, strong, and clear, or whether he found me weak and confused (as my father always saw me). Sometimes he seemed to be laughing at me. And just like with my father, I

126

felt a strong love from him sometimes, while other times I felt competition. It's still a puzzle.

As I was leaving, Maa brought me into the temple and handed me gifts—a beautiful silk cloth to put on my puja table, and artificial flowers from Walmart to surround my holy space. She gave me fruit for my journey home, which I shared at kirtan when I got back with my community.

Arriving back at Karuna, we passed around the slices of apple, and each person was surprised by the scent of Shree Maa's temple in the apple. I was delighted. All in all, this time with Shree Maa had opened my heart even more to the mysteries that lay beyond her form. I was in love with her, with Chandi, with the Devi Mandir. I could feel that I was beginning to love myself. I knew that Shree Maa would be arriving soon at my home and we would put on her programs in Northampton. I did not realize that when Shree Maa left Northampton, I would be traveling with her.

Three months later, Shree Maa returned to my home in Wendell for the Northampton programs. Again, she brought a caravan of sadhus and husbands and wives and children, and many of her followers who could not bear to stay behind. They set up tents in my yard and camped out on my rooftop. Everywhere we looked there were sadhus, kirtan, chanting, meditation, chopping wood, repairing harmoniums—a circus of joy, love, and happiness. The programs in Northampton were filled with people. At the first night's program, Shree Maa advised everyone to meditate, she sang, and then it was time for a blessing. All two hundred and seventy people who had packed into the yoga center got in a big line, and, one by one, came up to Shree Maa for some sandal paste on the third eye, a smile from a saint, and a blessing. It was a night of pure love.

The next day was Mother's Day. While we were preparing for that evening's program, my partner requested that since this was Mother's Day, Maa and Swamiji might offer a *Kumari* puja—a ritual dating back thousands of years in India that honors the divine mother in the form of a virgin girl child. A little seven- or eight-year-old girl is dressed up like a Hindu goddess and placed center stage in front of the satsang. Swami Satyananda sits in front of her and chants esoteric Sanskrit mantras for half an hour. Then he begins to give the girl sweets, and she is allowed to eat all she wants. The small girl is laughing, Swamiji is laughing, everyone in the room is laughing, and the kumari is stuffing her face with candy and cake. Even though most folks found the Sanskrit chanting alien, the joy emanating from the child, Swamiji, and, of course, Shree Maa, made the unusual night a success in the Northampton community.

One of Maa's jobs, given to her by Ramakrishna, was to create temples and puja spaces in people's homes. We lived in the woods and our meditation room had floor-to- ceiling windows on three sides, overlooking the forest. Maa moved all the furniture out, then took all the murtis in the house, along with most of the pictures of holy people, and created a complex mandala of flowers, pictures, statues, water, incense, more flowers, and candles. It was a work of art. Every morning at six a.m., Maa would sit in front of the Buddha murti and begin her chanting, while placing flowers in a very symmetrical, organized way, sometimes singing, sometimes silent. We sat in awe as we meditated around her, feeling the power of her sadhana. When she finished her chanting, we all gathered together and spent another several hours chanting all seven-hundred verses of the Chandi Path at breakneck speed.

Maa and her band of sadhus stayed with us for two weeks. We put on the programs in Northampton and we spent hours chanting the Chandi Path. Of course, there was also plenty of time for singing, walking in the forest, and hanging out with

128

these gurus. When it was time for them to travel on, I was invited to join them and play in the band. Even though my old Subaru's brakes were so worn that I had to say a little prayer every time I tried to stop, I joined Shree Maa's caravan. Swamiji organized our travels with walkie-talkies in each car, and we headed for Washington D.C.

In suburban D.C., we stayed at the home of two doctors, a very fancy house with a big backyard where we set up our tents and got ready for our first program at the Hindu temple. We gathered in the recreation room, where the doctors had filled one entire wall with a giant television set, more like a movie screen. Maa has a way of communicating a great deal with a smile or glance. It was clear she was having trouble with this television. Finally she turned to the group of sadhus and said, "We need to move this TV out of the room." Despite the doctors' apprehension, we picked up that huge TV and carried it into the garage. There was an immediate shift of energy and the recreation room quickly became Maa's temple.

Next morning we got up at our standard 5:30 a.m. and began chanting. Usually Maa was there with us, but today she was not to be found. It was a damp, rainy morning and, after not finding Maa in the house, we put on our raincoats and began to look for her in the yard. We finally found Maa in the back under a tree, where the doctors had placed a large stone Shiva lingam amid the leaves and dirt.

A Shiva lingam is a egg-shaped stone that represents divine regenerative energy and more. This one was about eighteen inches in diameter and four-feet tall, with a dome top. It sat in a tray that was shaped like a teardrop. The stone and tray together were a symbol of Shiva's lingam piercing Durga's yoni. On the highest level, the lingam and yoni together area symbol of the conjoining of creation with consciousness to form our world. The Shiva lingam is one of the holiest objects on the tantric path. If you look at a lingam as coming up through the yoni, you are viewing this penetration from inside the body of the Divine Mother Durga! In other words, our reality, our world, is the womb of Chandi Maa. This is one of the secrets of the lingam.

At 5:30 a.m. on a rainy morning, there stood Shree Maa using her sari to wipe the collected dirt and leaves from the Shiva lingam. How she knew it was there I do not know. We covered her with one of our jackets and helped her finish cleaning the lingam. I do know something about the intensity of her love for Shiva. Although she was old, sick with diabetes, skinny and frail, she stood in the rain and loved her Shiva.

I remember a time Maa warned us of the potential for upcoming cataclysm. She predicted that sometime in the near future many souls would have to leave their bodies, and after this cataclysm, we would enter the Golden Age, when compassion, truth, and love would rule the world. When she said this, a friend of mine went up to her and said, "Does this mean I am going to have to die, Maa?"

Maa looked into his eyes and said, "Why are you worried about that?"

Emmanuel, the disembodied spirit, put it this way: "Don't worry. Death is perfectly safe. It's like taking off a tight shoe."

A few days later we gathered at the Hindu temple to prepare for our evening program. When we traveled with Maa, each of us carried our own little altar. I had my statues of Durga, Lakshmi, and Saraswati, and some pictures and flowers. In the center of the temple there was a giant Shiva statue. We were all searching out spaces for our personal pujas when Maa instructed me to sit directly in front of Shiva. I set my space up as I usually did, with statues, pictures, and flowers. After a few minutes I looked up to discover Maa looking down at me. She knelt and began rearranging my statues. She brushed some dust and ashes from my cloth and neatened my floral arrangement. When she was done, everything looked so beautiful. She looked at me and said, "*Satyam, shivam, sundaram.*" *Satyam* means truth, *shivam* is goodness, and *sundaram* is purity, beauty or cleanliness. In other words, truth is goodness is cleanliness.

When a saint offers you a teaching like this, you have to be very careful to study the words and the meaning in your own life. In this situation I came to understand that the outer environment is a reflection of our inner state, or alternatively, the demons live in the cobwebs. The truth was that for most of my life I had not been truthful, I had not been good, and I had not been clean. As Bill Cleghern (a Sai Baba meditation teacher) taught me, I came from a tradition of liars. My mother was a compulsive liar. She was also a thief, even stealing from her children. My mother never even taught me to brush my teeth. Maa reminded me, in that moment, that it was time to let go of my Earth lineage story and to move towards free play. In other words, clean my room.

Over the next few days, Maa created the most beautiful altar where the huge TV had been. She took everyone to Walmart. It's always so interesting when Maa goes to Walmart. One time, when my friend Sadananda was there, Maa went to Walmart and filled three shopping carts with artificial flowers, cloth, and all kinds of sweets and junk food. When they went to pay, the bill was six hundred dollars. The woman who carries Maa's money said, "Maa, I only have forty-seven dollars here." Maa reached inside her sari and pulled out an old-fashioned purse. What do you think, she had the exact amount of money needed to pay the bill.

So Maa took everyone to Walmart and we bought all kinds of flowers and other items to decorate the puja space. Maa and Swamiji went into their RV and brought out statues and various holy objects to put into the sacred space. When everything was assembled, Maa stood looking around the room.

On one wall was a painting of a scene in India of women (some bare-breasted), sitting by the river with their buckets. Maa took out one of those classic posters she had of the goddess Kali and began using pushpins to put the poster over this painting. The doctors who were our host and hostess stood watching, aghast. Apparently this painting was done by a famous artist and had considerable value. Everyone in the room began to chatter, "Maa, please don't, it's valuable." Maa had this very strange smile on her face, almost like an impish child who is knowingly doing wrong. She took the pushpins and superimposed Kali over the Indian river scene. The doctors smiled. What could they do? Again and again, as I traveled with Shree Maa, I saw that she is free.

There is a story told by my friend, Devanathananda. He lives in Napa right near Shree Maa's ashram. Once, he picked up the phone and heard Shree Maa's voice on the other end. She said, "Devanath, I need to go shopping. Come pick me up." Devanath is without a doubt one of the worst drivers ever. He manifests the idea that "when it's his time, it's his time" by driving on the wrong side of the road, driving at very high speeds, and driving with his attention on seven other things. He is a very dangerous driver. This day, however, he was on his best behavior because Shree Maa was in the car. After a few minutes he turned to Maa and said, "Maa, would it be okay if I drove the way I always drive?" Maa looked back at him, and with absolute delight in her voice she said, "Go for it!" She punctuated her remark with a swing of her fist.

From Washington, D.C. we traveled north to Princeton, New Jersey. Our hosts in Princeton were extremely wealthy. We were staying at a farm owned by a corporate head who traveled to New York City each morning by helicopter. The farmhouse was two hundred years old and nearby was this football field-sized, three-story barn. The very beautiful main house accommodated all of us (with most of us sleeping on the floor).

Our plan was to camp out in Princeton and travel up to New York City for two programs—one at Integral Yoga, the second at Jivan Mukti studio. Integral Yoga owns a complex of brownstones in the West Village, with one building devoted to health foods and vitamins, a second is a bookstore, and the third building houses dozens of yogis and a complex of yoga studios and presentation rooms.

It was great to be back in New York City. We arrived early in the afternoon, unloaded our equipment, and had five or six hours to rest before the program. No way I was going to sleep while I was back in my old stomping grounds. I walked through the West Village to the East Village, where I hung out with my hippie friends back in the '60s, and ended up down on Houston Street watching the bocce players bounce their wooden balls off each other.

I had been living on a vegetarian diet, but staring at me from across the street was Katz's delicatessen. I could smell the pastrami, the pickles, my childhood, my traumas. I found myself standing in front of the sandwich man and slipping him an extra dollar so he would make my pastrami sandwich extra thick. I took the sandwich, pickles, and French fries to my table. I opened my mouth wide and took a bite. Something so foreign, so alien, so inedible filled my mouth. Good grief! What had become of my childhood yearning? What was I to do? I emptied the contents of my mouth into a napkin, took my punch ticket (New Yorkers know what I mean by that), paid my bill, and left.

Around seven o'clock that night we all gathered in a large room at Integral Yoga. Shree Maa sat in a corner; next to her sat Swami Satyananda; to the right of Satyananda was the band. I was the rhythm guitarist. We had spent much time at the ashram rehearsing Maa's songs and the band was pretty hot. At one point Maa began to sing one of her songs in such a deep devotional voice that one by one the musicians stopped playing to listen. Soon there was no accompaniment, only Shree Maa singing in complete absorption, her mind immersed in samadhi. When she finished the song, total silence filled the room. All two hundred of us were in a deep trance. Swami Satyananda was totally gone, eyes rolled back in his head, body like stone. The silence went on—five minutes passed, ten minutes passed, complete silence. Finally Swami Satyananda came back to normal consciousness, cleared his throat, and the program continued.

Later we asked Swamiji what had happened. He said, "Listening to Maa sing, I moved into a deep state of concentration and lost all body awareness. I floated in a world in which all was one and that same world was floating in me. Then I heard a tiny voice calling, 'Swamiji, Swamiji, come back, come back, we need you.' That voice was Shree Maa, so gradually I reentered my body and grounded my mind enough to continue the program."

Afterwards, Devanath, Deva Priya, Saradananda, a few others and I drove home in the van. We were all dressed in white, red dots on our foreheads, and we were all high from our experience. As we got off the highway, We saw a big sign that said "no left turn." All of us, that is, except the driver. He made the left turn and immediately lights started flashing on a police car behind us. The New Jersey policeman came up to our car, looked in the window, saw all of us seated rather tensely, red dots and all. "License and registration," he said. Devanath pulled out the registration and his license and gave it over. The big white van, called The Dodge Quest, was registered to the Devi Mandir. The California Department of Motor Vehicles, however, had translated the name of Shree Maa's ashram. The policeman read out loud to all of us, "This truck is registered to the Temple of the Divine Mother in Napa, California. You need to be more careful, sir." He handed us back our paperwork and sent us on our way. I can imagine the story he shared with his fellow policemen.

The next night was Shree Maa's program in New York City at Jivan Mukti yoga studio. In the morning, tractors hauled hay into the giant barn on the property in Princeton. We heard a rumor that Krishna Das would be performing in the barn that night. When we got together for the morning satsang with Shree Maa, we were told that Maa was not feeling well. Maa weighed eighty-five pounds and had diabetes; everyone worried about her health. That day her blood sugar was out of control, Maa could not get up, and the program for that night was canceled.

Chapter 8A

KRISHNA DAS

Later that afternoon, Krishna Das arrived with his band, our first meeting. We talked about Shree Maa, about Neem Karoli Baba, about kirtan. Turned out we had been born around the same time, within twenty miles of each other on Long Island; we were both alienated hippies; we both got into the blues when we were young. Of course, he went off following Maharajji while I went off following Muddy Waters, but that afternoon we sat around laughing at shared experiences and enjoying each other's sense of humor.

I asked him if I could sit in that night, and he said sure. How cosmic. The one night out of the last six weeks that we did not have some sort of a program with Shree Maa was the night I got to play with Krishna Das. We had a sound check around five o'clock. I met John McDowell, the master drummer, who had come down from the city to perform with Krishna Das. Then we sat in the kitchen of the main house and watched the cars arriving. Three hundred people found seats on the hay-covered floor of the barn.

I knew all of Krishna Das' material and had developed my own style of playing bhajan and kirtan on the guitar, so I was really looking forward to supporting him with the highest level of energy I could muster. As we began to play I felt my consciousness drift into the oneness that musicians, with our unique form of meditation, enter when the band unifies in the music. Krishna Das organizes his program so that the energy rises over the space of two or three hours. By the end of the first hour the unification transcended the band and all three hundred of us rocked *Om Namah Shivaya*. Right at the moment that the energy reached its peak, a giant flash of lightning, followed by a loud crack of thunder, filled the barn. A huge thunderstorm broke out, pounding inches of rain on the tin roof of the barn. With the thunder, the rain on the roof, and the presence of Maharajji, it was bliss.

While it's true that Krishna Das has a way of muting the PA channels of the people who sit in, he did tell me he loved the way I played. On the *Hare Krishna* kirtan, he kept going and going and I kept pushing and pushing on my guitar. John McDowell told me he thought I added a lot to the kirtan. At the time, I did not realize I would get a chance to be in Krishna Das' band, and get to know him as a friend. He is a true sadhu and a good man. After the kirtan, after our goodbyes to Krishna Das and his team, we sat softly speaking of the powerful love and the great gifts that one receives in the presence of one's highest self in the form of one's guru.

Krishna Das and Shubal

I got to know Krishna Das well during his regular visits to Northampton. He invited me to join his band for his performances in New England. It was always quite an incredible moment for me, sitting in front of five hundred sadhaks, next to

Krishna Das, accompanying him in his powerful kirtan. After the performance we would talk guitar. One of his early gurus was Mississippi John Hurt. I am well versed in John Hurt's music and we shared lots of stories about our encounters with him while he was still alive back in the Sixties.

One day I noticed Krishna Das was lusting after my guitar, a beat-up old Martin J40 that looked like it had been through the guitar wars. Finally he asked me if I wanted to sell it. I did not, but the next morning the two of us drove off to the local music store to examine a wide variety of Martin guitars. Krishna Das was determined to get a new guitar. He offered me my choice of any guitar in the shop in return for my guitar. The offer was such that I could not refuse, so I picked out a guitar exactly like the guitar I owned, but brand new. I took it for myself and gave Krishna Das my old beater. Even though the guitars were the same model, the new J40 Martin was a major improvement for me.

The previous year I had had to sell my 1961 Martin D28 in order to pay doctors' bills from the pancreatitis. I had worked all summer at a dollar and seventy-five cents per hour to earn the two hundred and thirty-five dollars this Martin had cost me in 1961, and I had carried it with me all these years. I grieved to part with it just to pay rent. But my life had to go on. Krishna Das knew the whole story. He had helped me out financially when I was sick, and he kept me in the band even though I was sick. When KD agreed to this trade, I felt this was the hand of Maharajji, still looking out for me, using Krishna Das as he does in so many ways to put into my hands an excellent instrument for my own mission.

Months later, we were playing at Kripalu Center. I arrived early and the two of us went into his private room to talk. A few weeks earlier I had sent KD my journal entries concerning my experiences with Ram Dass, including the perception of my "self" floating as a small cloud in the corner of my awareness. KD spoke of his time with Maharajji and of an experience where he found his "Krishna Das-ness" floating in the corner of his awareness. I jumped to the edge of my seat and I said, "Krishna Das, that was my experience also!"

He said, "It's a good thing I haven't yet read your story or you'd wonder." It was an intimate and revealing exchange. This reminded me of that remark from Ram Dass when he got back from Burma and said, "After three weeks I saw my sense of self floating in the corner of my awareness." This must be the way of Neem Karoli Baba; he gives this specific gift of detachment.

I had many opportunities to play with Krishna Das over the years. As he does with all musicians, eventually he decides to move on and one day he wrote me, "I love you, and I love the way you play, but I've now got David. He's playing with me."

I never asked him for work again, but our friendship is strong and we get to see each other once or twice a year when he comes to town. Last summer, during one of his visits to western Massachusetts, I took Krishna Das for a drive in the woods. We stopped in front of an open pastoral meadow and I turned on my digital recorder. We began to speak of his early life, his experiences that led him to his guru, and the road that includes wealth and fame on which he now travels. The interview was recorded for my radio show, "Pioneer Spirit," which aired weekly in the Pioneer Valley of Massachusetts.

As Krishna Das and I neared the end of the interview, we could feel the presence of Neem Karoli Baba so strongly. We stood together in the forest, hugging with tears in our eyes. The true meaning of the words Ram Dass once spoke to me became clear: "Time and space do not define friendship." The one sure thing that Ma Chetan Jyoti always said about Krishna Das was, "he is a true sadhu," to which I wholeheartedly concur.

To read the interview with Krishna Das, go to Appendix II.

Chapter 9

RETREATS WITH SHREE MAA

A world in the making can be likened to a great jigsaw puzzle whose parts have life and are capable of independent movement. The hand of God must move these pieces before the complete picture can be revealed. The way in which man can find his own place is to tune his instrument to the keynote of the chord to which he belongs. The chording vibration sounds in the innermost being of man and can be heard only in silence. When we go to that inner chamber and listen, then will the voice of God speak to our soul and we will know the keynote of our life. --Hazrat Anayat Khan

The next day we loaded up our caravan and left for Reading, Pennsylvania. We were planning a two-week retreat for all of Maa's devotees from around the USA. The event was to take place at the large home of one of her devotees, tucked away in the woods. We arrived a few days early at the strange-looking house, which was built around a swimming pool in the center of the home. We all slept on the deck that ran around the outside of the house. In order to set up our puja tables, we immediately took over the recreation room, moved all the furniture out, and each found a little space along the wall. We settled in for some days of regular sadhana before everyone arrived, rising at 5:30 a.m. each morning and chanting the Chandi Path for a few hours before breakfast. Then we spent the rest of the morning preparing for our guests. After lunch came siesta time. Shree Maa and Swamiji always retreated to their RV and locked themselves in until dinner.

One day after lunch, instead of napping I went to my puja table to sing a little kirtan quietly. I lit my candle (a tiny tealight) and incense, and after a little silent japa, I turned my back to my puja space and began to sing. After about ten minutes, my kirtan was interrupted by Swamiji. It was extremely unusual to see him between the hours of one and five in the afternoon. He turned to me and said, "Whose puja table is that?" I turned to see where he was pointing and found my candle had overheated and my puja table space was in flames. I quickly doused the flames before they could burn down the millionaire's house. Swamiji turned and left the room.

There were so many amazing coincidences around this man. I know that when consciousness turns into the intentional flow of the universe, when consciousness accesses the Akashic Records, very strange things happen. In this case, Swamiji's intuitive return to the meditation room saved much property and possibly even lives. The next day a memo went around to everyone advising them to only use votive candles in holders that were fireproof! That was known as the "Shubal memo."

People began arriving by the dozens after parking their cars way down on the dirt road. Tents were set up in the field and a big showering facility was established. Shree Maa insisted that everyone wash their bodies after every sitting visit to the bathroom, so we needed lots of showers. The cooks started preparing food for a hundred people. The rest of us devoted our time to seva—planning workshops on Durga puja, Shiva puja, and the Chandi Path, early morning meditations, afternoon kirtans, and evening cultural programs. We rose early in the morning for meditation, then did our private pujas until breakfast oatmeal was served. Late morning was siesta time. After lunch we broke up into groups and some of us studied the Shiva puja, some the Durga ritual, and others sang kirtan. Evening siesta and dinner were usually followed by cultural events.

For the second night program I organized a performance with the talented people who had come to the retreat. The show began with an Indian-style dance by Amy, accompanied by Damaru, a djembe player from New York City, who was a student of Ma Chetan Jyoti, and me. It became apparent immediately that Amy was offering a rather sexual dance, which was totally inappropriate in front of Maa. Very quickly we saw Maa turn her face away. This was not good. Next came Scott and William, puppeteers from GEP studios in New York City, who offered a semi-funny puppet show with a giant ventriloquist's dummy in the shape of an Indian guru. One of them asked the guru questions, and the other, in a pitiful Indian accent, responded with some totally lame jokes. This did not go over very well either.

The following night's cultural performance was a little different. The evening began with Swamiji discoursing on the nature of the Divine Mother and the systematic, scientific way to approach her. After he had talked for half an hour, Shree Maa asked me to lead a kirtan. A few months previously I had written a very personal kirtan to Shree Maa, which I began to sing. The chorus of a hundred people responded passionately to my words. *Shree Maa Jai Maa Mata Bhavani* (Victory to Shree Maa, the Mother of the Universe). The energy spiraled upwards, Shree Maa and Swamiji both went deeply into samadhi. In the end we kept repeating, "Shree Maa" over and over, louder and louder, with more and more love and passion, until we reached the peak and gradually slowed down until we were softly whispering her name. The greatest gift for a kirtan wallah is when his singing facilitates his guru's samadhi. I received this gift with humility, recognizing that I am closest to Maa in my kirtan environment, as well as closest to the real "me." It has little to do with the "me" I think I am. The level of oneness and love that we reached that night through kirtan came from when I asked Shree Maa to sing through me . . . and she had agreed. The next day at lunch folks told me of their experience during the kirtan. It moved me deeply to hear that so many had touched their innermost self through the chanting. I realized it was no longer my kirtan; it belonged to the power of Maa moving through me.

A memorable event occurred on the second to last day. After our morning sadhana, Shree Maa offered darshan to the entire group. Darshan essentially means "being in the presence of and receiving the blessing of a saint." In the case of Shree Maa, everyone lined up and came up to Maa one at a time. She touched each forehead with a little kumkum, and in some cases allowed a devotee to touch her feet. Sitting next to her was Swamiji, holding a small teacup in his hand half-filled with yogurt. With a teaspoon, he was depositing a small amount of yogurt in the palm of each devotee as a form of prasad. After we received our blessing and yogurt, I sat with my friend Sadananda, watching the proceedings. One by one our friends came up to Shree Maa and dissolved in peaceful smiles of bliss. One by one, they turned to Swami Satyananda and held out a hand to receive a teaspoon of the holy yogurt. We watched as they held their hands up to their mouths and ingested the prasad. Towards the end of the ritual, it suddenly struck me that Swami Satyananda offered a teaspoon of yogurt to a hundred people without ever refilling the cup! Horripilation coursed through my body.

The goings-on around a great guru are always very subtle. Swami Satyananda's siddhis do not necessarily indicate enlightenment. Siddhis—the power to read thoughts, the power to transform energy into matter, the power to manifest physical form in two places at once—come to individuals as the kundalini energy rises up the spine. Neem Karoli Baba and Ramakrishna taught that these powers come with spiritual development, but they are not to be used. In order to reach the final goal, according to these great teachers, you must focus totally on the goal and not be distracted by these various abilities. Nevertheless, sometimes a spiritual teacher will use these abilities to awaken, to heal, or to fulfill destiny, or even to impress the gullible. There are stories of Sathya Sai Baba, near the end of his life, using magician's tricks to pretend to have these abilities. Perhaps at one point in his life Sai Baba did have these abilities, but when I knew him, indications were that his focus was in a different area.

On the last day of the retreat, Maa and Swamiji held a fire ceremony in the backyard. We sat around the fire as Swamiji led us in a rapid chant of the Chandi Path. At the end of each of the seven hundred verses, we took a small handful of rice, touched it to our hearts, and threw it into the fire with a resounding *swaha! Swaha* generally translates as "I am one with god"—one way to end a mantra. Symbolically, we were taking those qualities that undermine our peace and happiness and throwing them into the fire of concentration to move ourselves slightly closer to reality.

I had now been with Maa and her sadhus for over two months. I had eaten only sattvic foods, slept little, offered hours of sadhana, led dozens of kirtans, and basked in the energy of this amazing enlightened saint and her wonderful little band of "dharma bums." As the retreat ended, I packed my bags and made plans to return home and begin my life again, if that was possible. I felt forever changed by the lessons I had learned and by observing the unique behavior of a soul freed from the bonds of psychology and attachment. Henry Miller said, "Peace and happiness are found only in infinite wealth or absolute poverty. Anything in between is a trap."As Leonard Cohensaid in one of his beautiful poems, "You ask if I will leave you. I will not leave you. Owning everything, I have nowhere to go." That's how it felt as I began to think about creating physical distance between my guru and myself.

Swamiji called me over for a short walk in the woods. I mentioned I had received the funds to be able to travel with him to Europe. I understood that most of the musicians were not following him, so I offered my musical talents to help support their programs in Europe. Swamiji said it would be more wonderful if I would come with them to India. I considered the possibility. Swamiji took me into Maa's RV and the three of us sat quietly for a few minutes. Maa asked me how I was, and I responded by saying I was a mess. I told her of my anger, my sexual obsessions, my petty jealousies and fears. Maa smiled at me so sweetly as I sat across from her. I said, "I just want to grow closer and closer and closer."

She said, "We are already one. What would you like to give up?"

"I would like to give up sexual objectification, obsession, frustration, and anger."

Maa said, "It will fade, and I will help." Then she looked directly into my eyes and pointed at me. "You are a man, you are a sadhu, stop this behavior."

I knew exactly what she meant. I remembered telling Ram Dass about a woman I had met. At that time he said to me, "Well, you don't quite see her as a bag of bones yet, do you?" We are all bags of bones. All that is born will die. Karunamayi had begun the healing with her delicious peaches and now Maa was giving me the tools to leave those behaviors behind.

It was time to leave. I loaded my bags in the back of the pickup truck, and Sadananda, Dona, and I headed back through Amish country, back to New England, back to Wendell. Like Steppenwolf before me, I had a new perspective, a new sadhana, and a new love, my sweet Shree Maa.

Because of business commitments, I was unable to go with them to India. I was sad because I knew this trip with Maa and Swamiji was a golden opportunity. There are many stories of their adventures while they traveled through Europe and India. The story that moved me most deeply took place in Benares. Swami had arranged for the group to spend a night in the great

Kashi Vishwanath Temple—a great honor because Westerners are usually not allowed in this temple. As the sun set, the priests escorted everyone out of the temple until it was completely deserted. At 8 p.m., Shree Maa, Swamiji, and her sadhus were locked in, with the doors locked both inside and out so no one could enter or leave until 4 a.m. the next morning when the priests would begin worship. They were completely alone. Each of Maa's sadhus set up their own small puja space and began to chant the Chandi Path. Sometime after midnight, a strange man came into the temple. He quickly walked around the perimeter, walked up to Shree Maa, offered his hands in the classic Indian prayer position, then quickly left. Everyone wondered where this fellow came from. No one except the priest had the key and he was asleep. There was no way in or out. Later Maa said, "That was Shiva. He came to give us his darshan."

Then, as they made their way to Rishikesh, the planes hit the World Trade Center towers and the world was thrown into crisis. Because of the tension, Maa and Swamiji decided to cut short their India trip and come back to the USA. In a sense, it was probably better I was not with them. The spiritual life tends to create the impression that the political world is like a comic book, until the physical suffering strikes home. Ram Dass always used to talk about the dilemma of whether to act or to sit and meditate. He would always refer to Frank Sinatra singing "do be do be do" as the best expression of this paradox.

A few years later, I arranged to attend the Shivaratri celebration at Devi Mandir. Shivaratri is the celebration of Shiva's gift to humanity. Swami Satyananda told us the following story:

Shiva disguised himself as a wandering naked sadhu. He wandered into a small village in India, went up to the town well, and spoke to the women who were collecting water. "May I have a drink, please?" said Shiva.

The women, seeing only his nakedness, shrieked and ran off to their husbands, the Brahmans who were sitting in the village square. The women said, "Come quickly! There is a naked sadhu by the well and he exposed himself to us, and we are greatly offended. Please go and curse this sadhu."

The Brahmans marched off to the well. When they saw the naked sadhu standing by the well, they also became outraged. They spoke harshly, "Sadhu, you have offended our wives. We have no choice but to curse you. Your penis shall fall off and lie on the ground."

Well, in those days in India, when a Brahman cursed you, you were cursed. There was no way to undo the curse except by the cursor. So Shiva's penis fell to the ground. Shiva paid no attention at all, he moved over to a nearby rock, sat down, and fell into deep samadhi.

As his meditation grew deeper, the blue sky became cloudy, the leaves on the trees turned brown, the crops in the field wilted, and everyone in the village became depressed. The Brahmans sat around the town square debating the cause for this terrible drought. After hours of discussion, it occurred to them that the cause might be coming from the sadhu meditating by the well. They went back to the well and again confronted the sadhu. This time, however, Shiva revealed himself to the Brahmans. Once they saw that behind the dirty naked sadhu was Shiva himself, they fell down in prostration and offered apology after apology. They said they would be happy to mitigate the curse if only Shiva would bring back the color to their lives.

Shiva said, "I will be happy to take back my penis. Here are the ground rules. During the new moon of every month, you must celebrate my name. You will call this day Shivaratri. On the new moon in February/March, you will celebrate Mahashivaratri. This will be the special yearly celebration of my gift to humanity." Then Shiva said, "I must offer hope to humanity." It is then that he *gave us yoga. "On the day of this yearly celebration, you will have a feast at sundown. Then you will fast and sing my name until dawn. At dawn you will again feast and remember 'the Consciousness of Infinite Goodness'* (translation of Shiva's name).*"*

The night before the holiday, we all gathered in the temple to chant the *Rudraskatam*, a long complex song to Shiva. I had never seen this prayer before, but I took the transliterated Sanskrit text and sat in front of the fire next to Shree Maa. I had always been a moderate-to-poor chanter, with mild dyslexia, and I was hoping to be able to keep up with or at least follow Swamiji and the expert chanters of the Devi Mandir. We began moving slow enough for me to be able to keep up. At a certain point I felt Shree Maa move her hand behind my head. Suddenly, the pace picked up, and I found I could chant this mysterious poem as accurately and as fast as the experts. We flew through the poem, my mind completely immersed and focused on the vibrations coming through my throat. Somehow, I had suddenly become excellent at reading transliterated Sanskrit.

There were about sixty of us chanting that night, and at one point I lost my place. As Swamiji led the group, chanting in his unusual style, I heard "verse 360." It is not clear to me whether Swamiji really said this out loud or whether he sent me a telepathic message. It was, however, exactly the information I needed. Judge as you wish, whether it was my mind shifting into a higher level of concentration or whether it was a miracle that Shree Maa vibrated through my form, I accepted it as a gift from the goddess.

As the sun set on the evening of Mahashivaratri, we had a feast. During the evening, along with kirtan, it is traditional to offer four pujas to Shiva. At the end of the first puja, everyone formed a long line and one by one we came up to Swamiji to receive a blessing. The prasad took the form of *bhang*— cannabis tea (not quite tea, bhang is more like chai, a delicious drink with coconut, cardamom, cinnamon, and cloves). One of the characteristics of Shiva is that he is always intoxicated on bhang, so the tradition is on Shivaratri is for worshippers to ingest cannabis tea. As each of us approached Swamiji, we received a small Dixie cup of bhang. There must have been two hundred people at this program; each one received a strong dose of cannabis, which set the tone for a very interesting evening. Shree Maa called upon me to lead kirtan. I chose a very simple *Om Namah Shivaya* and we began the back-and-forth bellows pranayama, chanting Shiva's name. The energy began to increase. Soon people were banging bells, wailing on tambourines (according to Dave Stringer, the tambourine is a lethal weapon that should require a license to play), screaming Shiva's name at the top of our voices, and dancing around the temple in an intoxicated cacophony.

Around two in the morning the room was quiet. Maa sat in a corner, softly singing her beautiful Shiva bhajans. A Bengali harmonium player sat next to her, trying to follow. There was a Western woman who had studied Indian classical singing and developed a technique to be able to sing a microsecond behind the lead singer, so it sounded like she was singing in unison. Together, she and the Bengali harmonium player were improvising very complicated ragas from Indian classical music. I occasionally joined in with my guitar, but much of the time I simply sat next to Maa listening to their divine music.

At a certain point Maa asked the harmonium player if he knew a certain song that she had recorded. The song was one that moved my heart so deeply, a song that brought tears to my eyes every time I listened to the recording. Maa was about to sing it right in front of me. As she began to sing, it became clear that the harmonium player did not have a clue, so I picked up my twelve-string and began to accompany her. The rapport that one develops as a musician, the ability to unify your mind with other musicians in order to create music, is a skill that takes a long time to develop. When I began to play, my mind united with hers and my music became one with her voice. She sang and I knew which notes were coming next; I knew where to place my fingers to create the most beautiful harmonies, the most wonderful rhythmic supports for her song. We played the song together, flying to the heights. It was the peak musical moment of my life. Tears ran down my face, and I stared into her eyes when the song was over. She gave me the sweetest smile. I felt, more than ever, that Shree Maa and I were, also, the same person.

After a while, Shree Maa got up to stretch her legs. Later, I was told that as she stepped into the night air, she turned to one of her devotees and said, "Everyone is always falling in love with me."

As the sun came up, we were served a large meal, prepared by Shree Maa herself. Again, we stretched out the dining cloths across the floor of the temple and sat cross-legged eating this holy food. We had been up all night, so each of us found a little space in which to stretch out and get some sleep. As I mapped out my territory, Swami Satyananda came over and sat down next to me. He took my hand and said, "You are chanting very well." With his thumb, he began to stroke the back of my hand. As he stroked, I felt this incredible ecstatic energy rising up from the pit of my stomach; it reached my chest and throat and I felt myself overcome with love. When his thumb stopped moving, I felt the energy begin to fall back. Then he began to stroke my hand again, and again the energy rose. I thought, "This man has anger, but his spiritual power is undeniable."

To illustrate the brilliance of Swami Satyananda Saraswati, an interview I did with him for my magazine, *Time And Space*, is in Appendix II.

Years passed. I corresponded with Swamiji by email. I opened my heart to him about my strengths and weaknesses. I clearly remember when he wrote back. "Shubal, cut the shit and do sadhana." The crudeness and coldness of the response hurt me. My partner and I had not been to the Mandir in a long time. We wrote Swamiji, reminded him of his offer to marry us and to initiate us, and we asked to visit. He invited us to a beginner's weekend retreat.

The retreat began with some of the senior devotees teaching the pujas that we had learned years ago. We had no contact with Maa or Swami except at the public programs. I began to feel less welcome. There was one beautiful intimate moment with Maa, however. Near the end of the retreat, we all gathered in the temple for arati. As we sang, I became overcome with love, and my voice grew louder and louder, more and more passionate. With tears dripping from the outside corners of my eyes, I sang with my full heart. At the end of arati, Maa got up to leave the room. As she slipped out the door, she turned back into the room, looked directly at me, gave a little wave and the most beautiful look of love. My heart expanded. Later that day the retreat ended.

As we flew home, I began to feel that my work with Shree Maa was coming to a close. There is only one sadguru, the one who awakens you, and that was RD/Maharajji for me. But Maa and Swamiji gave me so much. Swamiji is such a scholar, he taught me how to perform puja, the meanings of the *Navarna* mantra (the most powerful mantra of Goddess Chandi, *Aim Hrim Klim Chamundaye vicce*), and the secrets of the Chandi Path. He is the smartest person I have ever met, with his photographic memory and his twenty-two languages, and his fifty books and translations of the holy books. While Swamiji and I had our differences over the years, my relationship with Shree Maa has remained that of total love. When things are bad, when my voice is harsh, when my body is weak, I say, "Shree

Maa, you have to sing through me, I cannot do it myself tonight." And there she is, with her loving, silent eyes, and her aura spreading for miles around her.

Shree Maa is the most realized being I have had as a friend, but Bhagwan Ram began to call me.

Chapter 10

MA CHETAN JYOTI

Place the name of Rama as a jeweled lamp at the door of your lips and there will be light, as you will, both inside and out. --Tulsi Das

Ma Chetan Jyoti and Shubal

While I was playing in Krishna Das' band, he brought a friend of his over from India, Swami Ma Chetan Jyoti from Rishikesh. She was Canadian born, and had gone from being a topless waitress to becoming a swamini in just one lifetime. She was the greatest kirtan singer I have ever heard. Her parents were movie stars (she would never tell me their names), and her father won an Academy Award. She grew up in the company of famous artists and actors. When she turned eighteen in 1960, she left home to become a waitress in Toronto, where she hung out with John Sebastian, Bob Dylan, Ian & Sylvia, and other up-and-coming folk singers at the time. She used to say that she got through her promiscuous period very quickly; by 1963 she was studying with a guru in Toronto and starting her lifelong sadhana.

In 1973, she had a dream calling her to India. She had recently married, and had just found a lump in her breast, which had been diagnosed as cancer. She ignored her family's cries and took off with her husband to New Delhi, where she found an apartment. After three weeks of sitting there, she went to a local hospital. She joined the line outside the clinic for many hours until it was finally her turn. She walked into a room where there were three men in white coats. She showed her diagnosis to the first doctor, who laughed and showed the paper to one of the other doctors, who said, "Madam, today is your lucky day. I happen to be a world expert on breast cancer. I am here giving a lecture at the university and meeting my friend, Doctor Kumar, here. Come, let's do the operation now." Mataji had the surgery and all was well.

Years later, she had thyroid problems and needed an operation to remove part of her thyroid gland. After she was anesthetized and the first incision had been made, they discovered thyroid cancer. These doctors were not qualified to complete the operation, so they called a doctor in Delhi to come to Rishikesh immediately. The drive takes six hours, so a decision was made to keep Mataji under anesthesia until the Delhi doctor arrived.

After the doctors left the operating room, the orderlies heard a mysterious *Om Namah Shivaya*. They went running from the OR into the hallway, terrified. A doctor stopped them in the hall and said, "What's the matter here?"

"There's a demon in the OR chanting *Om Namah Shivaya!*"

The doctor laughed and said, "Don't you know? That is Ma Chetan Jyoti, the great kirtan wallah. "

For six hours, while unconscious with her throat opened, she chanted *Om Namah Shivaya*.

Krishna Das brought Ma Chetan Jyoti to America. She traveled with him and led a kirtan in each performance. When she came to Northampton, I was in KD's band and got to meet her. When it was her turn to lead, she chose one of the most complex kirtans I'd ever heard, a bhajan really, dedicated to Shiva. Not one person in the room could follow her, not even KD, except me, and when it was over we were friends. She invited me to Ananda Ashram to accompany her later in the month. The New York City group was there—Damaru, the drummer; Kamaniya (a local NYC kirtan wallah); Ray Speigel (master tabla player); and Sruti Ram (a Woodstock kirtan singer, blessed be his memory). In spite the rudeness among the musicians, I came to realize Mataji's true power: horripilation, tears, and shakti laughter.

The kirtan was well attended, and Mataji took off from the start. She had warned me that Ray Spiegel hated guitar, so I was on alert. Mataji raised the energy through the roof, and we all played and sang with great intensity. At one point, Ray turned around from his tabla towards me and lifted both hands in a "keep quiet" motion The kirtan, however, was undiminished by his behaviors, and we all came together and finished with high energy. Later Ray came over to me and apologized, saying he thought he was supposed to take a solo at that point.

I decided then to organize a retreat for Mataji. She had so much to offer, so much to teach. I had spent time with Robert Moses, a great yogi from the Shivananda lineage and owner ofThe Old School, a retreat center in New Hampshire. I rented his facility and scheduled a retreat. We had about ten people sign up. Kamaniya and Damaru were there, along with other talented musicians and singers. Mataji took Saturday to teach us from the *Srimad Bhagavatam* (stories of Krishna).She was completely in love with Krishna. She also taught from a book, *I Am That*, by Sri Nisargadatta (one of India's great twentieth century teachers in the very strict *advaita* school, based on the Vedic doctrine of "non-dualism." His book is one of the great spiritual works of all time.). We walked down to the river and sat under a summer sun, singing to Ram and Krishna.

Saturday night was the great kirtan with all the master musicians in the band. A hundred people turned out for the kirtan. Mataji had a gift for pacing the kirtans perfectly to raise the energy to the highest levels. After the kirtan, Kamaniya and I stayed up late, and I sang many of the spiritual songs I had written. It was a very blissful night. The next morning, we all went down to the local cafe and had pancakes and eggs. With Mataji, it was total laughter. She told stories, jokes, sometimes profound, sometimes bawdy; she kept us all laughing and crying. When we said goodbye, Mataji headed off with Damaru and Kamaniya for pizza while I headed off the other way, towards home, digesting all that I had been taught.

Over the next few years, Mataji and I became pen pals. I distributed her CD on iTunes, so we were in constant touch. I loved the intelligence and humor behind her correspondence, and I urged her again and again to come to the USA. I wanted to take her with me on tour. I told her I would keep her busy. Since we were all poor, we could not get the ticket money for her trip until Kalidas (Lawrence Edwards, a psychotherapist and mystic from New York) helped out and the trip was planned.

Mataji arrived at Logan airport in Boston. You could not miss her. She had an imposing presence at 5'10" tall, heavily built, with a shaved head and wearing the orange robes of a Hindu *sannyasi* (female renunciate). I saw her at the baggage terminal and approached rather awkwardly, not knowing whether to hug her or touch her feet. She seemed equally awkward and reached out her hand to shake mine, then introduced me to Shivananda, her young tabla player. We only had two hours to get to Portsmouth, New Hampshire, for our first program of the tour. I could see they were exhausted, but we got there, set up, and offered the large seacoast community an amazing kirtan. Mataji's voice had developed a gruffness that I hadn't noticed previously. She complained of a sore throat for almost her entire visit. We were told that she was in the hospital suffering exhaustion before she left for America. Apparently she got up out of her hospital bed to catch the plane. There was some concern.

After driving back to Western Massachusetts, Mataji, Shivananda, and I settled down to discuss future travels. I had planned the tour of New England, scheduling about ten kirtans during the three weeks she would be with us. She asked me if I would be interested in traveling with them through Canada after the New England tour. I quickly said yes. The next two months were clearly plotted out with lots of kirtan, many miles to travel, and plenty of excitement. Mataji made me promise not to leave her side during the tour. Although without a doubt it was a very uncomfortable seat, Mataji insisted on riding next to me in the truck all the way. During these travels, Mataji told stories nonstop. She told me about the Papa Ram Das ashram in India, where Ram kirtan goes on twenty-four hours a day. She had a recording on her iPhone so I was able to listen to some of the great kirtan wallahs of India singing Ram kirtan.

She taught me a great deal about leading kirtan. Mataji said, "I start the kirtan, and if the Goddess (or God) does not take over very quickly, I stop and change the kirtan. I sing in many voices. The voice of shakti comes out in varied ways." She gave me plenty of advice: "It is a precious privilege to be able to practice kirtan sadhana. Wear clean, neat clothing, clean your body immaculately, and wash your mouth thoroughly before ever taking the names of God on your lips. Before beginning a kirtan, pranam to your musical instrument, be it a harmonium, a guitar, a tabla, or an ektar. Stay in the love as long as possible before speeding up."

Ma Chetan Jyoti was, without a doubt, the most charismatic, egocentric, brilliant, musically-gifted, humorous, cantankerous, insightful, two-faced, gossipy, sarcastic, and loving sannyasi I have ever met. She tended to exaggerate, but her stories were always exciting and educational. She was a mass of paradox. She loved Krishna, and great tears would come to her eyes when she told his stories or when she sang about him. She also loved Sri Nisargadatta and the path of non-dualism.

Our kirtans in New England were extremely successful. Hundreds of people turned out and Mataji received much support her free school in India. Mataji started the Ma Chetan Jyoti School of Music with Shivananda Sharma as her master teacher. In India, the great musicians would usually say, "If it is not your karma to be able to pay my rates, you are not ready to play." She balked at the whole concept and so began to raise money for free education for children; the school is thriving to this day, run by Shivananda.

Our time at Ananda Ashram was exceptional. This peaceful hundred acres just north of New York City is a place where deer run freely across the campus, and many great Indian musicians use the ashram as a retreat center. Some actually live there. Many nights after our kirtans, the classical musicians gathered and we heard some incredible jam sessions. One night we even had a blues jam session. I remember Roop Varma, a world-renowned sitar master. I could see his smile as I played. Later, he told me he very much enjoyed my blues. Nothing is as meaningful to a player as a positive response from a master.

Mataji insisted that I arrive at her cabin every morning at 6 a.m. for chai, and she had me stay by her side throughout the day. She warned me that there were sharks about. I did meet those sharks—other kirtan wallahs from New York City whose competitiveness and condescension would have pushed my buttons had I not been under Mataji's care. We had great musical moments and sang kirtan right up until the moment our wagon train left for Canada. Before we left, though, Mataji told us a story about her experience with the great Indian guru, Anandamayi Ma, the "bliss-permeated mother."

Mataji was living alone in Rishikesh. One day she heard that the great saint, Anandamayi Ma, was coming to stay in Hardwar, the town adjoining Rishikesh. Mataji bicycled to Amma's ashram and made her way into the darshan room, which was filled with Indian women. As Mataji stepped into the room, they fell into silence. Anandamayi Ma pointed her finger at Mataji and said, "Impure Westerner, get out. "

Immediately all the mothers (the older Indian women) pushed Mataji out of the room and out of the building. Mataji was totally saddened by the event, but that night she fell into a deep sleep and saw the face of Amma beckoning to her. Mataji woke up instantly, and without a thought she dressed, got on her bike, and rode all the way back to the ashram. When she arrived it was the middle of the night, and as before, she crept into the darshan room where she found Amma sitting alone in meditation; all the ma's were asleep on the floor. Mataji entered and bowed, and instantly Amma's eyes opened. When they locked vision, an electric bolt was transmitted into Mataji and she immediately fell into *bhava samadhi*(the state where you are lost in love).They stayed locked in this intense vision.

At this point, the other ma's heard a rustling and woke up to find this Westerner back on the scene. Again, they crowded around Mataji and began to eject her from the room. But she and Amma were locked in this visual bond and they both moved their heads around so their vision could remain locked as the mothers dragged Mataji out of the room. Anandamayi Ma then said to the women, "No. She is very pure. Go bring her back." The group burst out into the street and before Mataji had time to bike away, they surrounded her and brought her back. The rest of the day Mataji spent in deep meditation within the aura of Anandamayi Ma.

When I brought Mataji to the Kripalu Center for Yoga & Health in Stockbridge, MA, she almost refused to sing. I loved what a purist she was. When she smelled fish in the cafeteria, well, that was too much. Kripalu Center used to be one of America's great ashrams. Swami Kripalu began a lineage that ended with a teacher named Amrit Desai, who was a direct disciple of Swami Kripalu. He arranged to purchase a nunnery and turn it into a magnificent ashram. Desai taught his students to practice disciplined hatha yoga, celibacy, kirtan, and meditation. Then there was a scandal and Amrit Desi moved to Florida. Kripalu became more of a business, a resort hotel for yoga and healing arts. It is a very successful institution, and it was always wonderful to offer my kirtan practice at this venue. I led kirtan there many years ago, when it was just Krishna Das, me, and a few others sharing the practice. Nowadays there are many varied kirtan singers evolving out of Kripalu.

But Mataji was offended by the fish. I could tell that her hackles were up from the start. When we walked into the cafeteria, the smell of fish was pretty overwhelming. Mataji turned to me and said, "We are leaving!"

I said, "No Ma, everyone is waiting to sing with you. We must do the kirtan." Mataji agreed to sing, and once we started, she became empty and the goddess sang through her; the night was blissful and powerful. We blistered the paint. But when she returned to India, Mataji wrote an angry letter to Kripalu.

After the busy New England tour, we headed for Toronto—Mataji, a heavy Hindu nun; Shivananda, a five-foot tall Indian man with hair to his waist; Satya, the Western woman who took care of Mataji; and me. This was the beginning of an exciting time, with every minute chock full of joy and love. Toronto was so much fun. We did kirtan and *abishekam* (a ritual

160

of bathing the deities) at the Hindu temple. We sang at yoga centers and homes. There is a large Indian Diaspora in Toronto. One day, we went to the home of an Indian family for bhajans. With the Sai community in Boston, I had been to many Indian homes and anticipated lots of fun at this Sunday afternoon gathering. Shivananda and I arrived to find the house filled with families. Men, women, and children were all there for the bhajans and the meal to follow. Everyone got a chance to lead a bhajan. Some were expert and sang with great beauty, some were well meaning, but I needed to move my capo up and down the neck of my guitar to follow them.

Then it was my turn. I could feel the skepticism in the room as I began to play. I was the only Westerner in the room. As usual, however, I threw my head back, opened my throat, and sang the Krishna bhajan, *Bhajo Manava*. In the silence after I finished, I could feel the relief. "Ah, this Westerner can sing!" Suddenly everyone was shaking my hand. I felt like Murshid Sam, who had been greeted with skepticism by the Persian Sufis until the heard him sing his wazifas.

We were staying at the home of one of Mataji's students from India, and the family was in grief about a recent family loss, so having four sadhus descend on this little Toronto house was a real burden. They were as hospitable as they could be, but it was uncomfortable. Our Brahmin tabla player found out that the family came from the shudras, the untouchable caste, and he wanted to leave immediately. On one level I understand that this is pure prejudice, as the caste system now is filled with racism and class consciousness. In its origination back in Vedic times, a more spiritual age, the caste system provided for a dharmic life. When you were born, there was no need to worry about dating or marriage, no need to choose a career as you were born into who you would become. You were free to practice sadhana. As Karunamayi said to me when I asked her about sex before marriage, "Different cultures."

There were many powerful moments that had nothing to do with kirtan during our Canadian tour. We went up the tallest building in the world in downtown Toronto. Actually, it was the tallest elevator in the world. Mataji and I traveled up to the top, stepped out onto a small platform and looked out over the entire greater Toronto area. The floor of platform was made of glass and it seemed like we were suspended in space. We hugged and laughed.

One day, Mataji was hungry for Indian food. Toronto has a major Indian population, but as we wandered around the city we could not find a single Indian restaurant. It was hot, and there is no AC in my Volvo. The more we drove, the hungrier and more frustrated we became. Finally, way down at the end of a street, we saw a billboard that said Discount Samosas. We cheered, this must be the place. We enjoyed a great meal there, but we could not stop laughing about those discounted samosas. It became one of our slogans for the rest of the trip.

Back in India Mataji had two little dachshund puppies. She had it in her head that Target Stores sold small biker clothes for dogs and she was determined to get outfits for her pets. We stopped at every Target we passed, but it turned out that the outfits were a winter item; this was summer. As we left each store, we created a little circle in the parking lot to dance and sing, "If you want to be free, be just like me, *Om Hari Sharanam.*"

One afternoon we jumped into my car and traveled to the house where Mataji was born. This later became a hauntingly mystical event. Back in 1965, my grandfather took me for a ride to the lower East side of Manhattan. My grandfather was kind of a mafia dude, running liquor for the mob in the 1920s; then he worked for the International Ladies Garment Workers Union, once the largest labor union in the U.S. He drove down East 6th Street to Avenue B and showed me the building where he had been born. I thought it was just a trip down nostalgia lane, until three days later he died of a heart

162

attack. Mataji also left her body shortly after revisiting her birthplace.

When it came time for our reentry to the United States, we took a hotel room at Niagara Falls and spent the day at the Canadian Falls, wandering through the rainbows and mists, through the tunnels and dampness, and out into the brilliant sunlight. There were no words necessary in the peaceful power of our union. Mataji and I later sat in the restaurant overlooking the falls and ate salad. We had been traveling together for almost two months. I loved her so much. Sitting across from me in this restaurant, Mataji took my hand and said, "You know what, Shubal? I once told you that you were a mess. I now see that I was wrong. From now on I will call you Shubh. This word means 'pure' in Hindi."

Journey Behind the Falls · July 12, 2007

Left to right: Shubal, Shivananda, Ma Chetan Jyoti, Satya

As we came through customs, they stopped us to check our luggage. Our car was filled with instruments, a three-

163

hundred-pound Hindu nun dressed in orange, a 5'2" black-skinned, long-haired Indian fellow, Satya, and me, the aging hipster. A typical officious bunch of Customs officers took an interest in us and asked us into the inspection room. They were far from friendly, and though polite, we could feel the coldness and hostility in the room. They pointed to Mataji's harmonium. The boss spoke, "What is that?"

Mataji said, "Oh, that is a musical instrument."

"Please take it out of the case."

"Yes."

"Can you play it?"

"Well, I can, but I have one rule. When I start a song, I have to finish it!"

And the trap was set. Watching this unfold, I thought of the Chandi Path and the story of Durga and *Shumba* "Self-Conceit" and *Nishumba* "Self-Deprecation"—the two greatest demons in the universe. (Durga say, I'd be glad to marry self-conceit but I have one rule, he must defeat me in battle first!) Mataji took out her harmonium and began to play the Hanuman Chalisa, a forty-verse song with a chorus between each verse. Mataji took her time. It took over half an hour for her to complete the song. At first the customs officials were giving each other sneers. After about ten minutes, they were smiling and snapping their fingers. By the end of the Chalisa they were dancing around the room, *Jai Jai Hanuman, Janaki Jivana Ram Ram*. It was a complete tribute to the power of Ram, and what a great blessing for those Customs guys. Mataji could push buttons until the bell rang.

We had a few more kirtans lined up before I was off to California and Baba Hariji's ashram. Mataji, Shivananda, Satya, and I had grown so close. Finally we landed at Satya's house and it was time to say goodbye. Mataji and I stood by my car. She took my right arm and tied an orange string around my wrist. I dropped flat onto the ground and touched her feet. She chanted

164

the Mrityunjaya mantra over my head and pushed a small package into my hand. With tears in our eyes, we parted. Later I discovered the package contained a small electronic tamboura. I had heard Mataji using one and had liked the sound.

A few months later I received an e-mail from India. Mataji had lung cancer. Then on April 20, 2008, an email came from Shivananda Sharma, her school director and master tabla player: "Shubal, bro. What to say or what not. Today is Hanuman's birthday and just today around half past 10 a.m. our Mataji passed away. *Jai Radhe Radhe!*"

Everything about Mataji was extreme. Her kirtan was not only the best kirtan I have ever experienced, she sang with the authority of one whose only desire is to be one with God. Mataji gave so much during her lifetime. We know she waited until the holy day of her beloved Hanuman (Hanuman's Birthday) to leave us, and we touch her feet one last time. I pray that in her last moments she achieved union with her beloved Krishna.

Chapter 11

BABA HARIHAR RAMJI & BABA BHAGWAN RAMJI

Midway between praying and relinquishing, I rest,
Bhagwan Ramji

Baba Bhagwan Ram   Baba Harihar Ramji

Baba Harihar Ramji, aka Baba Hariji, or just Babaji, is an Aghori Master. The historically ancient Aghor tradition in India goes back hundreds of years, back to the ancient guru known as Dattatreya. The Aghor tradition is the most extreme in terms of renunciation and adherence to a strict sadhana. They are devoted to the aspect of the Divine Mother known as Sarveshwari (the one who observes the function of all), and offer regular pujas to her. Some of the sadhus, who receive approval from their own gurus, live in India's cremation grounds and sit in meditation from dusk to dawn, sometimes making their asana on the body of a corpse. They are the sadhus who stand on one foot, with one arm raised toward God, for years. Their fingernails grow through their palms. The point of these extreme practices is to confront one's darkest fears, to bring light to the shadow. As Carl Jung once said, "Enlightenment is not great lights and visions. Rather, it is bringing light to the dark parts of the mind." In other words, Aghori sadhus develop dispassion by allowing great pleasure and great pain to be experienced without attachment or revulsion.

Tantra is a most misunderstood religion/science. *Tan* means to acquire or attain, and *tra* means to keep or retain. First you must attain, then you must retain. See God everywhere and treat every moment as sacred, holy, and you are a tantrika. The practices developed to achieve this are more complex. The four activities that define a tantrika are: puja, mantra, initiation, and guru. You meet the guru, receive initiation and a secret mantra, and learn to do puja. In Tantra, puja is a practice that we try to do twenty-four hours a day in every thought, word and deed. By transforming our experiences into celebrations and acknowledgments of the perfection and beauty of the gift of awareness, we turn our entire lives into a prayer.

The idea of left and right-handed practices is wrong. In Tantra, there are practices for the many, and then there are practices for just a few. The five "m's"—*madya* (alcohol), *māṃsa* (meat), *matsya* (fish), *mudrā* (parched grain), and *maithuna* (sexual intercourse)—are part of tantric sadhana. By the way, the world of "Neo-Tantra " has nothing to do with Hindu Tantra. From what I have seen, Neo-Tantra seems to be more about getting naked together and being sexual rather than working on self-realization. But in Hindu Tantra, students choose their sadhana from the world's possibilities. Another interpretation of the word Tantra is "to weave." One sadhu might use kirtan, Vipassana meditation, and self-inquiry, weaving them all together for a very personal spiritual practice. Ramakrishna once said, "There are as many paths to God as there are fingerprints."

Babaji's story is very simple. He was born with the name Hari. He was a young man, living in India, when his brother came to him and told him that he had met a great man. He urged Hari to come with him and meet this guru, named Baba Bhagwan Ram, the living master in the Aghori lineage that stretched back four hundred years. He is called The Aghoreshwar. There were many miracles and powerful transformations attributed to Bhagwan Ram. Finally, after much urging by his brother, Hari agreed to meet Bhagwan Ram. When Hari was brought before the great guru, the guru paid no attention to him except, at one point, he turned and looked into Hari's face and Hari felt a tingling throughout his whole body. Afterwards, his brother congratulated him on receiving such a warm welcome. Hari did not feel it was a very warm welcome, but he could not clearly understand the sensation that he experienced in the presence of this guru. He returned to be with this teacher again and again until a firm love developed between them.

Hari moved to California, set up a travel agency (Astral Travel), and begin to earn money. Bhagwan Ram urged him to continue this and to earn as much money as he could. At this point, Babaji had created for himself a wonderful lifestyle, with many friends, plenty of money in the bank, a nice new car, and a very successful business. Hari traveled to India often to be with Baba Bhagwan Ramji. Many times, he asked Baba, "How can I become a monk?" Finally, after many "not yet's," Bhagwan Ram said, "Sell and give away everything you own except your car. Fill your gas tank. Begin to drive, and when you run out of gas, get out, sit down, begin to meditate, and see what happens. If, after three days, you receive food, you will know that The Divine Mother has blessed you"''

Trusting his guru, he followed the advice explicitly. He sold his business to his second in command. He gave away his clothing, his books, his stuff. He got in his car and began to drive.

As he drove south from his home in Garberville, he passed a sign that said "Sonoma." When he looked at the sign, what he saw was *Sono Maa.* In Hindi, *sono* means listen, and *maa* means Ma. Baba Hariji immediately pulled off the highway. He drove into the center of town, parked his car, and walked into the town square. He sat and began to meditate. One day passed. Two days passed. Three days passed; no food, just a little water, lots of concentration, and quite a bit of uncomfortable body sensation. Hari finally decided to go over to the payphone and call one of his friends to come and get him, and to bring some food. He remembered, though, that he had no money for the payphone.

He resumed his asana. Hours later, a young man approached the sadhu, interrupting his meditation with an offer. "I've seen you sitting in the square for days; you must be hungry. I live near here. Please come for dinner." The mission was blessed! As Hari ate with this man's family, he told a bit of his story. The man offered the family's spare room and Hari slept in a bed for the first time in days.

The next day, the Fourth of July, his host took him to meet a friend, Patty, outside of Sonoma. She owned a retreat center and quickly Hari and Patty became great friends. Patty thought the best place for Hari to live permanently would be Father Dunstan's Benedictine monastery, Sky Farm, in the hills above Sonoma. When Hari and the Father met, a bond formed and Hari had a place where he could live. During the time he lived at the monastery, he taught yoga at the Sonoma Community Center and began to gather some of the people who would later become his devotees. There he conceived of creating an ashram and very quickly the funds arrived. He bought a small plot of land with a few buildings on it. Over the last ten years, Sonoma Ashram has become one of the most beautiful spiritual locations in Northern California. Sadhus, swamis, and sadhaks from all over the world come to stay there. Bhagwan Ram visited Sonoma ashram and blessed the ground.

Baba Bhagwan Ramji's kidneys were failing; he had been coming to New York since 1986 to receive medical treatment. Hari was asked to stay with Baba Bhagwan Ramji and help him through this crisis. Every day Baba Bhagwan Ramji walked to the local hospital with Hari. The people on the streets of New York began to recognize Baba Bhagwan Ramji, and as he walked by they would call out, "Hey Baba, how you doin' today?"

Baba Bhagwan Ramji and Hari became closer and closer. Hari rarely slept, as he was so busy taking care of Baba Bhagwan Ramji and the other devotees who stayed in the apartment. At one point, Hari was initiated and became Baba Harihar Ramji. During this time, Baba Hariji's brother left his body. Some people die in fear of the unknown, but Baba Hariji's brother left his body one-pointedly fixed on his mantra. Baba Hariji was filled with grief. Bhagwan Ram took him into a room.

Baba Hariji spoke, "I cannot forget my brother. I used to walk along the Ganges and talk to him about spiritual questions. I miss those times so much."

Bhagwan Ram asked, "When was the last time you saw your brother?"

Babaji said, "It's been many years."

Bhagwan Ram spoke, "That was then, and this is now. I will help."

As Babaji left room, he felt his heart lifting. The grief transformed into an awareness of unity and love, and he felt his brother's presence in his heart. Bhagwan Ram had removed the pain of his grief.

There are many stories of the amazing things that took place while Baba Bhagwan Ramji was on dialysis in New York City. On Baba Bhagwan Ramji's last day in his body, he had been sitting in *padmasana* (lotus pose) posture on the bed for hours. Suddenly, he departed this plane through his crown chakra. He used his yogic powers to appear to die from a cerebral hemorrhage. The greatest of souls depart while sitting in meditation, crown chakra wide open for departure. Many gathered for the celebration of his mahasamadhi.

After the cremation, Babaji returned to Sonoma Ashram and began to teach and initiate many into the Aghori practices, to grow a most beautiful satsang and a most beautiful oasis of silence. Babaji, however, does not ask you to sit on a corpse in order to face your fear of death. The system of awakening has not changed from ancient times, but the practices have been modified to conform more appropriately to the Western lifestyle. Babaji suggests that in order to face your fear of death, you could work in a hospice or a children's cancer ward. Babaji's teachings still lead you to face fear, but in such a way as to not upset the balance of good health and moral behavior. It is true that tantrikas face their pleasures and their pains with equanimity, and acknowledge that satisfying a desire is an efficient way to dispose of it, but the essence of the teaching is to transform your life into a prayer. (I am reminded of a phone conversation with Ram Dass when I said, "I feel my life is turning into a prayer." And he responded, "My life also is becoming a prayer.") When every thought, word, and deed is offered as a form of worship to the Divine Mother, you are practicing Tantra.

Babaji does not give free reign. He teaches you must stay within your dharma, your appropriate moral conduct, and suggests chanting the *Soham* mantra for a few minutes every day until you decide to receive *diksha* (initiation). *Soham* is a Vedic mantra meaning "I am That," so you identify with ultimate reality. You breathe in to the sound of *So* and breathe out *ham*. After you complete reading and studying (*biksha*), Babaji offers initiation into the Aghori tradition by giving you a personal mantra, which will become your best friend until you recognize that this mantra is simply a vibrational manifestation of your own highest self. Babaji once told me, "The Aghor tradition is simply japa."

A friend had been traveling the world searching for a spiritual path. When he discovered Baba Harihar Ramji's Nine Gates Mystery School, he saw an opportunity. This school sponsors workshops around the planet, bringing spiritual teachers from a variety of paths to join in a weekend of discussion and practice. My friend was so moved by Baba that he invited him to his home in Amherst, Mass, where I met him. Baba brought his assistant, Shivani, a tall, beautiful woman with an aura of love around her. Shivani was Baba Hariji's main organizer, manager of the ashram, and a teacher in her own rite. She always traveled with him, and she became my good friend over the years.

When I first entered the room, I saw Baba sitting on a small dais, his white *dhoti* (long piece of cloth wrapped around a man's lower half like a sarong), shawl, and cap glistening in the candlelight. The room was filled with many people I knew from kirtan; there was hardly an open spot left on the floor. I had my guitar with me, always anticipating a chance that I could offer a song to this holy man. I struggled into a back corner of the room, trying not to step on anyone. Babaji had apparently taken note of me because he immediately spoke up, "Please, come to the front, sit here near me." I was not going to wait for a second invite. I shuffled around bodies and folks in the front created a small space for me and my Martin. I found myself only a few feet from the dais. Baba began his simple discourse, teaching the *sadhaks* (spiritual seekers) about mindfulness.

He spoke, "There are many simple practices to begin your day. I suggest a practice of mindfulness upon awakening. In the morning, when you open your eyes, focus your attention on your breath. First step is to hold your hands in front of your face and wipe clean the veil of sleep. Then observe your breath, taking note of which nostril is less congested. Take three deep

172

breaths to honor your divinity and then step out of bed with the foot that corresponds to the nostril which is clearest. That way we start the day off on the right foot." Such a simple introduction to sadhana he offered. I thought, "Mindfulness, devotion, and puja all combined into three deep breaths."

As he spoke, he would occasionally turn and look into my face. After a few minutes, my perception began to shift. I felt myself floating. I felt the room and the people in it fall away. I saw only Baba's face; everything else in the room had changed into a deep purple glow. I felt a deep peace descend upon me, and I merged into a loving oneness with this brilliant teacher. He asked me to sing, and I sang for him. He invited me to come to his programs and sing, which I did.

He said he would be in New England for a few weeks and, if I wanted, I could set up a tour for him. What a wonderful opportunity! Baba traveled with me to all my kirtan stops, met the whole New England community, and shared his unique teaching with my family. We traveled up to Bethel Farm in Hillsboro, NH; into Boston at The Arlington Center; then Albany, Hartford, New Haven, Portsmouth, and more.

Time spent with a great being is filled with subtle teachings. One must stay very alert to catch as much as possible. For example, coming out of the Boston venue, Babaji was clearly tired. It was raining, and the traffic was chaotic. He was looking for our ride, and I noticed concern on his face. He turned to me and it was like the light went on, all tiredness and concern left him and his smile radiated a powerful burst of love and humor into me. He seemed to always be completely present in the moment. Simple, quiet, filled with love and peace, Babaji traveled with the grace of a holy man.

Another moment took place at Bethel Farm. We had a big turnout, a long discourse, lots of kirtan, and then darshan. It was past 11 p.m. when the last person was blessed. We were all starving, so we called the local Chinese restaurant and asked them to stay open late so we could stop in for a meal. We sat together in silence, enjoying the food, but even more enjoying the moment with Baba, Shivani, my partner, and I sharing intimacy and love. My heart soared.

This was the beginning of a wonderful love and friendship with Baba Harihar Ramji. During our travels, he seemed to know the level of my poverty and gave me all the donations he received. This was not only extremely generous, but also insightful, compassionate, and brilliant. This compassionate generosity was unlike anything I had previously experienced with a spiritual teacher. My experience with Karunamayi, with Sai Baba, and others was essentially the other way around. Especially with Karunamayi, there was an expectation that any expenses incurred around sponsoring them fell directly upon us. That Babaji was completely detached from money, and also cared enough about this stranger to teach him about unconditional love and the deeper nature of bhakti, stole my heart.

Babaji teaches that self-love is primary. To live a life of bhakti, you, through sadhana, learn to fill yourself with love. Once accomplished, you begin to share the overflow, until there is nothing left in the universe that you do not love.

Babaji wanted me to come to his ashram. I am a poor sadhu, living in a one-room cabin in the woods. I drive a twenty-year-old car and live on the donations of my community. There was no way I could afford a round-trip ticket to California, but I have discovered over the years that when a baba has a thought in his head, many times this thought will manifest on the physical plane. While it took more than just a thought to get me to California, Babaji bought the ticket and made arrangements for my partner and I to stay for several weeks at Sonoma Ashram.

After I dropped Ma Chetan Jyoti off at Satya's house in New York, I went home, repacked my bags, and headed off to Logan Airport. Cross-country flying is never fun. The seats are too small, my back hurts, the food is terrible, and it takes forever. But finally, late at night, we arrived at Sonoma Ashram. Babaji had reserved a beautiful apartment for us to stay in, so we unloaded our gear and settled down for a restorative night's sleep. Next day, I was up early and joined the satsang for morning darshan. Babaji spoke a few words and introduced me to the community. Then he took me on a tour of the ashram. One great thing about Babaji is that when he speaks, he speaks as a friend. There is no pretense about him, no guile, no "I am the teacher, you are the student." He is a real person, with real-life understanding of the West, offering a spiritually-developed perspective on the journey of life.

It took about five days to get into the rhythm of the ashram. Awake at 5 a.m., hatha yoga practice at 5:30 a.m., meditation at 6 a.m., then a delicious cup of tulsi tea, darshan at 6:45 a.m., 7:15 a.m. oatmeal, and then the work begins. There is much to be done at this ashram. Although it dwells within the city limits, the two-acre plot of land houses about fifteen people, a beautiful temple, a fire pit, and a large sustainable garden. Many of the devotees work in the garden—planting, weeding, and harvesting the food for the day. A great chef lives at the ashram and we ate tasty North Indian food like *maharajas* (great kings), and since Aghoris are not opposed to eating meat, an occasional Mexican feast.

Those not working in the garden are busy planting trees, cleaning and washing the living spaces, and generally policing the grounds. Babaji is always seen in his immaculate white dhoti, shawl and white cap, shovel in hand, hard at work with the rest of the devotees. During the construction of a small cabin, I remember seeing Babaji climbing the ladder in his dhoti, kneeling down on the roof, and hammering the shingles. This is definitely a hard-working guru.

In the afternoon, we would have a little siesta. Sometimes Babaji would sit by the pool (every ashram needs a swimming pool) and we would join him for some discussion. I remember one hot afternoon when Baba, Shivani, a few other devotees and I were sitting under an umbrella near the water. Babaji said, "You know, Shubal, you should have a CD."

I said, "Yes Baba, but it takes a thousand dollars at least to produce a CD, and I have nothing."

Baba said, "Let me make a few phone calls." He picked up the phone.

One fellow said, "Yes, I have two microphones." Another fellow said, "I have a small digital recorder." Slowly, we gathered scraps of equipment to finagle some kind of recording. As he hung up the phone, we heard a truck pulling into the parking lot. We saw a middle-aged Indian man step out and walk towards us. He seemed very excited. He said, "Babaji, the greatest thing. I have just purchased a fully-equipped mobile recording studio." This is the way things work around Baba. He has a thought, he puts out a suggestion, and quickly, in a variety of unique ways, we see a manifestation on the physical plane.

Near the end of the two-week visit, I felt very drawn to receive diksha from Babaji. I had been initiated into several mantras before, but had never received "guru" initiation. I really wanted a mantra of my own. Babaji's teaching is that an Aghor mantra is one of the most powerful mantras in Hinduism. I have discovered that this personal mantra is a "friend" until you recognize your mantra as *jivatma* (individual soul) in vibrational form. Baba invited us to stay for two more weeks so we could have the initiation ceremony.

I still was connected to Shree Maa and Swami Satyananda, and I needed to let them know my plans. I wrote to

176

Swamiji, who scolded me, saying I never really got into the sadhana of Chandi Path chanting, which was true. I could chant in Sanskrit, but not fast enough and not regularly enough to meet the standard of the Shree Maa Satsang. He blessed me to go ahead with my plans.

It is probably inappropriate to discuss the details of Aghor initiation. Traditional initiation, however, includes a ceremony where one offers a puja to one's teacher, with flowers, incense, and other ritual offerings. Then the guru will give a personal mantra. Sometimes that mantra is written on the tongue with a tulsi stick and honey. The power behind the ritual is essentially the guru transmitting shakti to the student. I can say that when I came out of my initiation, my feet hardly touched the ground. I felt myself glowing with the power of my new mantra. One woman came up to me and, although my initiation was a secret between me and Babaji, looked in my face and said, "I see by the light in your face that you have been initiated today." I guess it was that obvious.

It was my last day at the ashram and I spent the afternoon sitting with Babaji on his porch talking about sadhana and the lineage of the Aghoreshwars and the secrets involved in the application of the magical alchemical mantra. We took the midnight flight back to Boston and I settled in, allowing my mantra to penetrate my subconscious mind through repetition. As Baba said to me, "Aghor is all japa."

What an amazing summer it had been. First June and July spent traveling up and down the East Coast and into Canada with Ma Chetan Jyoti, and now a month in California at the Sonoma Ashram, living in peace in the arms of a loving guru and receiving my close friend, my Aghor mantra. It was shortly after I arrived back in Boston that I received the e-mail from Ma Chetan Jyoti saying she had lung cancer. We had a beautiful exchange of e-mails as she was preparing to leave her body (see Appendix II).

177

One morning in my meditation room, while chanting the *Siddha Kunjika Stotram* (the song that unlocks the key to perfection) with my friends, I was struck down with a brain seizure and rushed to the emergency room. An MRI showed a brain tumor, so I was shipped into Boston to one of the city's world-renowned hospitals for surgery. They operated, found the tumor was benign, but could not be removed. They put me on a very intense anti-seizure medication that reduced my IQ by at least thirty points and sent me home to contemplate my navel. I could not drive for six months, and in my confinement I spent much time working with my new mantra, and rereading the entire thousand pages of *The Gospel of Sri Ramakrishna*, unabridged!

I began healing work with a master healer named Tom Tam. He took my neck in his hands and squeezed hard. He said, "Massage this point. Your tumor will go away." I began regular acupuncture with one of his students. After a year of this therapy, my epileptologist (a neurologist who focuses on epilepsy) found that the tumor had disappeared. I was free from the "horror drug." The doctors could not explain how this happened.

I had been through a powerfully traumatic experience, not only from the illness, the surgery, but from my long and hard recuperation. Based on these experiences, I felt it was time for me to move out of my relationship and focus more on meditation and spreading people's experience of kirtan. I wanted to expand my travels teaching *namasankirtan*— chanting the holy Names. I needed to talk this out with Babaji.

When I boarded the plane for San Francisco, I realized this retreat was not only about healing from my trauma, but finding my way to my dharma. I arrived midday and Babaji met me at the gate. I received a long, loving, healing hug and a sense that this man understood what I had been through and how traumatized I was. We sat down together near the stream, a few others gathered around us. Suddenly I felt something break inside me. My eyes filled with tears and they flowed down my face. I felt the release. Up until this moment, I had been holding onto something so painful but could not let go.

Babaji said, "Shubal, go to the temple and sit alone." I followed his instructions, and as I sat there that first day, I felt jolts of energy that made my limbs spasm and my heart leap. Later that day I took out my steel guitar and began to sing. One by one people came into the temple and joined the kirtan. The chorus grew larger, the voices stronger, and my energy soared. Soon Babaji was sitting next to me in deep meditation while we sang to Durga and Shiva. By the end of that first day, my release was so deep that my sleep was equally deep.

The next morning I saw Babaji near the fence at the end of the ashram's property, talking to the neighbors. He came over and said, "The neighbors were wondering if we were killing cats yesterday. They seem to have heard a lot of screaming and squalling from the temple." I guess you could call it screaming, but to me it was a lullaby of awakening.

I spent two weeks in that peaceful environment. During the weekend, there was a benefit kirtan taking place in downtown Sonoma for the ashram. Jai Uttal, a devotee of Maharajji and an excellent singer and musician, had made many recordings with his jazz-rock-reggae-kirtan band, the Pagan Love Orchestra. When Krishna Das began to gain fame, Jai also began leading kirtan on the West coast. He had been paid $1008 to lead a kirtan to fundraise for the Sonoma Ashram Trust. People purchased tickets and the profit went to the ashram. Babaji asked me to come with him to the program. I said, "Babaji, every time I listen to another kirtan wallah, I hear something I like and I take it into my kirtan. I would prefer not to attend."

Babaji said, "You come!" So Babaji drove me to my first California kirtan.

As Jai began to sing, I noticed he was using an electronic tamboura, called a *raagini*. The one Mataji had given me was a toy compared to this one. Since the rather short , lackluster performance was only Jai and a drummer, the electric tamboura droned along with his kirtan and filled things out. I thought, "I want one of those." And there I was, caught again. I had gone to see a kirtan wallah and I had seen something I liked. One of the first things I did when I returned to New England was to purchase an electronic tamboura. When Krishna Das became popular, Jai began focusing less on his reggae/rock/jazz band and more on kirtan, and he has written some beautiful kirtans that I love to sing. He has become a major influence on kirtan in Northern California and his kirtan camp every summer has taught hundreds of yogis how to sing and lead kirtan. The raagini is still by my side.

One day, Babaji, some others, and I were sitting by the pool. Babaji looked at me and said, "How does it feel not to be experiencing daily abuse?" Another time we were sitting quietly in the garden and we spoke of my relationship. I told him how my time at the ashram had allowed me to process my trauma and, hopefully, to have found the strength to leave my relationship. I said, "Please do not give me advice. I know the right course for myself. All I ask is for my own inner strength to manifest and allow me to make this change in order to save my life, and deepen my relationship with my mantra and my guru."

The last night was spent performing a homa fire ceremony for my benefit. We chanted the mantras, and I *swaha-*ed my negative relationship. I took the sacred ash from the homa fire and marked my forehead, praying for strength to make the change.

On the day that I was leaving, Babaji sat with me on his porch. He said, "Shubal, now is the time of your life for you to sit quietly and think of God."

"Do you mean, Baba, that I need to take *sannyas*?" (Sannyas is the renunciation that a Hindu enters into at age seventy-five, working with celibacy, nonattachment, sadhana, and love. The fourth ashram of life).

Babaji said, "Shubal, you already are almost a sannyasin. You live with nothing, you offer your life to your sadhana, and you really love God."

Then it was time for me to leave, to return to New England and my relationship. While waiting for the limo to the airport, Babaji and my friends from the ashram stood around the parking lot with me. It was a sad moment, but I took with me the ash from the special homa Babaji and I had conducted the previous night—the ceremony to help me find the strength to go through what was coming. While I was putting my bags into the limo, Shivani came up to me, pressed something into my hand, and said, "Don't look at this until you are on your way."

Babaji said, "Here at the ashram we never say goodbye, we only say *namaste*." As the limo left the parking lot, I opened my hand and discovered five $100 bills. This not only covered my expenses for the whole trip, but left me with a little extra. Babaji's generosity is almost as powerful as his love. So I returned to New England, gathered my strength, and with the direct intervention of Kali and my mantra, moved away from my home and began my spiritual work in earnest. I did not realize it would be years before I returned to Sonoma Ashram. When I did return, all that had happened in the past months turned out to be preparation for the revelation of the power of Bhagwan Ram.

Chapter 11A

VASHI BABA &THE HRIDAYA HERMITAGE

Song and dance, kirtan, is the best way to extinguish low self-esteem. --Baba Hari Dass

After my return from Sonoma, I exited my relationship and expanded my travels around New England. I began to notice a young woman turning up at almost every venue. She introduced herself as Artemis and said she had seen me performing with Krishna Das. She had asked him where she could learn to be a kirtan wallah and KD mentioned me. Would I would be willing to teach her?

We began regular lessons and soon she was playing great harmonium. She also had this beautiful singing voice, so soon she joined the band as responder and harmonium droner. This began a great collaboration that has lasted many years. One thing led to another and soon we were lovers. We lived together for years, singing and building a life. After five years, it was time for her to move on from our personal relationship, while still keeping the kirtan band together. However, when she left, I became very depressed. I felt the loneliness of an ended relationship and, at my ripe age, I wondered if it was the end of other things. I felt the best thing for me was to head north to the Hridaya Hermitage in Maine and be with community.

Six months earlier, I had been leading a kirtan when this oddly-dressed sadhu entered the hall. His hair was up in a topknot like Shiva's, and he wore the clothing of a Tibetan monk—earth-colored *kurta* (shirt), dhoti, and shawl. After the sadhana, we talked. His name was Bhagwan Das and he lived at the Hridaya Hermitage (*hridaya* means the heart center).His guru, who also lived there, was named VaShi Baba (VaShi was Shiva backwards, so called because their sadhana was so difficult). When Artemis packed up to leave our home, I decided to travel to the Hridaya Hermitage and meet this baba. I wanted to see if I could take sannyas initiation, or at least find some peace from my grief. It was a three-hour drive through the north woods to Industry, Maine, then miles down a barely passable dirt road. The tall pines lining the road made it almost a regal journey. Finally, a wooden sign and a sharp incline up to the ashram.

I was greeted by Bhagwan Das and shown to a cabin. Everyone called Bhagwan Das "Shug" because he was "so sweet." Shug told me that the baba was on his own retreat and I would not be able to meet him over the three weeks I planned to be there, but he told me stories. VaShi Baba was a Westerner, one of a group of friends who decided to take a vacation in India. Without encountering any teacher, Baba was hit with a lightning bolt of awakening and everything changed for him. He began to lead his group of Westerners around North India. Everywhere they went, even though Baba was a red-headed kid in a hoodie, the Indians would pranam to him.

When he returned to Maine, he built the hermitage. Ten families came to live in the old buildings with no power, no water, and no heat. Out of this decay, they built homes for everyone, a huge darshan room, and a center for eating and teaching, though they still live without electricity or running water. This remarkable group cooks for twenty-five people on a wood stove, takes cold showers, and does sadhana—a strict hatha yoga and meditation that is working to change the consciousness of the planet.

I unpacked and took a stroll across the campus. As I began to walk up the main trail, I saw "Shiva" coming toward me. This being had a red-haired topknot, the same Tibetan robes as Shug, and a bright red beard that drooped almost to his knees. His eyes radiated a light that I had seen reflected in the great ones. It was VaShi Baba. He asked me, "Why are you here?"

This gave me that opportunity to let it all out. "My woman has left me, my age has caught up with my intentions, this physical world seems to be slipping away, I am seventy years old, it feels like it is time to take sannyas."

He thought for a while, then said, "This is a good time to take sannyas. You are here for some time, we will see. But using two Ambiens and a plastic bag is not a good way to kill yourself. It can be painful." I was shocked. This man had read my mind. I had not shared my favorite suicide technique with anyone. Yet, somehow, this fellow read the whole story. I had my thoughts "seen" by great souls before, and these words confirmed my initial impression that this man lived in the higher planes. He said, "I have a suggestion for you. Go back to your cabin and meditate. Try to find the answer to the question you have forgotten."

Again, VaShi Baba was overloading my rational mind. The answer to the question I had forgotten—what did that mean? I spent the next weeks thinking, like a good Zen student, what is the answer to the question, what is the question? As I sat meditating, I began to feel my personality, my sense of self, as nothing more than a house of cards. Originally, my world was "one" and then I called to my mother for milk and there was none and I became two. Each traumatic event colored the next one until I had a bunch of traumas known as "me." We remember at most five percent of what really happened and the rest is a memory manipulated by previous traumas. My sense of self—the small "s" self—was based upon memories that actually did not happen. I began to disintegrate.

Days later, Baba called me to his home. We sat for hours, talking of his vision for world peace. He believed that if folks could concentrate hard enough, they could impact the state of the physical world and bring about peace. He said that if it does not work, it does not matter, because intention is the key. I said,

"I have, over my time here, discovered who I am not. Now I must find out who I am."

Baba turned to Shug and said, "Many *vasanas* (old karmic imprints), not sure."

When it was time to leave the ashram, all the children gathered around me. I had fallen into such a bliss state that I hardly thought of Artemis, or anything really. I loved the kids and they loved me. One boy gave me a picture he had drawn of a dark blue sky with two white swans flying.

I returned to a home that had been emptied of the presence of my lover. Closets and cabinets were empty, as was my heart. Gnawing away at me were: what is the question? What is the answer? Slowly my home came back together and Artemis and I came to a peaceful readjustment. We continued to practice our kirtan sadhana together, traveling all over the Northeast, from yoga centers to concert halls to living rooms and temples.

About a year after my visit to the hermitage, I was called to lead kirtan at an ayahuasca ceremony. After the kirtan, the leader of the group invited me to stay and join the ceremony. I am not someone who uses psychedelics anymore. However, I had heard about the healing powers of the ayahuasca, the "Mother of the Forest," so I agreed. All sixty of us were in a yurt. The shaman leading the ceremony came to each of us with a glass of purple liquid, which tasted like the Peruvian jungle. I lay back and knew I was in for a ride. Next came a visionary explosion—geometric shapes of every sort flying through my mind, one after the other. I heard the sounds of sixty people vomiting, some crying, some laughing, some incoherent. Time seemed suspended. I left the yurt and walked past people vomiting in the woods. Fortunately, I did not get hit with the nausea or the diarrhea, and my head was filled with light. I returned to the yurt and lay back, reveling in the peace.

As the sun rose, the shaman asked me to sing. I picked up my steel guitar and began, without a thought in my head, to sing to the Mother of the Forest. The words were spontaneous, the melody came from nowhere. The song went on and on, and my voice filled the woods, "O Mother." When the song ended, there was silence in the yurt. A spiritual lightning bolt of awakening hit my head—sudden, thorough, and finally true. The answer to the question I had forgotten was, *We Are the Same Person!*

Somehow, over the long years of practice, things had become codified. I had become so absorbed in the concepts that veiled the truths I had forgotten. Maharajji, I forgot! Well, I did not forget, really. I had just gotten into the habit of thinking I was my thoughts. Again, I was filled with shakti laughter at the simple poignancy of consciousness versus awareness, and how wonderful it was to get back home.

Now, I was ready for Bhagwan Ram.

Chapter 12

BACK TO SONOMA

Finally, some big gigs came through and I had another opportunity to travel to Sonoma Ashram. Arriving at the ashram, I immediately caught whatever was flying around Northern California that week and took to bed with a stuffed nose and a cold. I was in a panic over a kirtan that was scheduled for three days later, and the stress added to my suffering when I pulled a muscle in my back. I lay in bed in agony. Each day at the ashram is so precious and they were slipping by in a haze of cough meds, sleepless nights, and stiffness. Finally, just in time, the cold abated and the back healed.

At my first darshan with Baba Hariji, I was so glad to see him. I love him so much, and it had been so long. I sat next to him. As the night went on with laughter and silence, a feeling came over me—my body felt light and shaky, and my mind slowed down. Whatever this was, it was beyond me. I pulled a shawl over my head for privacy, leaving open a space to watch Baba. As I turned my head towards him, I was shocked. He was a black silhouette, and coming through the blackness was a hurricane, a vortex, a tornado that was consuming me—a vortex of love pouring down on me. My tears and laughter and shaking pushed me higher and higher until I could not find myself. There was no thought, only love. *Bhagwan Ramji, the love is so strong, I can hardly hold my body together. You are a shining light; you are, I see now, you* are, *and I* am. *We are all the same person.* I saw that all the teachers have been sent by Maharajji, behind the scenes—the story behind the story.

The next night they asked me to sing. I did a kirtan that Anandamayi Ma used to sing. Ram Dass used to tell a story of visiting her in a darshan room that held a thousand people. She came in, sat down in a corner, and began to sing this kirtan. Ram Dass said, "It was like watching a lover, alone, singing to her beloved." Then he would sing the kirtan and it was as if *he* were alone, singing to *his* beloved. The words are simple: *Jai Om Bhagwan.* As I sang, the room grew quiet, and with more and more force I cried from the depths of my being, *"Jai Om Bhagwan!"* We grew closer and closer in our love for Bhagwan Ramji. Tears began to flow and the light changed. In the silence after I finished, Baba said, "Now THAT is *prana* (life-force energy)." Singing to one's teacher is the greatest darshan.

Days later we were in *mauna* (the practice of silence) and it was raining. Early in the day, I was on my way down the rocky path to the temple when I turned a corner and there was Baba. In his beautiful white dhoti and shawl, white cap on his head, broom in hand, he was sweeping the path. The sight overwhelmed me. I understood the love with which he swept in the rain, and I fell into the mud at his feet. In the traditional way, I stretched out and touched his bare feet with my fingers as the mud soaked through my white dhoti and the tears flowed from the outside corners of my eyes.

I rose, and as I passed him I whispered in his ear, "I love you."His face lit like a thousand-watt bulb, and, still in silence, he pointed both his thumbs toward the sky. Such a small moment it was. Ram Dass once told me, "There are many relationships deeper than the sexual." I can truly say that the experience of loving that exists between a guru and the disciple heals all wounds. I pray all get to experience this love in this lifetime.

On the day we were to leave the ashram, I spent a little private time with Baba, then went into the temple. I was alone, and sat in meditation for a few minutes. When I opened my eyes, I looked directly into the picture of Bhagwan Ramji and spoke to him, "I am tired of seeing only through these eyes. I am tired of negotiating the world through this psychological veil that I know is an illusion. I am tired of withholding my love. I am tired of this limited body. Alone, I cannot escape. I need your intervention. I need to be free, and I am unable to take this step alone. Bhagwan Ram, I need your help."

As I stared into the picture, a peaceful feeling came over me. The more I stared, the more presence emerged. I felt the vortex of love opening inside of me. Suddenly, the picture of Bhagwan Ram's face became three-dimensional. There was no movement, just a depth of vision that brought Baba to life. Silent tears poured from my eyes. *Tadastu*, the wish is granted.

I felt the presence of Bhagwan Ram deep in my heart. I left the temple, left the ashram, left California, left Boston. On my ride back to my mountaintop, I felt my heart dancing with the planets. Everywhere I looked I saw my reflection. The feeling has not faded.

Chapter 13

MIRABAI DEVI & NAMADEVA

One can realize God through kirtan alone. --Sivananda

During my "Shree Maa" period, I continued to host traveling spiritual teachers. One of the most interesting Mothers who crossed my path was Mirabai Devi, (Jane Bletcher). Throughout this time I led a regular weekly kirtan at Karuna Center (Shree Maa's gift). One night, as I topped the second staircase leading to Karuna with all my gear on my back, Mirabai Devi suddenly stood before me. Dressed in white, with long black hair braided across her shoulder, she seemed both beautiful and hideously ugly at the same time. She smiled at me; her smile was beautiful. I felt very warm and smiled back.

Mirabai Devi was born a South African Jew, and experienced bliss states from early in her life. As a teenager, she went to Germany to study with Mother Meera, one of India's great saints, who takes very few students. Mother Meera's offering to the world takes the form of darshan. Everyone gets in a long line and one-by-one they approach Mother Meera. First you bow to her, then one of two things happens: Meera places her hands on your head and, reaching in to find your blocks, she shifts things around. The second event is when she lifts your head up and stares directly into your eyes. With this second stage, she is opening up your heart, filling you with her light. One woman described horripilation when she met Mother Meera. Another friend, when staring into Mother Meera's face, began to repeat, "I love you, I love you, I love you."When I received Mother Meera's darshan, it was during one of my illnesses. She took me in her hands and loved me "real good." Mother Meera offers the world an amazing gift. She now lives in the United States, and each summer everyone has the opportunity to meet her and receive her darshan.

Mirabai Devi moved to Germany to be with Mother Meera. For ten years she took care of Meera, participated in the programs, and watched very closely. At a certain point, Mirabai decided she was ready to offer her own form of darshan. She began at home in South Africa. She grew a strong circle of friends and eventually traveled to the United States, to Northampton, and up two flights of stairs to Karuna Yoga and me.

On that first confrontation at Karuna, we stared at each other in the stairwell for almost a full minute before we exchanged greetings. The most recent kirtan is always the best kirtan, so the kirtan with Mirabai Devi was the best kirtan we ever had. This began a fine friendship. The next night, Mirabai was offering her own darshan at Karuna Yoga. I participated, sang the Tantric Devi Suktam from the Chandi Path, and all was a sea of love. The night was filled with great stories and great love. During the visit, Mirabai came to our house for dinner. I invited a few of my special friends. In my upstairs puja room, we sat in silence, such a refined atmosphere of love and presence.

Mirabai is a *shakti ma*; the spiritual energy that vitalizes the spine moves quite without obstacle in her. Just being around her activates that energy in others, just as a magnet will transfer its energy to an iron bar. When she gives her darshan, people quickly move into higher planes of consciousness. One time when I came up for her blessing, she touched me between the eyes and I began to laugh. I moved to the side but the laughing continued. It was this deep Shakti laughter that I remembered from Ram Dass' couch. Others picked up the laughter and soon the entire room was uproariously laughing, yet there was no joke. Shakti, as it moves up the spine, often causes fits of deep laughter and tears.

Mirabai Devi and I did many programs together. She developed a strong following in Boston, and we enjoyed many evening kirtan/darshan events. Some late nights, she would call me and we would talk endlessly about our lives, events, future, past, but always present. Mirabai and I had established an excellent collaboration and a fine friendship.

Mirabai asked me to organize a retreat in Western Mass for her and a friend, Thomas Ashley Farrand, known as Namadeva. Of course, I immediately said yes. I knew that part of my seva was using my organizational ability to bring the teachers of *Sanatana Dharma* (the "eternal path," the original name for Hinduism) to the spiritual community that had grown up around my kirtan practice. I found a beautiful retreat center, the Sirius Community, sent out the publicity, and very quickly filled all fifty beds. This was going to be a wonderful retreat.

Namadeva and Shubal

Namadeva wrote many books on mantras that have been published and distributed across the world. He was a trained *pujari*, a Vedic priest, and an excellent kirtan wallah. At the time, Namadeva was traveling throughout the United States offering

192

workshops and ceremonial pujas. He had written to me to say that he planned to offer initiation into the Gayatri mantra for anyone who wished. I had heard quite a bit about the Gayatri mantra from several of my teachers. Karunamayi had told me that initiation into this mantra required that several behaviors be in place first; it was necessary to have a regular meditation practice and a strict vegetarian diet in order to receive this initiation. I was concerned that I was sponsoring a program for someone who was recklessly offering initiation to unprepared seekers.

I wrote to Namadeva and I told him of my concerns. He replied, quite to the point, "Okay, I'm not coming." I realized I had overstepped my bounds, and also that Namadeva had misunderstood my reference to Karunamayi. I had a habit of putting my foot in my mouth, so I had to call him to explain and apologize, and he agreed to attend. My first encounter with Namadeva was a major teaching. When everyone arrived, the retreat center bustled with energy. The first morning of the retreat, Namadeva got up to tell a story about one of India's great gurus, Ramanuja:

Ramanuja was the student of a great guru. For many years he practiced meditation, renunciation, and seva in order to transcend ego and join the free play of the universe. Finally, the guru of Ramanuja spoke. "Ramanuja, I am about to give you a great gift. I am going to give you the secret mantra of enlightenment. This is a mantra that must be kept secret. Those unprepared might misuse it and cause great harm. If you dare to share it with the common folk, you will be banned to the hell realms. The mantra is . . ." The guru whispered the secret mantra into Ramanuja's ear.

Immediately upon receiving the mantra, Ramanuja left the guru's home and began walking towards the town square. As he walked, he called out to the people on the streets, "Come. Follow me. I am going to share with you a great secret." As he entered the town square, he saw that he was followed by hundreds of people. He climbed up onto a great rock and spoke, "I am going to share with you the secret mantra for enlightenment. Om Namoh Narayanaya." The crowd cheered, Ramanuja climbed down, and returned to his guru's home.

His guru was waiting for him at the door. He was furious. He shouted at Ramanuja, "How could you do this? I gave you a great secret, and you have desecrated it by spreading it indiscriminately among the masses. Now you will be damned to hell forever. How could you do this?"

Ramanuja spoke, "Well, Babaji, the way I see it, hundreds of people become enlightened and one soul goes to hell. That sounds like a good deal to me."

The guru fell at Ramanuja's feet. The guru spoke, "Ramanuja, you are now the guru and I am your student."

Finishing the story, Namadeva turned and looked directly into my face. I could not help but laugh. Later that day I received initiation into the Gayatri mantra from Namadeva. The retreat was a super success. Saturday night's kirtan drew hundreds of people. Namadeva was a wonderful kirtan wallah and the two of us raised the roof while Mirabai gave darshan to everyone. As I said before, there's nothing finer than singing kirtan to the spiritual teacher, and this night was no exception. We blistered the paint.

Both Mirabai and Namadeva made lots of money from the retreat and they were very happy. When it was time to leave I agreed to take Namadeva to the airport in Boston. We spent companionable hours driving to the city and then into the North End, where we had a delicious Italian fish dinner. Namadeva, among his other achievements, is a raconteur of good food and we had a true tantric celebration, which included delicious wine. Then we were off to the airport and farewells and the beginning of a strong friendship.

Namadeva often gave retreats at the Kripalu Center, and when he did, he always invited me and Bhavani (an old-time Kripalu kirtan wallah) to join him for his evening kirtan program. I love supporting Namadeva in his unique music. He was a devotee of Sant Keshav Das, one of India's gurus who used kirtan as his teaching tool. Namadeva had learned many kirtans from Sant Keshav Das, and he had written many kirtans on his own. It was not only great fun to play with Namadeva, but also educational. I learned many of the kirtans that Namadeva brought from Vrindaban in North India, the home of Krishna, Ramakrishna Hari, Panduranga, and on and on.

Later that summer, Namadeva traveled with me for a week around my kirtan locations and we got to know each other much better. He told me of his time singing with Al Jarreau, writing TV scripts in Hollywood, falling in love with Sant Keshav Das and renouncing that world to become a Vedic priest. He was also the Vedic advisor to Deva Premal, a famous spiritual singer. He dyed his hair, wore a tie, and perfumed his skin. He carried little boxes of vibhuti and kumkum in his pockets.

There is some irony in the mantra he gave me permission to teach. According to Namadeva, this mantra has the ability to heal damaged relationships and to attract the most appropriate next relationship if you are alone. I offered this mantra often in groups. My tabla player used it and within a few months she was married. The irony comes from my beloved Ram Dass. During his last years, Ram Dass taught everyone a mantra: "I am loving awareness." Namadeva's mantra is *Ahum Prema*, which means "I am divine love." The same...

In 2019, Namadeva contracted cancer. He chose, rather than go through the operations and the chemotherapy, to surrender to this last gift from the Divine Mother. He said, "I want to be with my guru. I am ready to leave." So Namadeva stayed home, and his friends and students gathered around in his living room. When he felt well enough, he would come downstairs and share his last few moments. I have seen some prepare for the final journey of their incarnation. Namadeva faced his death with astounding courage and equanimity. The night he died, he was scheduled to lead kirtan at Kripalu. Bhavani and I filled in for him that night and sang only his kirtans. Through Skype, we broadcast the kirtan into Namadeva's living room. We all felt his love and presence.

My job now is to keep Namadeva's and Sant Keshav Das' music alive and to pass it on to my students. Kirtan is an oral tradition that goes back at least a thousand years in India. Each generation takes the teachings of the previous one, adds its own sensitivity and creativity, and then hands it on. Those of us who understand the true nature of this practice focus both on the specifics of using kirtan to awaken, and the value of maintaining and passing on one of the world's most beautiful traditions.

Riding home from kirtan one night, I was struck with the most amazing pain, way beyond a ten on the pain scale. Somehow I got to the emergency room, where they discovered my pancreas had gone mad. They pumped morphine after morphine into me, which didn't touch the pain. Turned out I had pancreatitis as a side effect of my doctor increasing my Lipitor, a statin drug for lowering cholesterol. There was no cure for the pancreatitis, only the hope that it would not kill me. I lay in the hospital for a month fed only intravenously.

I was almost dead, but also deep in my mantra. Day after day, I lay in the most intense pain. Ultimately, the pain became my point of focus in meditation. Then came a vision: I saw the long chain of life, leading back into prehistory, each generation passing on the secrets to the next. I saw myself as one link in this long chain, and I honored all of my teachers and my teachers' teachers as well as my students. I saw that I had to remain in the body longer because there was more work to do. Deep in this experience, the tears flowed down my cheeks. A nurse came into the room. She saw I was crying and she bent close and said to me, "Are you terminal?" I thought that a rather odd question so I answered, "Yes, and so are you."

A final note about Mirabai Devi. The pancreatitis left me in dark pain for many months. During my recovery, Mirabai called. She was in California and heard of my illness and wanted to offer her love and support. We spoke about my experience, and the constant pain that had followed me from the hospital. It was so wonderful to hear from her. I was quite low with pain and depression, and was having relationship issues on top of it. We talked softly about me, about her, about healing and death. We ended the call with love and, as I hung up the phone, I noted that for the first time in three months there was no pain. In the process of our phone call, something had been released, and healing took place. For the first time since leaving the hospital, the pain had dissipated. We did not speak for some years after that. Mirabai is a Shakti Ma. People bristle with horripilation around her. She offers a rare insight into the character of the Holy Mother. She is a great blessing in my life.

Chapter14

SHIVARUDRA BALAYOGI and SHIVABALANANDA

When the kirtan is harmonious with so many people, it's a tumultuous beautiful sound. We can't hear just one voice during the chorus; or rather we do hear one voice. But that one voice is actually the sound of everyone's voice in harmony. That's our offering to God.—Radhanath Swami

ShivaBalaYogi   Shivarudra Balayogi

You cannot understand Shivarudra Balayogi without knowing about his guru, Shiva Bala Yogi. Shiva Bala Yogi was born in the first part of the twentieth century. As a young child he showed strange tendencies towards trance, devotion, and a strong love of God. At age twelve he had a dream in which God came to him and told him it was time to begin *tapas* (extensive spiritual work, sadhana)—and he should meditate twenty-three hours a day. So at age twelve, this young child began to sit. For twelve years he sat, unmoving, with his hands clenched in fists, twenty-three hours a day. At the end of this time, the kundalini energy finally reached his crown chakra, he merged with the divine, and reached enlightenment. He spent the rest of his short life offering his wisdom to others and focusing on the salvation of the human race. He had many great devotees.

A fellow named Yogeshwar was his attendant. Yogeshwar cleaned the rooms, prepared the food, and served Swamiji in all ways. Yogeshwar meditated for three hours every day and devoted the rest of his time to serving. His weakness was his sweet tooth. Yogeshwar loved candy. Every day or so, Swamiji would leave a piece of candy out on his table when Yogeshwar came to clean. Yogeshwar could not resist. Each time, he would eat the candy. When Swamiji came to the room and saw the candy gone, he would call Yogeshwar and scream in his ear for a hour about what a thief he was and how addicted to candy he was. Yogeshwar would sit there with tears of bliss rolling down his cheeks, as being corrected and scolded by one's guru is a great blessing.

Shiva Bala Yogi had many devotees, many of whom began teaching after he left his body. Shivabalananda even claimed to channel the guru. But when it was time, Swamiji passed his shakti on to Shivarudra Balayogi, known as Babaji. But first a challenge had to be met. After Shiva Bala Yogi left his body, he began to define Babaji's sadhana through dreams. He told Shivarudra Balayogi to sit facing north and meditate for twenty-three hours every day. He sat for three years in this position. Then Babaji was told to sit facing west for the same sadhana. Four times he sat for three years, until after twelve years of meditating, his awareness merged with the cosmic and he discovered the truth. He became Shivarudra Balayogi and, after a year of reintegrating, he began traveling the world, teaching his strict form of meditation.

Agastya from the Pacific Northwest has been a friend for a long time. I met him when he led the Shree Maa tour; he had left Shree Maa and now he studied with and worked for

199

Shivarudra Balayogi. When it was time for Shivarudra Balayogi to travel to the Boston area, Agastya asked if I could host him. I immediately began making arrangements. He would stay with my friend Brian in his huge mansion and we would hold programs at the Campe Studio in Northampton. The Campe Studio is a beautiful garden house on the property of a wealthy yogini, who allows the house to be used for special spiritual programs.

Babaji is about sixty-five years old, with a long gray beard, balding head, and bare feet. He dresses in a white dhoti and cotton shawl no matter what the weather. He is soft-spoken, has the kindest eyes, and a wonderful way of talking about imaginations—the fantasies of the mind—and circular thinking. His stories of his guru and the gods and goddesses are completely captivating. He is also a great kirtan wallah and plays tabla and harmonium.

I knew the Hindu traditions and when Babaji arrived we prepared a *pada puja*, a ritual washing of the guru's feet. Later that day, his devotees created their own ritual so as not to miss the opportunity to be blessed with the touch of the guru's feet. This is a great tradition in India. It is felt that the shakti of the universe connects with the guru's kundalini energy through the earth, through his or her feet. Devotees kneel down in front of their guru and stretch their fingers out to touch the feet and receive a small taste of shakti. It is also said that, in this process, the guru is given the opportunity to mitigate the karma of the devotee. Everyone always wants to touch the guru's feet.

The first day of Babaji's visit, we sat around together in Brian's living room getting to know each other. He told me that my kirtan mission was important and I needed to treat my body like a temple so that I could offer my practice for as long as possible. He had a pre-diabetic condition that he treated with a black powdery substance found only in India. Because of my illness, I also was pre-diabetic, so I was curious about this black

200

powder. He told me that he put a cup of it in a quart of water and drank it down every morning. He was sure this powder balanced his blood sugar. Then he gave me a brown paper bag full of the stuff as a gift. I went into the kitchen, poured myself about sixteen ounces of water, put half a teaspoon of the black powder into the water, and took a small sip. It felt like someone had thrust a red-hot iron rod down my throat. The burning began at the tip of my tongue and ended somewhere deep inside me. My nose began to run, my eyes watered, and I could not breathe. It felt more like drinking teargas than anything that would help my blood sugar. The Indian constitution is very different from the Western one. They develop abilities and immunities far beyond what we need here in the West in order to consume Twinkies and Wonder Bread.

The Campe garden house easily holds a hundred people, but the night of Babaji's program in late spring it was raining and the house was full to overflowing. Babaji's program began with forty-five minutes of meditation. Babaji comes from the tradition of Jnana Yoga—the system where you use the mind to transcend the mind. Some say it is like using a thorn to remove a thorn. There were many great gurus from India who used the Jnana system of yoga, such as Ramana Maharshi and Sri Nisargadatta in the twentieth century. Some call the system *Neti Neti,* meaning "not this, not that." With every thought, word, and deed, your intellect asks yourself, "Who is it that is committing this action, or having this thought?" We are obviously more than our bodies, more than our psychology, even more than our thoughts. When you eliminate everything that you are not, you are left with the awareness that everything is contained within you, and the essence within you is contained within everything.

Babaji began his discourse and talked about the power of meditation, and the greatness of his guru, and of the simple Jnana system that, if applied vigorously, guaranteed success. I knew from reading that during the tapas of Shiva Bala Yogi, he

201

sat with his arms extended in front of him with his fingers first outstretched, then curled around as if making an open fist. He sat like this for so many years in his tapas that for the rest of his life his hands were frozen in this position. I watched his hands assume the very same position that Shiva Bala Yogi had embraced during his life.

Shivarudra Balayogi told a story about what is more powerful: the arrow of Rama or the name of Rama:

Two very great rishis (Vedic sages), Vasishta and Vishwamitra, were having a discussion. Vasishta proposed that the name of Rama was the greatest force in the universe. Vishwamitra disagreed; he felt that the arrow of Rama was the most powerful force. The two of them debated and finally conceived of a plan to determine the truth.

Vishwamitra went to the kingdom neighboring Rama's kingdom and spoke to the king. "Oh great King, I have been told that Rama is gathering an army to destroy your kingdom. You must find a protector. I suggest that you find Hanuman, the strongest and greatest soldier from Rama's war with Ravana, and ask for his protection. But you must be careful. Hanuman loves Rama more than anything. You must ask for his protection without telling him that the danger comes from Rama." The king went to the Himalayas, searched out Hanuman, and received his non-refundable commitment to protect the kingdom against any marauder.

Then Vishwamitra went to Rama. He said, "Rama, the king of your neighboring fiefdom has been speaking ill of you. He says you are not fit to be king. He sees you as a threat. You must go and confront him with your army, and you must put an arrow into the heart of this evil-speaking king." Rama, being the essence of honor and a warrior, could not allow these types of statements to go unpunished. He gathered his army.

(It is not clear from this story how Vishwamitra could spread lies and get away with it. Probably it has something to do with the Gayatri Mantra)

So now all the conditions were met for this test. Rama's army crossed the border into his neighbor's kingdom. As he approached the city walls, he saw the king's army gathered. Standing in front of the army, in all of his splendor, stood Hanuman, the great monkey god. When Hanuman recognized Ram, he was horrified. He thought, "I cannot attack sacred Rama. In my lower self, I love him. In my higher self, I am him." So Hanuman dropped his weapons, settled into a comfortable meditation position, and began to chant Rama's name.

On the other side of the battlefield, Rama also recognized Hanuman. But the dharma of Rama is of the highest order. Throughout the Ramayana, *the epic poem depicting the exploits of Rama, Hanuman, and Sita, Rama is consistently confronted with moral dilemmas. He sees his dharma requiring more discipline than the average person. His reputation and his word are the truths by which Rama lives. In this context, Rama had no choice but to kill Hanuman. So he drew his arrow, placed it into his great bow, pulled back his drawstring, aimed, and he let the arrow fly directly towards Hanuman's heart. Hanuman was sitting quietly chanting, "Sita Ram Sita Ram Sita Ram."*

As the arrow flew through the air towards Hanuman, suddenly it transformed itself from a death missile into a garland of lotus and marigold flowers, and fell gently around Hanuman's neck. And so the debate was settled decisively. Vishwamitra admitted that Vasishta was correct: the name of Rama is without a doubt the greatest force in the universe.

Then Babaji sang in a small, high-pitched tenor. He led some bhajans his devotees knew and things really began to rock. I got to accompany him on guitar. He sang a version of Shankaracharya's *Shivohum* ("I am Shiva") that could be a hit here in America—pentatonic and fast, over and over, the words *Chidananda Rupa Shivohum Shivohum* (I am the eternal bliss, I am the consciousness of infinite goodness, I am Shiva). He is a great musician and supporting him was a great honor. He loved the way I sang *Rama Rahima* ("Only your name can carry me across the great river to the truth"), so I put it on my first CD and named it the same.

One morning, Babaji called my partner and me in for a private meeting. Babaji would never allow himself to be alone with students, so four of us sat in a circle on the floor. He talked about relationship and tried to give us some strong advice. "There is an ideal for adult relationship. Once past childbearing age, the reason for intimate relationship is to provide the optimal environment for each other's awakening." Then he looked into me and my partner. His eyes got very intense as he said, "See the god and goddess in each other and always keep that in mind during negotiations." Finally, he said, "Your work is loving support for each other's truth" (or as David said to Absalom in the movie version, "May the Lord shine in your heart as you shine in mine.")

When it was time for Babaji to leave, we stood alone outside his door. As is the custom in India, I laid my body out flat in the dirt in front of him, stretched out my arms, and touched his feet. He said, "Shubal, you are a very pious man. Your work is clear. Dedicate yourself and you will do well."

Babaji and I correspond now, and when he does come to the East Coast, we meet up and I sing his favorite bhajan, *Rama Rahima*. He is truly a great man, who clearly has done the work. He travels the world, teaches meditation, and tells stories of the glories of his guru.

Shivabalananda

Shivabalananda, called, Swamiji, is also a devotee of Shiva Bala Yogi. He was a scientist with the Indian space program, while meditating five hours a day. When his guru left his body, Swamiji began meditating twenty hours a day, and he began to allow Shiva Bala Yogi to speak through him. I have watched his hands form into the frozen state that Shiva Bala Yogi's hands froze into after twelve years of tapasya.

I met Swamiji in Northampton during a bitter cold February and sat next to him during his program at the Campe studio. Shivabalananda came from his car dressed in a simple dhoti and shawl, no shirt, no coat, no nothing. This little eighty-year-old man walked through the slush in his sandals. He took his seat on the *takhat* (wooden platform) in the front of the room and we all sat hushed in anticipation. He began with a silent meditation for thirty minutes. Sometimes, in the presence of a holy person, meditation can go very deep, and this was one of those times. When I returned to normal consciousness, Swamiji was asking everyone to get in a line and one-by-one come up to ask personal questions and receive a blessing.

I went first. "Swamiji, how can I deepen my sadhana?"

His answer was simple. "Just meditate, my son, just meditate."

Since I was the musician, my seat was next to Swamiji's, so I was able to watch the next person come up and ask him, "Swamiji, I have migraine headaches. Can you offer some techniques for relief?"

Another simple answer, "Just meditate, my dear, meditate."

The next person asked, "Swamiji, I cannot get my kids to behave. What can I do?"

"Just meditate!" was his response.

Everyone in line got the same answer. I was beginning to get the message.

Then Swamiji opened it up to group questions. Everyone was silent, so to get things rolling I asked, "We're headed for Armageddon. Is there anything we can to do avert catastrophe?"

He said. "If everyone on the planet would meditate, we could be saved."

I said, "Then, in other words, we're doomed!"

He rose up out of his chair and said, "It IS possible!"

Someone from the back of the room called out, "George Bush will never meditate!"

Again, Swamiji said, "It IS possible!"

In that moment I finally got what he meant. "Shut up, stop asking questions, and meditate." OR, the medicine for your illness lies in the space between your thoughts.

After the discourse and darshan, I was called upon to lead kirtan. I did not have any specific kirtan in mind and my mind was pretty blank from all the meditating, so I just closed my eyes and began to sing. The first phrase that came out of my mouth was the name of Shivabalananda's guru, Shiva Bala Yogi.

I sang "Jaya Shiva Bala Yogi" over and over, with more and more intensity. I felt energy invade my fingers and my spine. There was definitely a strange force in the room that was captivating all of us. The more spiritual emotion I put into the singing, the more the chorus responded in kind until there was lightning striking throughout the room. When it was over, we sat in silence for quite a while. It was clear to all of us that Swamiji had gone into samadhi during the kirtan. A while later I received an e-mail from him: "We made a recording of your kirtan that night in Northampton. Your kirtan is a treasure at our ashram."

The next year, Swamiji came back to New England and we had a private dinner with him. He is ancient. He walks with a stoop, speaks very slowly, and is very hard to understand. We talked about the United States, about his guru and his mission. I sang a little, we ate and he began to talk. He told us the whole story of the *Ramayana*. It took a while, but that was okay, I enjoyed hanging out. He blessed us and sent us on our way with love.

Swamiji does not claim to be enlightened. He claims to go into trance and channel the disembodied consciousness of his guru, Shiva Bala Yogi. I have seen this, but I remain skeptical. It's hard to figure all this stuff out—disembodied consciousness, channeling of other souls, etc. My sense is that when God wants to talk to you, She speaks directly to you. We do not need any intermediaries in our conversations with our "God-Guru-Self." He taught me with his sweet graciousness, the brilliance of his old age, and his peacefulness. And he taught me, yes, it IS possible.

EPILOGUE

"Our work is to joyfully participate in the woeful suffering of the universe."-- Buddha

As I sit in my cabin at the peak of Bear Mountain, in the center of the Massachusetts State Forest, I watch winter transforming into spring and I cannot help but think back over my life. I have finished writing the stories of all the great souls I've met. It is interesting how each one of these beings offered a slightly different gift, or tool, for creating a little more freedom in my life.

Neem Karoli Baba, and through him, Ram Dass, gave me the greatest gift of all—the vision of God/Guru/Self.

Sathya Sai Baba taught me bhajans and kirtan, and gave me a whole series of amazing quotes. "It's okay to be born in a religion, but it's not okay to die in one." "There is no free will, but to make it work we must act as if there is." "Before you speak, ask, is it the truth, is it kind, and does it improve upon the silence?"

Karunamayi took me on a journey into my anger towards my Earth lineage, into the way I relate to women, and helped me see my attraction to women as a form of worshiping the Divine Mother.

Swami Satyananda Saraswati taught me much about Hindu concepts, the nature of the higher planes, and the nuts and bolts of worshiping the Divine Mother. He taught me how to be a pujari.

Shree Maa taught me how to cry out from the depths of my being with love. She taught me how to be a man.

Baba Hariji gave me my mantra. After chanting the mantra intensely for years, I discovered that this mantra is simply a vibrational form of my own self. I offer Ramana

Maharishi a slight correction. God-Guru-Self-Mantra, all one.Bhagwan Ram opened the Vortex of Love and sealed the deal.

And then there was Ma Chetan Jyoti. She gave me many of the secrets of kirtan and taught me how to use kirtan to worship my guru. She taught me that ego-centrism, arrogance, narcissism, untruthfulness and spiritual intensity are not mutually exclusive.

The others, Shivarudra Balayogi, Nealon (she said, "You can't think when you sing"), Shivabalananda, Mirabai, Namadeva, Henry Miller, Herman Hesse, Rudolf Steiner, Muddy Waters, Sheldon Kopp, Nisargadatta, Ramana Maharshi, Paramahamsa Ramakrishna—they are all signposts. To paraphrase Ram Dass, there is only one *sadguru*, the true teacher, and everyone and everything else is an *upaguru*, a teaching. I touch their feet and the feet of their teachers. Shree Maa says "there is only one sadguru, Shiva". She means, when you see your guru as being one with Shiva, eureka and excelsior! You have found it, ever upward.

Sometimes I try to understand what kind of karma allowed me, a most unworthy soul, to meet these great beings and have these intense experiences. The first forty years of my life were spent in the borderland, with untruthfulness, addiction, and loneliness as my only friends. The second half of my life, at least so far, has been immersed in the search for my own divinity, some kind of karmic compensation for my earlier suffering. Maybe, in the giant bead game of my incarnation, the scales of justice are coming into balance.

A group of Russian mathematicians recently developed a mathematical model for the expansion of the universe from the Big Bang until present. At the same time, they developed a mathematical model for the expansion of social media like Facebook and a model for the expansion of consciousness and awareness in the human brain from birth to maturity. They discovered that all three mathematical models were identical. As the universe expands, so does our consciousness. Perhaps my incarnation is simply a metaphor for the incarnation of humanity as one living consciousness, from the birth of time until the infinite conclusion.

We start out innocent, unified and pure, then one day our breast milk is denied and the one becomes two. The dynamic nature of that split is essentially the Big Bang. This is the gift of Kali. She breaks us in half for her own amusement, and then nurses the split until the higher planes are attained, where the split is healed. This is where we finally become someone, on the road to becoming no one.

The pain and suffering and grief I've experienced in my life—the bad relationships, estrangement from children, unsuccessful business career, time uselessly spent grieving the loss of something I never had (Earth lineage mother love)—turns out to be the grist this sadhu has been grinding to consume as much karma as possible in as short a time as possible. Karma is not created by the painful events of our lives. One of the basic laws of the universe is the inevitable disruption of easy times in our destiny (within the incarnation), leading to pain and dissolution. Karma is created by our reaction to these disruptions.

To the degree that we can surrender to our inner divinity, to the degree that we can accept the events of our lives as gifts, as opportunities for puja, for worship, to the degree that we can maintain loving equanimity through these inevitable turbulent experiences, to the degree that we can see the face of God in everything and everyone we encounter, to the degree that we can recognize that the medicine for our illness lies in the space between our thoughts—to that degree we can find some happiness in this vale of tears.

APPENDIX I
ALL ABOUT KIRTAN

True singing is a different breath, about nothing. I wish to be with those who know the secrets...or else, alone.--Rainer Maria Rilke

Kirtan is singing of the lord's glories. The devotee is thrilled with divine emotion. He loses himself in the love of God. He gets horripilation of the body due to extreme love for God. He weeps in the middle when thinking of the glory of God. His voice becomes choked, and he flies into a state of divine bhava. –Swami Sivananda

I
BHAJAN and KIRTAN

Bhajan (BUH-jun) is Hindu devotional music, employing Indian *rag* and *taal* (scale and rhythm) and complex Sanskrit phrases. Kirtan (KEER-Tun) is a form of bhajan using only the names of God (*namasankirtan*) in Sanskrit, sung in a group in a call-and-response style with very simple melodies.

The essence of the spiritual practice known as namasankirtan has its roots in Indian prehistory. In the earliest days of the Sanatana Dharma, the "eternal path," Brahma gave birth to hundreds of rishis. The community of the three worlds consisted of gods and goddesses, rishis and *munis* (saints), and *asuras* (demons). Man was also around in some form. In those days, the rishis and munis composed sounds that became the foundation of Sanskrit. These sounds were developed to vibrate in sympathy with the various chakras, to awaken kundalini and move this energy up to the crown of the head where it explodes into cosmic consciousness. These sounds combine to form mantras.

In Sanatana Dharma, history is divided into long segments of time known as *yugas*. The Kali Yuga is the period we are in now—a time of the lowest consciousness, with gross materialism and body awareness. The wisdom taught by the *Bhagavad Gita* (Krishna's treatise on love, karma, and selfless service)—and by many sages and saints since Krishna's time—says that the only way for mankind to awaken kundalini and attain cosmic consciousness in the Kali Yuga is to use simple mantras (and the names of the gods and goddesses), and to repeat these mantras all day long, even when the mind is occupied in other matters. This is the practice of japa, which sometimes uses a mala of a hundred and eight beads on which you count your repetitions back and forth, using your thumb and second finger, and never passing the "guru bead," but reversing directions with a mental sound of *HRING* when that bead is reached.

In 1273, an avatar was born named Jnaneshwar. When he was six years old, he was sitting on the porch of his home giving teachings to the villagers. They would come to the boy and ask him to heal illness, or to tell the sex of an unborn child, and even ask for spiritual advice. The local Brahmins heard about this boy and called him in before the court to find out if he really was capable of teaching. They said, "If you are what you say you are, make that cow over there recite the *Bhagavad Gita.*"The boy looked at the cow. He said, "The cow and I are one" and, as he began to recite the Gita, the cow joined in with him. The Brahmins looked at each other and said, "Okay, we guess you can teach."

When Jnaneshwar was twelve years old, he realized that only the Brahmins could participate in bhajan singing. The average person was not educated in Sanskrit, nor in the ways of classical music. He decided to remove all the verbs, adjectives, adverbs, prepositions, and pronouns from bhajan practice, and leave only the names of God. He called this practice namasankirtan. It spread throughout India like wildfire during the golden age of Hinduism. At the time there were dozens of enlightened saints living in Bombay (now Mumbai). They would all gather at Jnaneshwar's house to sing for three or four days without stopping. This young boy transformed the prayerful practice of bhajan into the meditative practice of kirtan.

When Jnaneshwar was sixteen, he stood on a street corner in Bombay and translated the *Bhagavad Gita* into Marathi, the language of the common people. As he translated, he discoursed on the meaning. There was a scribe getting down everything Jnaneshwar said and compiled these discourses into a book called the *Jnaneshwari*. Even though these words were spoken eight hundred years ago by a sixteen-year-old boy, the book is still used in every Indian public school as one of the two definitive commentaries on the *Gita* (the other is from Shankaracharya).

When Jnaneshwar reached his twentieth birthday, he decided "enough is enough" and dropped his body. He was buried sitting in lotus asana, and a shrine was built above his grave. It is said that his body has not decayed and he is still sitting there, spine straight. It has become a major pilgrimage site.

A hundred years later, the Moguls had taken over India. They were destroying the temples and giving everyone the choice of converting to Islam or dying. Most of India's Hindus converted. But the Divine Mother has a way of preserving the great culture of Sanatana Dharma. A new avatar was born in Bengal, named Chaitanya. He was such a great devotee of Krishna that some thought he WAS partly Krishna. Chaitanya taught that by singing the names of God you could reach a state of yoga and have great experiences of higher consciousness and bliss along the way. He was the first great practitioner of bhakti yoga. He transformed India, reawakening the Hindu traditions that were under oppression from the Mogul empire. Chaitanya traveled across India, spreading his gospel. Everyone who heard Chaitanya sing the famous *Hare Krishna* mahamantra became reawakened to their Hindu roots.

The Mogul police heard about Chaitanya and decided he had to be killed. They called him before a judge, who said, "Before I sentence you to death, Chaitanya, I will grant you one last request." The trap was set. Chaitanya said, "Yes judge, I do have one last request. I request that you chant the Hare Krishna mantra with me just one time." They only got halfway through the mantra before the judge putdown his gavel, threw off his robes, and went dancing down the street with Chaitanya, lost in an ecstatic Krishna samadhi.

Chaitanya is the root of so many lineages in India, the most famous of which is ISKCON (the "Hare Krishnas" of airport fame). He initiated and proselytized the practice of kirtan, which Americans have learned to love so deeply.

One of the great twentieth-century gurus was Swami Sivananda. Swami Satchitananda and Yogaville are part of his lineage. He had a fine understanding of namasankirtan. Here are some of his great words:

"Kirtan is one of the nine modes of bhakti. Kirtan is singing God's Name with feeling, love, and faith. In Sankirtan, people join together and sing God's name collectively, accompanied by musical instruments, such as the harmonium, violin, cymbals, mrdangam or khol, etc.[and guitar].*Kirtan is an exact science. One can realize God through kirtan alone. This is the easiest method for attainment of God-consciousness. Great divine persons—like Narada, Valmiki, and Suka in ancient times, and Gouranga, Nanak, and Tulasidas in recent times—have all attained perfection through kirtan bhakti alone.*

"The harmonious vibrations produced by singing of the Names of the Lord help devotees to control their mind easily. They produce a benign influence on the mind, elevating the mind at once from its old ruts or grooves to magnanimous heights of

divine splendor and glory. If one does sankirtan from the bottom of his heart, with full bhava and prema(love), *even the trees, birds, and animals will be deeply influenced. They will respond. Such is the powerful influence of sankirtan.*

"Kirtan is a very effective method of devotion for another reason. Humans are erotic beings. They love and love. They cannot help but love the things of the world; but their love is only passion and not pure divine love. They want to hear sweet music, want to see beautiful objects, and want to witness the dance. Music melts the heart of even a stone-hearted man. If there is anything in this world that can change the heart of a man in a very quick time, that is music and dance. This very method is made use of in kirtan bhakti, by directing the attention toward God instead of toward sensual enjoyments.

"Man's emotion of eroticism is directed towards divinity, and his love for music and singing is not destroyed; sudden destruction of such a sentiment will not prove successful in making him perfect. Kirtan is sweet and pleasant, and easily changes the heart. Do sankirtan daily. Disseminate sankirtan bhakti far and wide. Develop Vishwa-prem(God love) *through sankirtan. Establish Sankirtana* mandalis (circles) *everywhere. Bring Vaikuntha* (Vishnu's home) *to Earth in every house by doing sankirtan! Realize the state of Sat-Chit-Ananda—total Existence, total Consciousness, total Bliss."*

--Shivananda Swami Shivananda(*Bliss Divine,* Divine Life Society, 1955)

The way kirtan is practiced in North India, in Rishikesh on the Ganges, is that the harmonium is passed around a circle; each member leads two kirtans, reaching great heights, with each kirtan reaching higher than the last. The circle goes around and around all night long. Some ashrams have kirtan going on twenty-four hours a day. The monks and nuns attend kirtan as their schedule permits, and the kirtan goes on and on. This is

215

also true about the environs of saints. Many of the great saints of India have kirtan as part of their regular practice. Anandamayi Ma always had kirtan going on within earshot. Sathya Sai Baba had a minimum of two hours of bhajan singing each day at his ashram. And Maharajji always had kirtan going at his ashrams.

Because of the easy way that kirtan creates one-pointedness (concentration on only one thought), it has traveled around the world. You cannot think when you sing! Nowadays, wherever spirit gathers, whether it be Sufi or Buddhist or Hindu, Jewish or Christian, you will find that singing God's names is part of the practice. You will also discover the similarity of the names of God from all these different religions: Christianity has "Yeshua," Judaism has "Ha Shem," Buddhism has "Buddha," Islam has "Allah," Hinduism has "Ishwara." You can hear the consistent seed syllables throughout the names.

The "secret" of kirtan is that when your mind is focused on getting the words pronounced exactly right, and learning and singing the melody exactly as the leader sings it, combined with the group experience of singing together (like the Pete Seeger Christmas Concerts in the '60s), the vibration created by the vocal chords when pronouncing these sacred seed syllables, the bhava created by the beauty of the melodies, the intensity of calling to God with your innermost being as loudly as you can—all this leads to God answering your call. It happens in varying ways, but it always happens. When you put your heart fully into singing kirtan, close your eyes, throw your head back and open wide, your soul soars with the birds and the space is created for God to come and sing Her response in your ear. Music is God's great gift, and kirtan is the meaning of music, a meaning beyond concept.

II
Kirtan Sadhana

The most difficult and important aspect of any sadhana is routine. Whatever sadhana you choose—meditation on a mantra, or watching a flame, or hatha yoga, or kirtan—the key to success is repetition. The first thing to do is choose a location, some spot in your home that is quiet, secluded, safe, and private. It should be big enough to hold a small table, some wall space for pictures, and room for you to sit on the floor (or in a chair).

Get a comfortable cushion that only you will use, with maybe a special blanket or sheepskin underneath. This is your asana, your seat (as Swami Satyananda says," it's what you put your ass on"). As you do your sadhana on it, it will grow in power and shakti. When you sit there consistently, it will eventually assist you in awakening your dormant energy. Now you can create your own puja table, your altar. On the table should go pictures of loved ones and teachers, statues of the gods and goddesses (if you're into that), mementoes of special moments in your life, a candle, a stick of incense, and flowers. Spread out your favorite spiritual books around you.

Now you are ready to begin. The ritual you use is completely up to you, so make up a good one. A suggestion might be to begin with three deep OMs, then see who you want to honor that day (from a list of all your friends and family who are sick or angry, or people from work who are out to get you, etc.) and offer a quick prayer to your higher power that healing be given to all ("healing" is not the same as "curing"). May they be happy, may they be peaceful, may they be free from suffering (Buddhist lovingkindness meditation). You might then place a flower at the feet of each of the pictures and statues on your puja table, and thank each one silently.

Then, if you are on a kirtan sadhana, you look into the eyes of a picture of Krishna or Rama or the Divine Mother, or

217

your guru, and you begin to sing softly, telling of your love and your heart opening. Letting go of other thoughts, sit singing softly to God for a while, maybe five or ten minutes, but make it the same minimum amount of time every day.

Kirtan is part of the practice of bhakti yoga, the yoga of love and devotion. The practice is enhanced when guidance from a guru, and love for a guru, is included. At this point it is important to say that there are many false gurus in the world. For every hundred you meet, ninety-nine of them will be *teachings* rather than *teachers*, "almost there's" or wannabees offering practices and initiations before they have completed their own work.

Meeting a true guru is a transformative experience. I strongly suggest that you take every opportunity to meet every teacher you possibly can. You never know when you will meet the one who resonates with your soul and awakens a consciousness within you that you cannot even imagine. As my friend Chris says, "Open Heart Open Eyes." Or as the bible puts it: "Now I see though a glass darkly, but when that which is perfect is come, then I see as I am seen." The glass being our desires, our psychology, our persona, our projections, the veil in front of our eyes that keeps us from seeing things as they are. All that is in your way must go. It is the key to the relationship with the guru.

As Shree Maa says, "As long as you have a body, you have more to learn." But there are a few beings that have found completeness in themselves and, therefore, do not want or need anything at all from the outside. These beings are deep in the awareness that there is only One, that we all are waves in an ocean of consciousness. So these beings, wanting nothing, seeing only oneness, have complete unconditional love for you, as they do for themselves. When you meet a being who is very close to this perfection, as the bible and Paul continue, "I see as I am seen." This is the essence of the practice of *shaktipath*—an

218

exchange between a student and a teacher who lives in this oneness. Shaktipath is India's great open secret. Many, including myself, have had their lives changed and their hearts awakened by this practice. When the resonance is right, you are given a glimpse of reality through the teacher's eyes. This glimpse puts you on the path. It dispels doubt, heals many wounds, and gives the strength to heal the rest. This secret miracle of India is something to be held in great awe.

The guru is a reflection of your own highest self (since they project nothing, they are able to reflect accurately back to you your own divinity, the polished mirror). Here is one way the principle works: when I wanted to learn how to play guitar like BB King, I went to BB and asked him, "How do you do that?" When I wanted peace of mind, happiness, personal strength, and love for all, I went to someone who had it and asked, "Will you show me?" That is only one aspect of the value of a guru. The guru is a remover of darkness, and there is only one way to remove darkness, to bring light.

Kirtan naturally leads to meditation, so after a few minutes of chanting, sit quietly on your cushion and watch your thoughts. At this point, you may employ any of the varied types of meditation—watching your breath, chanting a mantra, focusing on your third eye. The obvious goal in all of this is to develop one-pointedness, the ability to focus on just one thought. Once concentration is achieved, there is a natural pull towards meditation, or being able to focus your mind in awareness without any thought, a kind of blank mind. When you can focus your mind thus for fifteen seconds or three minutes or three hours, you begin to experience meditation.

While in the state of meditation, information normally inaudible because of the noisy thought process begins to pour into the brain. Much of the function of the brain is still a mystery to the scientists. There are many theories as to how the brain functions, including a very valid holographic theory. The

219

Koppographic Theory of Brain Function theorizes that aspects of the brain and spinal column actually exist in dimensions not perceivable by our limited sensory organs (and consequently unknown by Western scientists). Hindus define these aspects as nadis (spiritual nerves) and chakras (the energy centers along the spine). When the kundalini energy activates the chakras, they begin to act as sensory organs receiving data from the higher dimensions. The brain begins to receive and interpret the data from these spiritual sensory organs in the same way it does when it receives data from our physical sense organs.

You may have heard of the string theory in quantum physics. They say that the smallest particles constructing our entire universe look kind of like violin strings. These violin strings are smaller than electrons and quarks. Depending on which way they vibrate, different forms of matter or energy come into existence. The first epiphany is that the entire universe is vibrating. It is MUSIC! The theory says these strings are vibrating in at least ten dimensions. We are limited by our sensory organs to perceive only three of these dimensions.

There are seven chakras, energy plexuses, in the human body. As your consciousness moves through the chakras and the kundalini energy begins to rise in the spine when thoughts are stilled, you perceive the information coming from the chakras, and each one gives a deeper understanding of the universe. As the energy moves beyond the first, second, and third chakras, you are healed of negative instinctual behavior, sexual obsession, and the need to "be someone." At the fourth chakra, you become quiet and feel a deep compassion for humanity rise up.

When the energy reaches the fifth chakra, you enter into states of higher consciousness. Swami Satyananda Saraswati explained it to me like this: "The first stage of samadhi is called *bhava samadhi*, where the deep compassion swells so that all that exists is you loving everything and everyone in the universe. It is you and your love relationship with your beloved, the object of your overflowing love." As the energy reaches the sixth chakra, more information is perceived that moves consciousness into the second stage of samadhi, called *savikalpa samadhi*. Again, from Satyananda, "In this stage, you look at your beloved (the entire universe) and see that you and the universe are one. You see your beloved and say 'we are the same person.' The relationship dissolves into oneness, just you and the beloved as one."

In the final seventh chakra, we find the universe within us and discover the holographic God. It is called *nirvikalpa samadhi*. No longer do you say "I and my beloved are one." In this state the "I" dissolves and you become the beloved. No one talks about this final stage.

The great nineteenth-century sage of India, Ramakrishna, tried to speak about it. He sat his students around him and said, "When the energy reaches the fifth chakra, you have knowledge of God, and when it reaches the sixth chakra, you have the vision of God, and when it reaches the seventh..." At this point, like iron filings to a magnet, he was drawn into nirvikalpa samadhi and could not speak. His students sat there for twenty minutes until he returned to normal consciousness. Then he tried again, "The fifth chakra, and the sixth and the seventh..." and again he was drawn into that highest state. Finally when he returned to normal, with tears running down his face, he said, "I want to tell you about it, but the Divine Mother will not let me!" But he did tell this story: "There was once a salt doll, and it wanted to know the nature of the ocean, so it dove in. Naturally, it dissolved."

Swami Satyananda says that in this highest state of consciousness—the state that the world sees as "enlightenment"—there is no longer a relationship, or even a "you." All there is is the Beloved. You actually dissolve in the oneness of the beloved universe.

There are scientists who propose the theory that the universe is a hologram. A hologram is created by shining a laser at an object, and then bouncing another laser off the first beam onto a photographic plate or film. Then, when a laser shines through the film, a three-dimensional picture of the object is created. If you take the film and cut it in half, you have two complete pictures; if you cut it in sixteenths, you have sixteen complete pictures, and theoretically on into infinity. If you look at the film without a laser, it seems to be nothing more than various waves of frequencies.

There was an experiment in the 1970s where a scientist found that two electrons, great distances apart, both instantaneously reacted to stimulus applied to just one. In other words, the message was apparently traveling faster than the speed of light, which Einstein said could not happen. Another scientist, David Bohm, theorized that the only way this could happen without violating Einstein's law was for this apparent reality to be a hologram. Since then, other experiments have contributed to Bohm's idea. If the universe is truly holographic, then each particle in the universe contains the entire universe. Each of us is a shard of glass in a great (perhaps broken) photo plate of the holographic universe. Within each of us is everything, and when our crown chakra begins to send its perceptual information to our awareness, we finally see the whole picture. This explains how Krishna could open His mouth and thus reveal the entire universe to His mom. This explains why a young child like Jnaneshwar could at the age of six recite the holy books of India, and at sixteen could write a definitive commentary on the *Bhagavad Gita*.

But back to kirtan sadhana. Namasankirtan means to sing the names of God in a group. At home there is no group, so it is important to get together with like-minded friends and practice as often as possible, even if it's just a few of you. A great saint once said that if you take all the pleasures of the world and put them into one, they would not equal the pleasure of satsang, spiritual community.

After meditation, you can make some offering to the gods, goddesses, ancestors, or whoever you like. There are many forms of ritual offering that all contribute to the opening of the heart into its great flowering. In India these rituals are called pujas, and you honor, bathe, clothe, and feed your personal form of divinity and then you sing her praises. You create your own personal religion and then let it self-destruct as you move closer to your very own inner God.

III
How to Lead Kirtan

It is interesting how over the last ten years in the United States the practice of kirtan has become so popular. Many singer-songwriters saw the popularity of kirtan growing and thought they could establish a performing career by leading kirtan. There are many Krishna Das "cover bands" competing for performances at yoga centers all across the USA. I've spoken about this with Krishna Das, Wah!, Dave Stringer, Bhagavan Das, Ma Chetan Jyoti, and many other serious kirtan wallahs. They are all consistently in agreement with Krishna Das, who I paraphrase from our interview, said, "If your motive for leading kirtan is anything other than creating the environment where you are closest to your guru, then sing in the fucking bathroom."

It is true that in India kirtan is sung in the homes, the mother leads, the daughter plays harmonium, and the rest of the family is the chorus. This is the true essence of kirtan. There are a few *harikathas* (storytellers) in India, as well as the Bauls, who travel and lead kirtan as their personal sadhana. But yoga center kirtan is something unique to America. It is important to have all your mala beads in a row if you intend to lead others in the singing of the names of God. There are many beliefs, attitudes, and opinions on everything, so I will speak from my own perceptions and experiences, as well as from the perspective of the great ones with whom I have discussed leading kirtan. Below are some of the principles I've been taught by the great masters.

Leading kirtan is not a performance. More than an art, leading kirtan is a sadhana. There are many forms of sadhana, but kirtan comes from the school of Bhakti Yoga. In order to truly express the fullest possibilities in the kirtan experience, the leader must be a person to whom all that matters is love (in other words, a bhakta). The leader must be doing regular sadhana and have had initiation with a guru. The leader must be able to keep excellent time and sing on pitch with a lovely, pleasing voice, and they must master a musical instrument.

So the first requirement for a kirtan wallah is that consistent sadhana needs to be in place. Sadhana includes meditation, hatha yoga, japa, puja, reading holy books and the words of holy persons. If you presume to lead kirtan, you must be on the path of bhakti yoga and have a personal relationship with a realized guru. This may be considered a hard line point of view, but remember Gandhi and the sugar. A woman came to Gandhi and said, "Please tell my son not to eat sugar."

Gandhi told her to come back in three days. Three days later, she returned and Gandhi said to the boy, "Don't eat sugar."

The woman said, "Gandhi-ji, why did I have to come back? Why didn't you tell him three days ago?"

Gandhi said, "Three days ago I had not yet stopped eating sugar myself!"

In order to lead kirtan you must walk the walk, not just talk the talk.

This, of course, recognizes the very special role the kirtan leader performs for society. It is a great sacrifice in kirtan to keep track of the rag and taal, to keep the words straight, to balance the energy of the room—so many thoughts must a kirtan wallah keep in their head. To be in the chorus is great bliss; you can fly, nothing holds you back. Within the narrow practice of kirtan, surrender to the names frees you to rise above.

The second criterion is to be an excellent musician and singer. Nothing inhibits the experience of kirtan more than a leader who sings "not good" or a musician who plays out of time or hits wrong notes. As Wah! told me, you must be a great musician to lead kirtan. Kirtan does not require lots of instruments and great solos. You should know music so well that it is second nature, and what comes out of your instrument should be beautiful. However, when I was in his band, I once asked Bhagavan Das whether I should play melodies or chords on the guitar, and he said, "I don't care what you play, but keep it simple because I don't want anyone listening to you." In other words, musicians must be so good that they can support the group and raise the energy without bringing attention to themselves.

The third criterion is experience. Ma Chetan Jyoti (the world's greatest kirtan wallah until she left her body) told me that she sat in the chorus for twenty years before she ever attempted to lead a kirtan. What she meant was that a kirtan leader must be completely conversant in Sanskrit, must have learned many kirtans and bhajans, and must have learned from a master by sitting in the chorus and watching and singing. When I mentioned this to Krishna Das, he said, "Twenty years? No! Twenty lifetimes!"

The role of kirtan leader is not a career opportunity. It is a form of seva. One sacrifices personal bliss to provide this environment for others. There is no room for selfishness, or for career orientation, or for monetary gain. My kirtan guru, Ma Chetan Jyoti, once said, "Rather than charge money for kirtan, go work at a regular job in the daytime." She lived by the principle of dakshina, and she taught many American kirtan wallahs to follow her principles. Dakshina is essentially donation. But Swami Satyananda had this definition. "If you attend a spiritual event that you feel is valuable to the world at large, you make a donation to give the event the energy to get to the next venue. In other words, this night together was funded by the group we sang with last night. The gift you give tonight is to the next community tomorrow night. That's how dakshina works. It is a different way to look at money. If you are meant to be leading kirtan, Lakshmi will provide.

According to Ma Chetan Jyoti, a kirtan leader should put on clean clothes before starting, wash their mouth carefully (the names of God, the holy vibrations, will come from this mouth), pranam to the harmonium, and salute the other musicians. Then, when starting a kirtan, if the goddess does not take over in thirty seconds, it's time to choose a different kirtan (I've seen her do this many times).

Since the kirtan wallah is offering holy sadhana, they can keep the vision of their guru before them (I always ask Shree Maa to sing through me whenever I begin). They can try to stay as one-pointed as possible, and must not let the motive of reward, financial, emotional or spiritual, enter their consciousness. Ram Dass once told me, "Ram Dass loves everyone, but Richard Alpert counts the house." If concentration and motivation has not reached this point, you should continue to sit in the chorus until ready.

The important thing here is to use this practice, whether in the chorus or leading, to discover who you really are, and to expand your love until there is nothing left you do not love.

Kirtan Charts

Chamundaye

Amba Parameshwari

Gauri Ganesh

Bolo Bolo Submil Bolo

Gopala Radha Krishna

Govinda Narayana

Hara Hara Mahadeva Shambo

APPENDIX II
INTERVIEWS

For one who chants the name of God, neither yoga or yagna *are needed. The injunctions of "duty" do not pertain to him. He transcends all illusion.* –Jnaneshwar Maharaj

SWAMI SATYANANDA SARASWATI

Time and Space magazine, January 2010

Swami Satyananda Saraswati

Shubal: When there is a group of serious seekers, searching for union with the universe or God, what principles need to be honored to create harmony and mutual respect?

Swamiji: The question is extremely subjective, and there is no one answer that will fit all the time in all circumstances. However, we have all observed that there are four main elements in each of our disciplines: attention, knowledge, devotion, and service. These four are present in everyone's discipline, no matter what path we choose to practice. But the emphasis is constantly shifting for us all. At one time we are more a student, another time we are called upon to be a teacher, sometimes we are engaged in deep meditation, while other times we are called to serve. When we realize that our balance is always changing, and the needs of our associates and community are always changing, then we find that in acknowledging the elasticity of our paths, we create greater harmony and mutual respect. In giving up our dogmatic nature, we build bridges of harmony which demonstrate respect.

Shubal: What is the proper attitude for living in an ashram? What is needed in terms of behavior and attitude to gain the most from contact with the saint?

Swamiji: Sincerity and humility. A guru is an example that we wish to follow. In order to become a disciple, it is required to have a sincere desire to follow the example of the group. Disciples are people who make changes in their lives. They do what the group does, worship the way they worship, cook and clean as per the example provided. We must have the capacity to work with others, and the ability to harmonize and negotiate. Remember, a group attracts a following from many diverse experiences, from various social and economic backgrounds. Disciples will need to celebrate the differences among the ashram family and cultivate the tolerance to work together to achieve the ashram goals.

If we do not have the humility to admit that our former ways of life were not satisfying, then we cannot seek to make changes for our new way of life with sincerity. It is not important to find the best group. What is important is to become the best disciple. Remember, it is not about performing spiritual practices. The goal is to lead a spiritual life. Practices are only important insofar as they help us to remember that the objective is to lead a spiritual life! Spirituality means giving more than we take.

Shubal: What do the days look like at an ashram? What are the regular daily activities at the Devi Mandir?

Swamiji: Shree Maa says that God means "Go On Duty." God gave us twenty-four hours a day so that we can work eight hours a day for God, eight hours a day for our families and communities, and eight hours a day for ourselves. We believe that the person who accomplishes twenty-four hours of work in a twenty-four-hour period stands still. In order to gain the benefit, one must accomplish twenty-five hours of work in a twenty-four-hour period. Then there is gain. Sadhu means efficient. Sadhus become so efficient at everything they do that they don't waste time or resources. Then they don't require the repetition of actions that are incomplete. They get it done right the first time.

Our days begin with worship and they end with worship. Throughout the day there are structured breaks for worship. The length of the worship varies according to the activities that we are performing. Those activities vary according to the needs of our community. But the most important remembrance of living in an ashram is our sense of purpose: to keep God in the center of our lives, to serve God, to serve the guru, to serve each other.

Shubal: You are responsible for maintaining the structure called an ashram. How does that support and how does it conflict with your personal sadhana? What sacrifices are needed to be a "leader" or "servant" of the aspirants living in the ashram community?

Swamiji: First we must remember in Hindu philosophy, a *yajna*, or sacrifice, is a privilege to unite with God through specifically-defined actions. It is not sacrifice in the sense that we give up something we don't want to give up in order to get something else. That is a business contract, and that is not what living in an ashram community is about. Therefore, the ashram community does not conflict with my personal sadhana. It is one of the expressions of my sadhana. It is a result of my sadhana. Love is such an experience—you have to give it away in order to make it grow.

There are three things that are necessary for leadership: pure love, inspiration, and appreciation. Pure love accepts you the way you are. Inspiration motivates you to make changes. Appreciation expresses gratitude for every effort. These three are the necessary ingredients for inspiring participation. I believe that is the only way we can serve. There is always a balance between too much and too little to be maintained, and I consider it my privilege to have an ashram community to assist me in making those decisions. Like every family, we have a limited amount of resources, and we are constantly working to adjust the allocation of those resources so we can accomplish the goals of our community in the most efficient manner.

Shubal: What is the proper attitude around money? I never see fundraisers for the Devi Mandir. Can you talk a little about dakshina and how it works in India and here in America?

Swamiji: Money is a form of energy that we are all accustomed to using. But we all know that it is neither the most important energy nor the most efficient energy. It is only one form of energy. When we fall in love, money is relatively unimportant. In fact, when we fall in love, food and sleep also become relatively unimportant. Now we all know how little effort is required to fall in love. It just happens of its own accord. What is difficult is how to stay in love. That requires effort, understanding, communication, and surrender.

Dakshina means that which is given without effort, because of our understanding, in order to communicate the intensity of our surrender, a token of our respect that demonstrates the sincerity of our love, and how much we appreciate what your being means to me. Dakshina is not an agreed-upon business transaction. It is not a fee levied for the performance of a religious ritual, nor tax collected by a guru or an ashram in exchange for teachings or initiations or participation in religious functions. Dakshina is offered as a privilege to support what I believe in, to honor the conveyor of knowledge, in all humility to share respect, and to enable the recipient to do more in order to make this world a better place. In Devi Mandir, Shree Ma and I believe in the functions of nature. We see that it is both the commitment and the privilege for the flowers to give their nectar to the bees. It is both the duty and the privilege for the bees to take the nectar from flowers. If we will only exude our wonderful fragrances, the bees will come of their own accord. We are only responsible for fun raising.

Shubal: How does an ashram relate to the larger community? Is there any responsibility or contact with the larger community, or is self-sufficiency the goal? Does an ashram have a responsibility to perform seva in the larger community?

Swamiji: As many as there are seekers, so many are the paths. Each individual and each ashram has its own goals and relationships with the larger community. Some ashrams have one or two devotees, others have thousands, and this is by no means a measure of the success of the ashram. It is rather an expression of the intentions of the participants. Some sadhus want to fundraise and engage in social service projects, while others want to stay home and perform sadhana. In either case, there will come a time when we want to give back to our communities. Even Heraclitus, after years of wandering on the mountain tops naked, left a copy of his book in the Temple of Apollo. No one stays on top of the mountain. Either they do not find what they are looking for and are required to return to society for the needs of the body, or they do find what they're looking for and feel they must share it.

Shubal: When you lived in India, were you a loner or did you live in an ashram? What were some of your experiences traveling alone and in community in India?

Swamiji: From the beginning of my search I learned that a guru is an example of how I can perfect myself in the disciplines of life. So I always searched for teachers with whom I could develop a personal relationship. I could never derive that kind of relationship from an institution. As a result, I never felt comfortable with the concept of institutionalized religious experience. I was seeking a personal experience that could change my life, a personal relationship that would inspire me to change. So I often found myself in smaller ashrams, where the guru lived with one or two or a few devotees, and we interacted together as a family, and the situations of daily life were the curriculum.

The years I traveled in India, both alone and with other sadhus, were filled with so many experiences that I could fill up many volumes telling stories. The experiences themselves are not so important as to what kind of person I became because of having had them. Many years ago I stopped writing adventure travel logs and focused on translating scriptures. I felt it was the highest occupation of my mind to contemplate the same thoughts that the ancient rishis thought, and to do the same sadhana as they performed.

Now I am seeing that the India I had traveled with such innocence and wonder can't even be conceived from the perspective of today's current events. The ancient culture is all too quickly receding and evolving to meet the demands of modern globalization. So let me share some stories of what I was doing years ago, when the villages of India welcomed visiting soldiers with respect.

My guru was performing the Sahasra Chandi Yajna for a thousand days—three years of reading the Chandi Path in Sanskrit in front of the sacred homa fire, often as many as nine times in a day. We lived in the Birbhum district at the time, a few miles away from the nearest village, in a very remote tribal area of West Bengal, just at the foot of the Santal Parganas Mountains at the Bihar border. Subogh Mondal was a farmer and he loved to sing. He had a bullock cart, and every so often Guruji would send us out from village to village to collect ingredients for the yajna.

Pachu played the drum, and I played the harmonium. We visited every farmhouse in the region and sang kirtans and songs in their courtyards. All the neighbors would gather and people asked us what we were doing, and everyone contributed a big bag of dal (lentils) or some rice or container of ghee for the yajna. We walked around the countryside for a week or more at a time, and then, when the cart was full, we would bring the collection back to the ashram and prepare a feast for everyone. Sometimes we would feed as many as ten thousand people! Every day I would recite the Chandi Path, do yoga exercises, study Sanskrit, meditate, and walk around the countryside. That was the India I fell in love with!

One time I joined a family of shepherds grazing their flocks along the mountain paths of Himachal Pradesh. I stayed with them the whole summer as we followed the goats from Bilashpur to Lahul to graze the fresh grass through the monsoon season. These people knew every tree of the forest and were completely self-sufficient. The family worked together and lived together with such harmony there. It was one of the most memorable experiences I shared.

I walked the Himalayas along with my guru, alone, and with other sadhus, stopping to chat in every temple, singing and joining in village festivals, sharing stories in every tea stall. My stories are too numerous to share. But I have crossed the Himalayas from West to East, from South to North, by bus, by jeep, by force, by foot, and I am sure that many of our friends who have visited the Himalayas with me will attest that many of my old friends still remember me.

Shubal: What is satsang and what is its purpose?

Swamiji: Satsang literally translates as "community of truth." Satsang is a gathering of spiritual beings to share inspiration. In satsang we come together with our community to share knowledge gathered from our various disciplines. Sometimes we talk, sometimes we sing, sometimes we sit in silence. The important ingredient is that we come together with no other motivation than fellowship in godliness. Neither do we look for the status of being a leader, nor the income of being a provider. In the true community of truth there is no other motivation than the fellowship in godliness.

Shubal: If ultimately the journey can only be walked alone, how can community facilitate that journey? Is community necessary for the sadhu? Householder?

Swamiji: Yes, community is necessary. Even if we allow only the most primary requirements, community is essential. To perform sadhana we require at least three things: a physical location, the ingredients of worship, and the supply line to restock our necessities. This is the minimum needed to perform the discipline by which we can have a spiritual experience. After we have experiences, we will know how much is required to share our understanding according to the authority that God and the group gives us. They will define the scope of our mission to share for us. Once we have our mission defined, we are required to give back. Again the community becomes involved. There is no one who is free from community.

Shubal: Can you offer suggestions for bringing the larger community of America and the world into greater harmony? What can one do?

Swamiji: Show respect through your every action. Be the Giver. The spiritual! Don't only focus on your spiritual practices. Lead a spiritual life!

MA CHETAN JYOTI

From an Interview in November 2005

Ma Chetan Jyoti

Mataji Speaks:

I went to India for the first time in the early Sixties. I was brought there, pretty much unwillingly, by my first guru, an eccentric and little known tantric named Swami Devananda. I stayed with him thirteen years. At first I was overwhelmed by the diversity of activity and the sheer amount of it! The colors, smells, the poverty, lack of sanitation. Thousands of people were living openly on the streets—washing clothes, having baths, children, kitchens, TVs, even pets! I had never experienced anything like it in my life. I was awestruck, I must say! Then I began to notice how happy everyone was. I wondered deeply what could be the reason everyone was happy despite all the crowded conditions and lack of comfortable living standards like I was used to in the West.

I loved the thousands of attractive temples with their beautiful murtis and I marveled how they were packed full of people coming and going day and night! It was such a contrast to the empty churches I had seen all my life. I became a real fan of the tea shops, which are never more than a kilometer or two apart, and the delicious Indian chai with boiled milk and sugar. In fact, my first guru told me never to drink water in India, only drink chai! I am still following this advice up to today with great success!

During the 1960s and early 1970s, I visited India several times, including the 1971 *Kumbha Mela* (a spiritual event that attracts hundreds of thousands of people who bathe in a holy river at an astrologically-calculated time). Each time I came to India I wanted to stay more and more. Finally in 1974 I moved to India permanently. My first guru had purchased some land in Northern India at Hardwar, which is a pilgrimage center, and I moved in there. Conditions were very difficult. My husband, who was still with me then, contracted hepatitis and had to be hospitalized, and I tested positive for breast cancer. We had a terrible ordeal that lasted several years! In fact my whole time in India since the last thirty years has been a chaotic mixture of spiritual bonuses and terrible ordeals! India is tailor-made for this combination. Spirituality and mysticism go on in India pretty much exactly as they have done since many thousands of years, at the same time a population of a billion people bounces around between ancient traditions and the latest technology second to none. There is never a dull moment. It is a different world all together from the West.

I met my sadguru soon after moving to Hardwar and lived with him in his ashram for thirteen years. From the very beginning I was keen to sing spiritual music. In Canada, too, I bought cassettes and spent hours singing along with them. I even purchased a Western-style harmonium in Toronto. After moving to India one of the first things I did was to purchase a harmonium. Gradually I picked up bits and pieces of simple kirtans and persevered, practicing on the harmonium five or six hours a day. Gradually I actually developed an ear for picking up Indian melodies and taals. I spent many hours sitting in kirtans with Indians. Key to it all was gradually understanding and speaking Hindi.

Kirtan refers to the call-and-response style of singing. Actually I am singing Namasankirtan. In the Hindu scriptures it is stated very emphatically that in the Kaliyug (the Age of Ignorance, when, as it says in the *Srimad Bhagavatam Mahapuran*, there is no essence left in anything) the only way to enlightenment, or self-knowledge, is by chanting the names of the Divine. It also says this in the Bible, Koran, and Guru Granth Shabad. "Naam" is usually translated as name. But this is not really the meaning. Before there were forms, the munis and rishis formulated the subtle vibrations in creation into sounds that human ears could hear and human tongues could speak. As the bible says, "In the beginning was the word, and the word was with God and the word was God." When these names were chanted, forms emerged out of them, or were created perhaps by the repetition. In a way, the names of the Divine are more powerful than the Divine itself!

By chanting, we get darshan of the Divine, which is compelled to come to us by the chanting of the Name. In other words, this is the path of devotion. By constantly repeating the name of the Divine, He comes to us, intervenes in our lives, answers our prayers. As it says in the *Srimad Bhagavatam:* where the names are chanted every day, Kaliyug will not even come! "San" is the root of sing, meaning in the company of others as opposed to meditation or silent repetition of the name (japa). Kirtan, which is the medicine of the Name wrapped up in the sweetness of the music, as Krishna Das says, is so inspiring it opens the heart right away by the compelling appeal that beautiful music and devotion make easy. By singing not just anything but these *naam* or formulated vibrations, or "sacred syllables" as I call them, first the heart chakra, then the throat chakra, and then all the chakras are opened in a very natural and vibrant way.

How often I have heard people's voices completely change, including my own, halfway through a kirtan as devotion kicks in and transforms heart, mind, and throat! Any kind of kirtan is better than no kirtan at all, at least they all give a kind of joy, but ones that have a more serious intent or a greater understanding of Naam actually transform the participants. And transformation is what spirituality is all about. You can have the most amazing spiritual experiences, you can have the highest knowledge, or powerful siddhas, even overcome death (for a while!) but if it does not transform you, then what was the use of it? There is nothing like informed kirtan to awaken the devotion we all have in our hearts. And there is nothing like sincere devotion to transform! Devotion IS the transformation. Tears flow, the chest swells, the lips smile, faith blossoms. At that moment we know who and what we really are! Guru Nanak Dev says we only have tongues to repeat the Naam.

I spent almost six months in America this year after thirty years only leaving India once before when I visited many countries in the company of my Gurudev. I was very struck by how popular kirtan has become (largely due to the persistence of Krishna Das, who chanted practically alone in Jivan Mukti for ten years) but really due to the Kaliyug when music and the arts become very popular. I guess to ease the sorrows that we are going to have plenty of, in fact already do, in the Kaliyug. But I was also saddened to see how, like most things in North American society, it is being manipulated in order to become one more means of making money; as all things are inevitably converted into in the West, in other words "commercialized" or gobbled up by the desire for money. *Tsch! Tsch!* I am also struck by how little knowledge is given along with the yoga and/or chanting. Ignorance reigns.

I began talking more between the kirtans in order that everyone would have the proper and correct knowledge of what we are chanting. How many people told me that the Shiva lingam is a penis and the *jaldhari* (water catcher) is the vagina. Very sad it made me to hear this! I began taking a mercury Shivalinga around with me. The mercury Shivalinga is the most auspicious Shivalinga to worship in the Kaliyug, according to the Hindu scriptures, which include the Shivpuran by the way. I began talking about what the Shiva lingam is and how to do proper worship, and why, etc. Now whenever I am singing I give proper explanations according to Hindu scriptures.

I mostly am familiar with the *Srimad Bhagavatam* written by Vyasa after he wrote the *Mahabharat*. It explains the incarnations of Vishnu that we are so familiar with, with Lord Krishna in greatest detail. And Sri Tulsi Das's *Ram Charitmanas* (his translation of the *Ramayana,* written in Sanskrit by Valmiki), the story of Lord Ram, his brothers and the rest of his family, including his wife Sita and famous devotees like Sri Hanuman, the very embodiment of devotion. All these scriptures are available in simple translations to us now and I started reading extracts from them in order to end ignorance. Now I am keen to do more readings of these scriptures. In fact, I would love it if some institution would invite me to read the *Srimad Bhagavatam* for six, seven hours a day for a week like they do in India. Really immerse ourselves in the world of the Hindu scriptures. After all, yoga, kirtans, pranayama, all the paths to self-knowledge, all the commercialized, merchandised "yogas" and much more came after these scriptures, which are full of fascinating and revealing stories about how creation itself came into existence. It's a real eye opener to read them!

I have been invited by several organizations back to the States and Canada from next April to September for more kirtan workshops and teachings as well as singing and I intend to do even more reading as it is so wonderful to give firsthand knowledge! It is so empowering. In my kirtan workshops I do whatever anybody wants of me. Sometimes I spend the time talking about the actual meaning of the chants, including a look into Sanskrit, and lots of stories about the names we are chanting. Often the name itself is associated with or emerged out of a story. They are also associated with certain rhythms and musical instruments. Sometimes I spend the time talking about the music, how Indian music is structured. It is quite different from Western music and gives my kirtans its character.

I have helped a lot of people already leading kirtans by pointing out timing, taals, pacing, and interacting with other instruments. How by merely changing the key the whole kirtan comes alive. Rag and taal (melody and time) and pronunciation are important in kirtan. Imagine how you feel when a foreigner sings a Christian hymn mispronouncing the words and getting the rhythm wrong! We can acknowledge his sincerity, but wish he had learned to sing it right! Does hearing "Cheezaaz" evoke the same devotion as "Jesus?" Sanskrit is a very spiritual, precise language, which is meant to be chanted in a particular rhythm.

How to find one's "sa" (Sa is the "Do" of the Indian music scale) that they talk so much about in Indian music? It's about finding your most effective range and pitch. But mostly how to sing with your heart in your mouth and on your sleeve! How to have that courage. My own brand of kirtan philosophy! I've lived in India now since thirty years, up to now, ninety percent of the time with Indians. I'm an Indian citizen myself and had to apply for visas to come to the West. Now, perhaps, a change is taking place. I feel happy to be with Americans and Canadians, sharing with them what I have learned through the years. Sometimes my workshops end up being hang-out sessions listening to my million stories of all the amazing things I have experienced in the wonderful land of India, living and traveling with my Guru for thirteen years and now on my own!

INTERVIEW with KRISHNA DAS
September 2012

Shubal: Krishna Das, welcome to Pioneer Spirit. We're happy to have you here. I've known you for a while, and certainly I've known Maharajji, and the history of the satsang. I'm wondering, you were very young when you found your way to the spiritual path. Many of us were hippies back in the '60s. I found my way into a blues band. Somehow you found your way into a spiritual life.

KD: Well, I was very depressed. I was probably someone who wasn't going to make it unless I found something. I had heard about Ram Dass from some friends and first I wasn't interested in seeing him, but then I decided to go see him. He was living on his father's estate in New Hampshire. I drove up there and when I walked into the room where he was sitting, without a word being spoken all of a sudden inside I knew that whatever I was looking for—and truly I don't think I could have told you what it was—but whatever it was, it was real. It could be found. It was in the world, so it could be found. Obviously this had a very deep effect on my life. Up until that point, I had read books and met a few swamis. I didn't know that it was real; *it* being whatever it is we're looking for. After that I knew it was real and it gave my whole life a different orientation. Without really doing anything on my part, I was simply moved and turned into a different direction from that point on.

Shubal: And you contacted Ram Dass, who had the energy of Maharajji.

KD: Well, at first I thought it was Ram Dass, because he was there. But after I spent time with him I realized it was his guru coming through him. Then after a year and a half I decided to go see him in India. I had already had dreams of Maharajji and knew that he was my guru. I knew that. So I went to India in August 1970.

Shubal: What was your first meeting with Maharajji like?

KD: Completely amazing! On one hand, it was hard to relate to that physical body. I had been feeling his presence for years after meeting Ram Dass. I had been feeling his presence with me all the time, or any time I thought of him, I felt he was there. So to see this body wrapped up in a blanket was almost disorienting, but at the same time you could not take your eyes off him. It was just amazing! He was very gracious to us and allowed us to stay. Of course, I became completely attached to his physical body after that. And then when he died, I had a horrible time for many years.

Shubal: You kind of fell in love with him.

KD: I fell completely in love emotionally and every way. You know the name Mohan, which is the name of Krishna that means "He who causes the whole universe to become attached." But in the case of Krishna, that attachment is really love. And that love, that attachment to the highest love, is the program that removes all other programs from your being over time. It dissolves all the other attachments. It cleanses the mind and the heart. Because all you want is that love, even when you forget and look somewhere else you're always disappointed because it's not that love. So there it is again. The longing for that love is what pulls you through all the time. It cures you of your attachment to the external physical plane.

Shubal: Ultimately that love is oneness, samadhi. Once the love merges into oneness, there is no attachment, or let's say we become permanently attached to everything. I know that when Neem Karoli Baba took you in, he really took you in. You became a pujari for him. Can you tell us the story of how that happened?

KD: You know, he took everybody in. He loves everyone equally. He played with us and he would show one person more attention at a time and then another at another time. He had enough juice for everyone in the universe, so there was no question that he took anyone in more than another. It was all according to the karma you had with him. What were your needs. The history you had with him in your previous lives.

Shubal: So everyone got a different sadhana from him?

KD: Everyone had a completely different Maharajji. Forget about a sadhana. He would manifest for each person exactly what that person needed in order to move deeper into themselves. Everyone has his own relationship with him. He showed each person what they wanted to see. In the *Bhagavatam*, it says, "Krishna loved each one of the gopis exactly the way they wanted to be loved in their secret hearts, all at the same time." Maharajji was doing that same *lila*, the same play. He showed each one of us our beloved. Our perfect beloved. Each one saw him in a different way, but the love was the same.

Shubal: He made you his pujari.

KD: He had built the Durga temple. They brought in a priest and after a couple of days they caught him stealing from the donation box, so they sent him away. They brought in the second priest, and caught him stealing. They brought in a third priest, they caught him stealing, too! The temple trust came to Maharajji and said, we can't find a priest that won't steal! What can we do? And he goes, "My priest won't steal!" They said, "Your priest? Who is your priest?"

251

Maharajji said, "Krishna Das is my priest." So I was called from the back of the temple where the Westerners spent most of their time banished to inner darkness, waiting to see him. I was asked to sit in the temple and be the pujari. But he was so sweet. The temple was right opposite the window of his room where he sat inside before he came out to see us. Every day I'd be sitting there at the temple and without even knowing my eyes would look up towards the window and he would be watching me. The minute I looked, he would slam the window closed and he would come out. Every day! And every day I would forget to look until somehow unconsciously I would turn in that direction and I would hear the windows slam. Every day! What a lila. It was so great. So I sat there at the Devi temple and I thought, well, I always loved the Mother so much, especially when I was getting started in this stuff. I had read Ramakrishna about the goddess Kali, and his devotion to the goddess, and I would cry. I knew what that devotion was. So there I was, worshiping my own private Durga. I learned some mantras and pretended I knew what puja was.

People ask me, "How can I become a kirtan wallah? How do I share my chanting with the world?" I always say, "I don't have a clue! You think I did this? You think I even wanted this? You think I even knew I wanted this? This had nothing to do with me." And I'll tell you something else. Siddhi Ma said to me, "Maharajji made you the pujari of the Durga temple, and asked you to give out the charanamrit, the water from the worship of the goddess. (Every day the people would come, I poured some water in their hands, they took a sip, and I gave them some prasad from the temple.) When he asked you to distribute the water, the charanamrit, he created this lila." Then Ma said, "Krishna Das, nobody understands Maharajji. Nobody can understand what he was doing when he was in his body or what he is doing now." She says to me, "Why you? Why you, the big kirtan wallah?" She teases me like that and I say, "Ma, I don't know! You tell me."

Shubal: I think that Maharajji used Ram Dass for so many years in the West as a teaching tool. Then when Ram Dass had the stroke and couldn't travel, and couldn't offer teaching at the same level, Maharajji chose Krishna Das as his puppet, as his teaching tool. It may be a different language than Ram Dass used, but it is the same message. Ram Dass used to see himself as Maharajji's organ grinder monkey. I think there is a monkey in you, too.

KD: You know, I joke with Ram Dass now, and when I speak to him, I say, "You finally have become what we thought you were thirty years ago." He is in such an extraordinarily beautiful state now. He really is immersed in the ocean of love. It is quite amazing. I have never met a Westerner in this state of openness and heart-felt availability. It is extraordinary.

Shubal: That's so wonderful to hear. Ram Dass was instrumental in my awakening thirty years ago. I sat in his living room and watched him transform into Neem Karoli Baba, and Maharajji allowed me to touch his feet. I watched him begin to transform my life into a prayer. Back then I asked Ram Dass if he would be my guru. He said he would play the game, and it sounds like now he is becoming the game. I truly hope someday to go to Maui and see his beautiful shining face one more time.

KD: Go soon. (Ram Dass left his body on December 22, 2019.)

Shubal: Near the end of Maharajji's time in his body, he sent you back to America. Could you talk a little bit about that experience?

KD: Well, when I left America for India in August 1970, I planned never to come back. I had no intention of returning to the West. I gave away and sold everything I had. I never said anything to my parents, of course, but I never had any intention of returning to the West. I was in for the duration and he allowed me to stay for two and a half years. One day he looked at me and said, "Okay, you have to go back to America. You have attachment there, you have to go back." I said, "But I'm just learning Hindi." He said, "Too bad. Go. *Jao!*"

So he sent me back in March. Then, I think in June, he was sitting around with some of the Westerners and he asked Chaitanya, "Where's Krishna Das?" Chaitanya said, "Baba, you sent him back to America." Maharajji said, "Oh, write to him, tell him to come back. I want to hear him sing."

I got that letter and I was so happy. I couldn't believe that he even thought of me, and he wanted me to come back. But it took me too long to get it together to go back. I was trying to get some money so I could stay there, according to his instructions. I had applied for a long visa according to his instructions. So instead of getting on a plane right away in the state I was in, I wrote to India and I said, " Chaitanya, ask him if I should wait for this stuff, or should I come now?" This was in July. I got a letter back saying, "Maharajji says come in December." I said great, by then all the paperwork should be done. But then he died in September. I never forgave myself for not going back.

Shubal: What an amazing moment. The guru says come back, and you say when should I come.

KD: I was buying time, because I was getting laid for the first time in three years. I did not want to give that up right away. I had been celibate all the time I was in India. Maharajji would joke around with me. I would say, "No, I don't want to get married." So he sends me back to the West. Finally, after months, I was able to get it on with someone. I had forgotten how to touch somebody with lust. I'd been away from it for so long I couldn't remember how to do that. So it took me a long time, and then I finally figured it out, so to speak. I was enjoying it in a way that I had never enjoyed it when I was younger.

You know, we think we're great disciples, great devotees. We say, "Just tell me what to do, Maharajji. I'll do whatever you say." You know, we're so full of shit it's ridiculous. Because we say that, but the guru asks you to do something, and you don't do it. You might not even recognize that he's asked you to do something because our samskaras, our attachments, are so strong, we don't even see these things clearly. We have so much unprocessed desire, so much hunger, so much attachment to the world and to who we think we are, that sometimes we are unable to hear his call. I was unable to hear his call. I heard it in my head, but I did not hear it in my heart. If I heard it in my heart, I would've gone. But my own attachments, my own illusions, prevented me from really hearing the call and as a result I didn't get to see him before he died.

Shubal: How was that resolved for you?

KD: He, himself, resolved it for me. I was unable to overcome that sadness. I was unable to live. I was in despair. I had blown the only shot I had. The only time I've been happy was with him—in that special kind of unconditional sweet love that I never tasted anywhere else. And then it was gone, as far as I could tell. I lost my connection and it was getting worse and worse and worse. I was unable to help myself. I could not do anything about it. I was in terrible despair.

I went to India in 1984, eleven years after he left his body. Siddhi Ma called me into the room where she was sitting. When I walked into the room, I was actually knocked down by a thunderbolt right in the center of my chest. My heart exploded and I was lying on the floor weeping uncontrollably. In that instant when I got hit with the thunderbolt, I saw every second of my life from the moment I heard he had left his body to that moment. I saw it from a completely clear and simple place. I saw why I had done everything I had done. I saw why I was feeling the way I was feeling. I saw that he had never left me for a second, but I had not let myself feel him because of my own shame and guilt. But he exploded my heart, he opened my heart again. At that moment I understood it was okay to live again. It was okay, I could live, I could be happy. I hadn't blown it. It was possible to live. It was like being born again. And this was the beginning of me trying to get my feet back into my shoes, to get back on the ground.

I came back from that experience and I started to go to therapy, to counseling, trying to work out some of the issues that were fucking me up. It was a new beginning for me. I saw that I could do this, because the other thing I saw in that instant when he hit me with that thunderbolt was that I had built a wall around my heart. Every brick on the wall had a neon flashing sign, shame, shame, guilt, guilt, fear, fear, greed, greed, selfishness . . . I saw the wall, but I also saw that I could take this wall down. All I had to do was look at the stuff. I could not pretend that it did not exist. I could not pretend it wasn't there. I had to deal with it, but if I did deal with it, it would go away. Little by little, it would begin to go away. And then I would be able to feel again, and in live again in a good way. And that was the beginning of where we are now.

Shubal: Ram Dass used to say, "You have to become someone before you can become no one." You have to integrate the split. How beautiful. The guru is the remover of darkness. Carl Jung once said, "Enlightenment is not bright lights and great visions, but rather bringing light to the dark parts of the mind."

I wonder if we could come more into the present now. One of India's greatest kirtan wallahs was your friend and my friend, Ma Chetan Jyoti. Mataji used to tell me, "Krishna Das is a true sadhu; all he wants is to be one with God." And now, here you are living in the most materialistic country during the most materialistic age. As you travel you receive adulation, and the potential for all kinds of attachment. My question is how do you stay centered in your dharma, focused on the goal, in the face of this potential snare?

KD: First of all, it's all his grace. If he wants me to be lost, he will look the other way for a minute, and I'll be lost in a second. It's all his doing. It's all his lila. You can't prove that to anybody, but I don't care. I don't take it personally. I'm actually able to enjoy the fame and enjoy the adulation and enjoy the love. Because, what am I famous for? For jumping up on stage and singing my baby left me I feel so bad? No, I'm famous for doing my practice with people. The purpose of a practice is to keep you from all your stupid stuff. And so that's what I do.

257

And those moments of singing with people are the most intense moments of my practice.

It's built into the system that by his grace I'm able to use this energy and the situation to be with him, which is what I want in this life. If I'd gotten this kind of attention when I was younger for other things, it would've killed me, no question about it, but what most people don't understand is that I gave up singing about seven months after I started. Absolutely quit. I went back to India and I said to Maharajji, who had been out of his body for quite a while, "You have to fix this, or I'm not singing." Because I could see what was going to happen. I could see the attention that was coming my way, the attraction that was coming my way. I could see the situations that were developing and there was no possibility that I would not misuse the situation. I would not use these situations to serve my own lower instincts. There was no possibility. None, whatsoever.

So I gave up because I could not do that to him. I was supposed to be singing to him, and here I was luring women into my bed, or about to. There was no possibility that was not going to happen. So I said, I am out of here. I am not going to keep singing unless you fix this. I was in India for three months. This was in 1995. Three or four days before I had to leave, nothing had happened. Nothing has shifted in my heart, it was the same. But just before I left he actually did something, and he saved me. I was able to come back, and I was able to sing and I was able to give one hundred percent or aspire to give one hundred percent by his grace. Otherwise I could never have done it.

I was so horrified by my impurities; they were preventing me from doing the very thing that could save me. My own stuff was preventing me from doing the very

258

thing that would save my life. It was a horrible, horrible, terrible place to be. The despair was so unbelievable. But he came back and took me into a place and showed me the way things are, and he showed me that it had nothing to do with me. (Sweet laugh.)

Shubal: That is how you do it. That is how you stay centered, quiet, equanimous, and happy. You appear completely surrendered, and completely in love with God and your teacher. A true bhakta.

KD: By his grace.

Shubal: Many years ago you told me that once you surrender to Maharajji, he will supply your sadhana in the form of the events of your life. When you feel you want to meditate, you begin your meditation practice.

KD: When he wants you to meditate.

Shubal: When people would come to Ma Chetan Jyoti and ask her what does one need to do in order to become a kirtan wallah; she would say you must sit in the chorus for twenty years. What advice do you have?

KD: I'd say sit in the chorus for twenty lifetimes. I don't want to be a kirtan wallah. I want to be with God. I want to be with Maharajji. I have no desire to share what I have with people. I'm not trying to get anybody off. I'm not trying to help anybody. I'm not trying to save anybody. Who am I to do that? Only he can do that. I'm singing to him. He does everything else. If you want anything other than to sing to your guru completely, you ought to give up. You want to stay home and sing in your fucking bathroom. It is not a career. It is not to be used . . . Well, you use it anyway you want. Everybody's got to learn their own way. I can only talk of my own experience.

People think I'm rich. In reality, I have just enough money to keep singing. If I stop singing, we go into debt. And that's fine all around because I have to keep singing for the sake of my own heart. This is what transforms me, what helps me. So this is what I want to do. The desire must be to surrender completely to that love. It can't be about you. Otherwise all you do is get more ego. Look at me I'm such a great kirtan wallah. I never think that. I don't even think I'm the best singer out there by far. I'm certainly not the best musician by far. But it's his grace. He touches people through the chance. And so it happens. I can't claim that this is mine in any way whatsoever. It's his doing, and as long as he wants me to do this, I'll be doing it. If he decides to change the program, what can I do?

Shubal: Krishna Das, you have moved me so deeply with your words. I love you. Thank you so much for your time, and for your practice, your love, and your seva.

KD: Ram Ram

MA CHETAN JYOTI
Email Correspondence with Shubalananda

Mataji and I corresponded via email for five years, growing more and more intimate until she came to visit in 2007, before she left her body in April 2008. Here are some excerpts from her emails.

6/20/05 Krishnaya Namah

I feel so happy to see you are back! It makes me miss being with you all and I wish I could be over there for a few weeks. Is it possible to start thinking about a possible program(s) next summer???? I'm just feeling like a dose of that love! Sing until all the minds present simply burst and get replaced by the perfect, blazing heart of devotion in the kirtan! In divine love, CJMa

9/4/05 Krishnaya Namah

I'm just back from a month in Europe. Mixed feelings about it all as usual, but I did have a great time giving a ten-day retreat with 50 people in Terre du Ciel, a beautiful center near Lyon, France. It was a quiet protected environment, especially suited to meditation and kirtan where I could really "hang out" with everyone and do all sorts of fun stuff! Like, one day I took everyone over to a neighbor's house and invited her to do a gypsy dance in the next kirtan. She was really great and it really rocked after that!! Well, you know me! Still really do love a great rocking kirtan! Always fascinated to read your crazy schedule, man, you do have energy!!In divine love CJMa

10/25/05 Krishnaya Namah

Greetings, I pray this finds you both well and happy! Here life is good, opening a small music school next Monday with some wonderful VIP heavy-duty musicians (you might know one of them, Pandit Barun Pal, sans veena), there'll also be puja and children and food, of course! Initially, we will be teaching guitar (by far the thing in most demand here in Rishikesh!) and sitar. Name: Sri Krishna Kripa PLAZA Music Academy (in Hindi: sangeet kendra). Also, I will have my newest CD ready by that day so will have its "opening" from the hand of Barun Pal and two other top Indian musicians. Auspicious start!

I will be sending you a box of them soon - hope you like it! I've been working on it for months although it was interrupted in August when I went to France/Italy. Also this is the traditional time in India to clean house and even paint it too (because the monsoon is finally over and the weather is nice and sunny again). I've been doing some of that as well, mercifully it is going fairly peacefully this year. There's also been a change of guard with my boarders which definitely changes the vibes and routine in the ashram. I like it as it keeps things boiling and also is a constant test for attachment! Just when you get to know someone and really like them, they leave! Anyways life is good, I mean, good and busy these days! In divine love CJMa

1/6/06 Krishnaya Namah

Yes of course when I record a kirtan it becomes everyone's to do with as they want, you included! I have, however, been deeply hurt that people are recording my original kirtans on their own CDs and not even mentioning my name! (i.e. Shyamdas, the Vrindavan school of music Amsterdam, Shantimayi sangha, and some guy in Germany called Onkar Ananda I think - and God knows who else). I just cannot understand this attitude between kirtan singers. In India they are so proud to announce where and who from they learned their kirtans and who composed the kirtan. But in the West everyone wants to pretend that they are the best and only one, I guess. I am completely different in this. Even in my own private diary of kirtans, at the top of every page I have proudly written details of where and how I learned the kirtan, it makes me happy to remember where I learn kirtans. If you take the time you will notice on my notes onmy CDs I talk a lot about where/how I learned each and every kirtan. I think it adds to tradition and continuity of kirtan music in fact. That's how they look at it in India anyways. In divine love, CJMa

2/4/06

Shubalananda wrote: Namaste Mataji:

Mataji, Krishna Das has referred me to a group in Vermont who put on kirtans and they asked me to come up for kirtan but they want to charge $10 a seat rather than use dakshina. So far, dakshina has been paying my rent, and I feel it is a violation of a principle to charge for kirtan. We have to travel about 6 hours to get there. What do you think about all this? The scene here is crazy, and the practice has been disguised into gross commercialism, but I'm driving a 20-year-old car, and am getting older, what do you think about this charging? Love Shubal

Mataji writes: Krishnaya Namah

I think you stick to your heart's principles as long as you possibly can. Unless there is some very very good reason to break what one's heart is telling them (especially surrounding kirtan)then you should never never do it. I have sacrificed possible name and fame (translate big income, or at any rate some income!)by not coming back to the US just for this reason. I was so happy just singing on my roof to Ganga Mata all by myself! I should be whipped to death if I ever sing for money.

Anyways this is my opinion. Tell them NO TICKETS. If they don't like donations, well, that's too bad. I do this here with very famous international artists that I invite to Rishikesh. Some come, some don't.....so be it! Well, you ASKED me my opinion!!! I really appreciated what you wrote me about sitting on the stage playing with KD and looking out at those people! I feel so happy that at least there is someone else who feels as I do. Kirtan is not my job it's my sadhana. Better you get a part-time job at the post office and sing kirtan for love. I did - now I rent out rooms in my ashram to get some income. In divine love, CJMa

2/26/06Krishnaya Namah

I've just had a really wild three days hosting a wonderful sarangi player from Delhi with his tabla player. Well, you've arranged enough programs to know what a roller coaster ride it is caught between the artist(s), the technicians who are on the spot, the owners (or the heads of the institutions) of the venue. The artists are all characters with many quirks. I get a hundred shocks a day with them! Now its 10 p.m. on Shivaratri night with a storm raging! I'm supposed to be singing at 10:30 in the temple at Shivananda but instead am preferring to watch all the incredible "shows" the big mahatmas are putting on TV (here we have four religious channels 24 hours of satsang, kirtan, temples etc. etc. and also ALOT of pomp and showing off!)

3/12/06 Krishnaya Namah

Yesterday was the 6th anniversary of my sannyas. In the morning I fed people and in the evening there was a bunch of my friends enjoying music on my roof, including a fantastic professional classical music Slovakian violin player. Unbelievably good playing Paganini and Bach beside the magnificent view of Gangaji and the Himalayas. Afterwards he sang the Divine names with us with gusto. Life can't get any better.

In divine love, CJMa

9/14/06 Krishnaya Namah

I thought you would enjoy hearing that a friend invited me to nearby Dehra Dun where she was staying in an ashram. So I went and met no other than Shivarudra Balyogi and spent two days in his ashram. When he saw me walk in he laughed in surprise because, of course, he already "knew" me from my CD which no other than You had given him! Then I recalled the email you sent about how a Balayogi was coming to NH and you were going to spend the weekend with him, you had heard he was the real thing but you didn't know him at all etc. etc. Small world.

First night he did kirtan and second night I did kirtan. I had three fabulous musicians with me (which was why I had agreed to go in the first place) and I don't know about anybody else, but I had a great time with them!). Shivarudra seemed very moved when he thanked us as well. Before leaving we had a chance to sit together and we spoke about you and the whole subject of spirituality especially kirtan in the West as opposed to India etc. We seemed to agree...He gave me his CD which was produced in Malaysia and I was very surprised how over-produced it was and definitely not live kirtan! How did you feel? He said you had tears in your eyes when he was leaving. Don't get me wrong, he was sweet, sincere and polite, his kirtan in the ashram was very nice. I and my musicians were treated extremely well in his ashram. After his kirtan he gave a talk in Hindi (there were about 12/13 people in the hall) and I liked his talk.

He told me he likes going West because the Westerners are interested in meditation unlike the Indians. I don't know if I entirely agree with this. It's definitely easier, because in the West it's already organized into a "retreat" and there's a ready-made group sitting quietly there only to listen to the teacher. Over here it's far less clear. Normally whole families just arrive and they have many agendas. For one thing they want to do seva in the ashram. They want satsang and quality time spent with the teacher as well as spiritual instructions on exactly what they should be doing in their sadhana plus they want their children to be blessed and assurances of protection from the teacher/guru for all their various problems. Many of these demands are not there with the Westerners.

But, I note that here in India, when an ashram holds an actual organized "retreat" Indians come too and behave not much differently from the Westerners. It has occurred to me several times that perhaps the teachers (i.e. the gurus)in the ashrams take their Indian devotees too lightly and don't bother to teach them meditation! For instance, in my own guru's ashram there are FOUR one-hour meditation sessions every day! Plus satsang/darshan. One has hardly any spare time for anything else. Yet, every year more and more Indian devotees are flocking to my guru. There were about 2,000 Indians this year at Guru Purnima. I think it shows that indeed, Indians are very interested in meditation!

I feel a transition coming on, yet another one!!Rains are getting less, more sunny days. Luvya, In divine love, CJMa

3/27/07 Krishnaya Namah

As I write this an exquisite herd of Bambi deer are delicately walking along the edge of the water on the beach opposite my office window, drinking and ambling. Their golden bodies are perfectly reflected in the water! How lucky am I to be looking at this scene, how lucky am I to be looking at this Ganga Ma, how lucky am I to be looking at the vista of these Himalayas? Oh Kali Mother, save this helpless child who runs here and there not knowing anything! This child of ignorance and foolishness who prattles on and on and needs constant care and who foolishly denies the wonder and beauty of your maya!

I just received this very minute this cry of sadness from one of "us," a sincere devotee of sankirtan, who comes to India

266

every year, who lives in a Kali Ma temple in America, who is a sannyas like me, who is full of integrity and devotion to the Divine and who even knows the Divine. Here is an excerpt..... (I've included the little quote from Swami Ram Das he puts at the end of his emails as well.)

"Mataji, I am really horrified and saddened by what is happening to the kirtan scene in America. It has lost its innocence. It is now almost only performance, name and fame, with no interest in real worship. Wine is being served at kirtans! Over the years I have become more and more outspoken about the modern kirtan wallahs, but now I have to leave the room when someone talks about what they saw or heard at a kirtan "concert." It has become a self-legitimating cycle of spiritual selfishness. I learned about kirtan from Swami Sivananda, Swami Ramdas and Srila Prabupada. Who are the new kirtan gurus? My own reaction is to sing lots of straight "unsexy" kirtan and read and lecture every week on the *Srimad Bhagavatam*, where real devotion is revealed. Interesting enough, most of the Western devotees do not attend; it is mostly all sincere Indians."

"By constantly repeating the name of God who resides in our heart, gradually we become conscious of Him. That consciousness purifies our heart, fills our mind and senses with a strange and powerful light of the Divine, which eradicates all the low desires lurking within us. Ultimately, we become perfectly conscious that God is dwelling within us. This is the greatest gain." --Swami Ramdas

So you see Shubal there are a few of us around, still here after all these years!!!

In divine love, CJMa

5/28/07 Krishnaya Namah

Well I didn't make it to Paris so I'm in Cahors just now - and it's foul weather, freezing cold wind and rain since five days! Leaving for Granada today - sure hope they have some sun stored up there for us! If I go to Paris I'll never leave as there are many friends there with yoga centers retreat centers etc. etc. What's the use to leave India just to be in Paris? At least that's the way I look at it. Instead I accept invitation to visit friends who live in small places all over Europe. This way I get to be driven around in beautiful countryside as well! In divine love CJMa

Shortly after I received this e-mail, Mataji arrived in the United States. After our travels in the USA and Canada together were over, Mataji retreated to Ananda Ashram and I went off to California and Baba Hariji's ashram. When I got back from CA, her email was waiting for me. She and Shivananda had returned to India. Both Mataji and I were headed for some very dramatic experiences on the physical plane.

8/20/07 Krishnaya Namah

I hope your recording went well in California, and you were welcomed to MA by your great kirtan sangha! They must be glad to have you back. I wrote Kripalu an email commenting on their newsletter about the great "yogic" food they serve in their ashram! (I couldn't believe the article!); I just couldn't resist commenting on their serving meat and how their ashram stunk of stale fish the day I was there! They didn't acknowledge my email, which is OK. I noticed Karmaniya also wrote them an email on this subject as well. Requesting them NOT to serve meat if they wish to be considered a spiritual yoga ashram. I hope they got LOTS of feedback about this! Hope all is well with you, here is "down time" as we all have summer colds! In divine love, CJMa

8/24/07 Krishnaya Namah

Beloved Atma Shubha, Hari om, Nice to hear from you! Today or tomorrow we sent off by "speed post" 100 copies of the reprint of "The Thief." There are already orders waiting for them. I'm so glad you had a nice time in Calif. and I'm glad you got to record some of your songs. I am assuming it was your songs that you sing that you recorded? Some of them are sooooo beautiful and deeply touching. Are you actually going to produce a CD now?

For me, recording is the quick easy part. Getting <u>ready</u> for the recording is the long part and the long, <u>expensive</u> part is the mixing/mastering, art work, printing, labels, printing and/or burning the CDs, packing. whew - recording is a walk in those redwoods! Although, the dramas of all the people/musicians(?) who one inevitably has with them at the recording studio is definitely long and tedious. Today I took the first tentative step to yet another CD which will involve all of the above and some new surprises as well because I'm going to do it with the kids in our school. Today we had our very first sit down together. Musically, it went amazingly well. They pick things sooooo quickly. But we were all so stiff and uneasy with each other - I don't think that's going to change much either! It's going to be a long, interesting journey!

Things are finally settling down here after my whirlwind return home which had lots of drama! There were so many people staying here when I arrived back. It's nice just to have three of us actually living here now, with the lady cook coming in during the day. And of course, my two sweet dogs. Tomorrow five/six young pandits will come and we will have chanting of the Sunder Kand which takes about three hours in the temple and a feast afterwards. Some neighbors might wander in for a while, Shivananda will play. This morning I went to the bazaar and bought some new clothes and surprises for dear Hanuman to wear tomorrow! I bought a frame for our "Niagara" photo -

happy days. I've hired a second teacher for the music school fulfilling a long-time wish of mine. I have new living quarters now in the ashram which were prepared for me while I was touring. Much better than before and much, much more spacious. It's taken awhile for me to get used to having so much space in my own ashram! but I'm feeling more settled this week.

My throat and chest are still bothering me and don't feel up to normal yet, it'll take more time. I've been enjoying time away from kirtans and visitors and teachings etc. but this Sunday, which is always open kirtan day at the ashram, I had promised a group from Rome (with a Canadian teacher)they could come before I left for my tour, so they're coming. I realize I would prefer if they weren't coming, and I didn't have to sing for anyone. Interesting new feeling. But in fact, I feel that I am entering into a new level of consciousness, or, perhaps, already have (haven't figured it out yet!). I have new, deeper(?) sensitivities and new signposts that I don't recognize. This has been coming on since the last two/three years and now, it appears it is here. Wonder what's going to happen?

Maybe a symbol of this change is that I lost my japa mala and its bag somewhere on the very last day in Europe. Perhaps just left on the plane. I've had it since thirty years and one of the malas (it was ten malas strung together) was the original mala that my Gurudev gave me. I'm grieving for this loss still. But, I've had a new one made and new bag and I'm off to my Guru's ashram next week for a couple of days and will seekHis blessings of the new mala. I feel this is going to bring some changes as well. Or, maybe not. Sing like an angel. In divine love, CJMa

Then the terrible news arrived: Mataji had lung cancer. It became apparent that the cold Mataji was suffering from when she traveled with us was not a cold, but rather the onset of the cancer. I expected Mataji to demonstrate great fear, but instead all she did was love me.

10/25/07 Krishnaya Namah
Beloved Atma Shubh, Hari Om

Chemotherapy is going on. There is a lot of uncertainty about what is going to happen as far as treatment. This is terribly difficult mentally as it's a real roller coaster ride so far. Pray for me. Rest, morning program of meditation/kirtan/satsang is still going on with a few students. This weekend is the third anniversary of the music school Plaza Music Academy. It's a miracle to see these local poor children who three years ago did not know what a violin, sitar was, let alone a raga, play beautiful beautiful music together. Really they are heroes! Shivananda is very very good with them and deserves much praise, and I am the visionary of this unique concept here in Rishikesh (i.e. children's classical music orchestra), plus the financier. So many visitors are arriving and musicians. There will be a lot of music and workshops all free for the children. Never been done before! I am so looking forward to hearing the children. It will be so different for me this year as I am hardly participating in any arrangements as I have to rest a lot. November first I have a big kirtan at a big program in memory of Swami Rama of the Himalayas. Hope I have enough strength. Well, some great musicians will be sitting in with me and I plan to have them do a lot of solos!!In divine love, CJMa

11/20/07 Krishnaya Namah
Beloved Atma Shubh, Hari Om

I'm so shocked to hear this sad news [about my (shubal's) having a brain seizure and surgery]. When I read your email I immediately held you in my arms, think that I am there all the way holding your hand! Well, this body and the creation that it makes to support it, is itself the expression of imperfection. And so, we inevitably suffer sorrow, fear and pain even though we are essentially joyful, trusting and bliss. We spend most of our time tossing in-between. What a month! Mohan Das, one of the NKB Das's and great friend of KD and Shyam Das, was in Delhi and decided to have a check-up only to discover that he needed open heart surgery immediately - which he has just had in Delhi. I myself live each day trying to figure out the balance in life when death is so near. Making my last will and testament has weeded out lots of unnoticed attachments which has been painful and liberating at the same time!

Let's be together again. In divine love, CJMa

12/5/07 Krishnaya Namah

I want to tell you that right now, as I write this, I have six pandits chanting Mrityunjaya Mantra for your complete recovery in the Virbhadra Temple. Virbhadra Temple is one of the oldest most famous and revered Shiva temples in India and to my great good fortune is just near my ashram. They will be chanting every morning from 8-10 a.m. until Tuesday. This will have a great, invincible power to heal you. We look forward to hearing the news of your successful operation. You know that I love you. In divine love, CJMa

12/8/07 Krishnaya Namah

Om
Triambikam yaja mahal/sugandhipushtivardanam
Urva rukamiva bandanam/myrtchormukshiya mamritat
In divine love, CJMa

12/9/07 Krishnaya Namah

You are probably in hospital being prepped for your operation and won't see this for some time, but I just wanted to connect with you over cyber space as well as over intuition space (which is spaceless!) and tell you we are just off to the Virbhadra Shiva Temple one of the oldest and most revered Shiva temples in India which so fortunately is near to my ashram, to offer an abhishek (Shiva puja which includes bathing the Shiva lingam in various substances like milk, honey, yogurt) and chanting two hours of Myrta Mantra which was started for you last Thursday. Om Namah Shivaya, In divine love, CJMa

1/8/08 Krishnaya Namah

So much silence from you. I hope things are going well for you. Over here, so much silence as well. The ayurvedic treatment had a setback when the tumor suddenly almost doubled in the last two months. I'm in Delhi in the hospital, very depressing. Probably starting chemotherapy very soon. Except I'm NOT depressed, only I feel like I *should* be depressed as it's sooo yukky. Remember jamming in your living room while Durga rustled up some great grub?? Remember jamming all afternoon at the coop in Ananda? I love you guys!!!! I miss you. Remember Saraswati Das who was cooking up a storm with Durga in the kitchen in the coop? Now he's SitaRam and has been staying with me since the last five months. He's a candidate for receiving sannyas initiation from me! He and another sewak Jai Pal are sharing this dismal experience with me - bless them! In divine love, CJMa

273

2/3/08 Krishnaya Namah

What can I say? I am so overwhelmed by your love and caring. The mantra will help me so much. I am deep into chemotherapy. I feel weak and tired but pain is less and recent x-ray showed reduction in lesions, but x-rays are misleading and the mid Feb. CT scan will tell the true story. By the Grace of the Divine chemotherapy is being all done right here in Rishikesh. In fact the clinic I go to is also right on Gangaji. Every day is different and we have had many crises to pass through. I have an angel as my doctor who has bravely taken on the task of an unconventional chemotherapy, an old one which worked better than the modern ones, but has gone out of fashion creating so many difficulties for him. Every day I battle all sorts of side effects. Friends and well-wishers continue to surround me with love and help and hope. Last three days have been "good" in the clinic and yesterday we all watched a Nisargadatta Maharaj movie while chemo was going on. Today we are going to watch 14th Tai Situpa Rinpoche teachings videos if all goes well. But, how are you doing? I don't hear much from you and Durga about yourself. I remember you every day and pray you are recovering well.

If you don't sing kirtan for the sole purpose of worshipping, acknowledging, adoring, sharing with gratitude, and pleasing the Divine *who is your own real Self* - then you are already a dead man and nothing else matters. I am praying for you, love you and keep you in my heart. In divine love, CJMa

INTERVIEW with WAH!
March 2013

I met Wah! when she first came up to Northampton to lead kirtan. She invited me to play with her, and we met for lunch the day of the performance. She had her family with her, and they were bickering, so I gave them space until the evening. That evening, we gathered at a local yoga studio—Wah!, her husband, an amazing African drummer, and me on guitar. She is a very powerful woman. Wah! actually walks the walk; she is a great bass and violin player, and she sings great. It was a full house, the music was high. Wah! raises the energy, and so do I, so between us things got hotter and hotter. It was a great session and we became friends. When she would come through New England we would often see each other. When I was publishing my magazine, Time and Space, *I interviewed Wah! and got some great stories and advice.*

Wah!

Shubalananda: Namaste Wah! Thanks for doing this interview.

Wah!: Thank YOU. But before we start, please tell me, what brings you to interview me? What is your history?

Shubalananda:I've been leading kirtan for more than twenty years, first with Maharajji, then Sathya Sai Baba, and now Shree Maa. I've developed a mailing list of three thousand names from doing kirtan around the Northeast for the past five years. I have traveled with Shree Maa, and played in her band for a few cities on her tour, and got to know a lot of people there too. I met Ma Chetan Jyoti, a great kirtan wallah, and got to interview her, so I thought the best way to use it would be to start a newsletter.

There is something happening with kirtan in this country. People are finding that this is an appropriate sadhana for them to investigate. A community is forming, people are joining this "kirtan family." I thought it would be interesting to bring the wallahs together, to review CDs, to let people know what is happening around the country and in their community, and also interview people like you who many are interested in, people who are actually living the historic "kirtan wallah" lifestyle.

Wah!: Each group that was formed in the late '60s and early '70s has spawned a different kirtan wallah. Osho's devotees, Shree Maa's devotees, Maharajji's devotees, Siddha Yoga devotees—there are singers from each of these groups out on the kirtan circuit. And now it's no longer about a particular group, it's about coming together. It's beyond the groups, and for me it's a moment I've been waiting for.

Shubalananda: What led you to follow an inner path?

276

Wah!: Nothing was available through my family life. Neither of my parents have a spiritual path. I was born to a college professor and a professional musician. I had a longing, even as a young child, and I didn't know where to develop it. Having feelings of longing when you are seven and not being able to explain it puts you on a search. So I went to Africa when I was seventeen, and lived in Africa for some time. I really enjoyed it. I stayed at a psychic and healing shrine (in the hills in the north of Ghana) where they train shamans and healers. They have a gathering each sunrise where they drum and go into trance. All community problems are presented to the leaders and worked out while they are in an elevated state. There is a great sense of community. Eventually I realized that the African experience was not from this incarnation but a previous one, and wasn't appropriate for this lifetime. I came back to New York, moved into an ashram, and started doing yoga.

Shubalananda: I heard a little bit about where your music came from, because one of your parents is a professional musician...

Wah!: Yes, my mother is a professional violinist. She plays chamber music, string quartets, and such. When I was growing up, instead of getting together for parties, they invited people over to play music. There was this feeling that music was always in the house. Music was a great way to meet people and also a great way to spend the evening.

Shubalananda: Can I infer that maybe there was something missing in parental love which you searched for and it turned out to be God love? Was that the connection between spirituality and music?

Wah!: I don't think you ever find it from your parents. There is a natural generation gap. You choose your parents, and they give you the gifts that they have, but God's love you need to find on your own. You need to find a teacher, put your efforts there. It would be unfair to expect that from parents.

Shubalananda: Can you talk a little bit about Ammachi and your relationship with her? Do you have any good Amma stories that you could share with us? What is your relationship with her, and how does she figure into your sense of self?

Wah!: Amma has a gift for picking up the stragglers, orphans, seekers who don't fit anywhere else. She doesn't build temples, She doesn't create organizations, She urges people to network. In most towns she urges people to have satsang in their own homes. She's different from the other teachers I've met in that she's not trying to create an organization, She's simply trying to uplift people in what they're doing.

For me, I had been on another path and was basically finished with it, but I didn't know where to turn. I was living in Santa Fe at the time, and a man was taking machining lessons from my husband. He said he had been asked by his guru (Ammachi) to make a CD. He was an electrician, and had no experience in the musical field. He said to her, "O my God, how am I going to do this?" Amma said, "Have devotees do the singing and hire professional musicians to build the tracks." So my husband and I were standing around the machine shop and this fellow says, "Do you know of any professional musicians who have a little bit of a spiritual background?" We all laughed because that was me. I came to Amma under the guise of helping. I came in and

278

helped them out and realized after several years, I was the one benefiting. I've been helping them out every year since, doing their annual CD.

Wah!: The responsibility for engineering and producing the annual CD was eventually given to a man who lives in LA. He also ended up producing my latest album, *Opium*, done with Macy Gray's band and some of Alanis Morrissette's musicians. The Ammachi English Bhajan CDs are like listening to "my history."

Shubalananda: It's a good history. All those Santa Fe bhajan tapes were a clear cut above the standard English bhajan tapes.

Wah!: This is how Amma works. She brought us all together to work in a selfless way. It's unusual. Not everyone has had an experience like this. Most musicians get paid, or get some kind of image enhancement, and the Amma CD was never like that. Everybody worked on it in a very thorough way, and nobody got any credit. There are no musician's credits, no vocal credits, nothing. But still we had to work it out—who sang lead, how the arrangement was, and so on. It exposed everybody's egos.

Shubalananda: A lot of those early Ammachi tapes were actually kirtans that she was incorporating into her satsang as she was building her own portfolio of bhajans that she and her musicians had written. Is that how you got more into the kirtan form, or was there another source?

Wah!: When I started doing yoga at age seventeen, we were supposed to do extended meditation, either hour-long meditations or two-hour-long meditations, so I asked if I could make a tape recording of mantras. Instead of singing them monotone, I sang a melodic version and put it on a tape. This allowed me to sit at sunset and put the tape on, and not have to watch the clock or anything. When the tape was over, my meditation was over. So even as a young adult, I was making music with mantras. I think what Amma did freed things up. It didn't have to be perfect, the energy could shift, the tempo could shift, the music was dictated by the energy. So for me it grew into a really improvisational style. I was working with a lot of jazz musicians at the time, and they were very comfortable with that improvisational approach.

Shubalananda: How is that versus the more orthodox kirtan wallahs who feel that part of the experience of kirtan sadhana is doing it in classical raag and taal and sitting straight on your cushion. Some people might say you need to have that "Indian" feel in order for the kirtan to work.

Wah!: I studied for five years with one of Ravi Shankar's disciples, Roop Verma. I went to Oberlin Conservatory in Oberlin, Ohio, and Roop came out there to teach raga to any musicians who wanted to learn. We were asked to learn on our instrument of choice. So I learned on violin. We had bassoon, French horn, guitar, quite a wide variety. And I also learned on voice and continued to learn ragas for a number of years, even after I graduated.

Shubalananda: So you digested that traditional style.

Wah!: Well, I went into it. I think it's proper to understand the technique of ragas to see the music as worship. Every note is a deity. You come to the music with a respect that each note you sing evokes an energy. The way you go up and the way you go down is defined, you can't just do whatever you want, because it will change the energy. So with a respect for that you can move forward into something that is perhaps more improvisational. I think the ragas are really important to study so you can know where the music is coming from, and what the purpose of the music is.

Shubalananda: I hear in your style so many different influences. I hear Jamaican, Indian, African, I even hear Appalachian sounds and some Memphis thrown in.

Wah!: It's true, I was born in Alabama.

Shubalananda: I hear all the roots, and I am wondering how that style evolved. I know you spent time in Africa, you studied Indian music. What did you listen to as you were coming up musically?

Wah!: Jali Musa Jawara (Gambia), and Bhai Chatter Singh (India), and Bob Marley (Jamaica). My CD *Krishna* has a lot of Bob Marley in it.

Shubalananda: I read somewhere that that reggae is really an Indian folk style?

Wah!: It's called Bhajanee style. Bhajan is the folk music of India, and yes, it does resemble some of the Jamaican beats. At some point in your life, I think you let go, and all of the things you have learned and experienced come together. You open your heart, you release it all, you look at it. It's kind of strange maybe, having it all out there like that, but there it is. Even *Opium* changed my style. After working with pop musicians from Macy Gray's and Alanis Morrisette's bands, it changed my approach yet again. Incorporating the whole pop style forced another period of growth for me. The new CD we're working on (*Jai Jai Jai*) sounds like Natalie Merchant doing Sanskrit. Whatever we're working on, whatever we're listening to, it just seeps into who we are and it naturally comes out in our singing and expression.

Shubalananda: Great musicians chant in their own language. Duke Ellington said, "Everyone prays in his own language and God understands them all."

281

Wah!: Yeah. Great musicians are great musicians, and that is a divine expression, for sure. Listening to a great Qawwali group, you sit there and appreciate it. It's so amazing! For the kirtan artist, I think it's a matter of continuing to perfect the style, the musicianship; that will make whatever style comes forward great. I don't think it matters what the style is, as long as you've got chops.

Shubalananda: You mean the heart, the bhava?

Wah!: No, I mean musical skill. There are people out there leading kirtan that haven't had the chance to study musically, and they haven't had a chance to perfect their instruments, whether it's their voice or whatever they're playing, tamboura, or guitar, whatever it is. I think it's really important to have some musical skill to bring to the table because it gives you that much more capability.

Shubalananda: Do you see the kirtan leader as a servant in a way, developing these skills and techniques in order to facilitate the kirtan experience for others?

Wah!: Look at Ammachi. She sits there and channels divine energy, and she uses the music to transmit that out to the audience. The band, the swamis, and everybody who is backing her up, they really practice. Who gets to play tablas is really a big deal. They work on their musicianship. There's a real thirst for knowledge and I think that's important.

Shubalananda: Some people approach kirtan as a spiritual practice, a form of sadhana. Some sages say that kirtan can take you all the way to one-pointedness and samadhi. Could you describe your experience of kirtan as a spiritual practice, and what practices might you suggest to people who want to approach kirtan from that angle? Have you seen how kirtan is practiced in India and could you tell us a little bit about it?

Wah!: There are three spiritual practices in my life: hatha yoga, kirtan, and meditation. I think all three are important. I joke with people, "Do yoga until you get injured, then chant until you lose your voice, and then sit quietly and meditate." I think all three of those practices are important. Kirtan by itself is an acceptable path, and any path can take you there. But because you store experiences in your body, yoga is necessary to break up the blockages and release them. Chanting and meditation are also good practices. If chanting is your path then you'll know it is your path. You won't be able to do anything else.

Shubalananda: Do you recommend a formal approach, or based on inspiration. In other words, do you get up at 6 a.m. and chant Krishna for forty-five minutes, or do you chant as the desire comes?

Wah!: I think different sadhanas are appropriate for different times in your life. When I was young, living in the ashram, we did two-and-a-half hours of practices before sunrise, and then we did some more practices for two hours when the sun set. We all worked regular jobs during the day. Most ashrams have a group practice before the sun rises, and they also have some sort of sunset program. The discipline of that will give you an experience. You have to be disciplined about some things in order to gain the full benefit.

As you go through your life, there are going to be different schedules appropriate for different times. After my daughter was born, I continued all of my practices in addition to having a child. I became depleted. I had to give it up. After fifteen years of doing a certain practice in a certain way, giving it up wasn't easy. But to release it is sometimes necessary. Buddha was only able to renounce it all after he mastered it. He was one of the

283

greatest yogis of all time, and after he mastered it, then he said, now I release it. You can't renounce something that you haven't had. Our sadhana now is our touring. Every night it's chanting. If it's 8 p.m., we must be chanting. Yoga and meditation happen in the morning whenever we wake up.

Shubalananda: Have you led kirtan in India? Can you tell us what that is like?

Wah!: My experience of singing in India is through the temples. That's the way it is organized. If I compared it to the temples here, I would compare it to the gospel churches. "You hear the house band over at the Westside Church? That band is HAPPENING! You've got to go check it out." And you go just to get the energy of the band. The temples in India are just like that. There's competition for having the best slot, for being the best kirtan group or bhajan group or whatever. There's also the more informal situation when you go to someone's house. They'll say ,"O please sing us a bhajan. Won't you make some offering of music?" and you might say, "O no, thank you, I really don't play," but they won't take no for an answer! When you go to somebody's house they say, "Please offer a song, a blessing," and then there you are, having to offer some kind of song or share your worship on an informal basis with the people.

Shubalananda: In a sense, God has given you a gift, which is to facilitate this energy through your voice and spirit. Part of the responsibility of having the gift is to share it.

Wah!: Yeah, take someone like Amma. She leads music, and hugs people, and it almost doesn't matter what she's doing, it's the transmission of the uplifting energy. She gives to everybody.

Shubalananda: Just sitting in the room you experience that.

Wah!: It's important to know that you can't pick who you will help.

Shubalananda: A very wise statement.

Wah!: Did you see Mother Theresa's interview in *Time* magazine? Her interviewer said, "What do you think about having fed the poor, having fed all these people?" And Mother Theresa said, "I am not feeding the poor." The interviewer was perplexed, "Who are you feeding?" "Jesus" was the answer. To her, the person accepting the food is not "the poor," it is Jesus. If you do it for your Lord, your Beloved, people will get what they are supposed to get.

Yes, I have a responsibility to share, but it's also an opportunity for the people leading to evolve. You can only be a student for so long. As I move into the role of teacher, the rules change. How I interact with people, that also changes. Many things I have experienced have come about only because I am in the role of teacher. I wouldn't say it otherwise. I sat in a room for fifteen years by myself, just listening, getting to a certain place, and now I'm talking with you, talking with new seekers, people who have been on other paths. I learn something from it. The first stage is when you perfect something— where the discipline comes in, where knowledge and learning come in. Then at some point in your life you graduate, and whatever you've learned, you have to give back. Everybody is at a different point in their life, but before you die you will get to a place where you have to give back. For me it uncovered all kinds of aspects of myself that needed to be worked on.

Shubalananda: I know you're off to Chicago next week, you seem to be traveling the world. How, in the context of that traveling, do you stay centered and present at each kirtan? Is there a practice that you use?

Wah!: I always pray to the deities before we start. It's the deities that do it, I am just their vehicle. Keeping your attention focused is very important because you are allowing yourself to be utilized for the group. As far as keeping myself together, I use a combination of yoga and chanting and meditation when I'm on the road. You know, sometimes my band members are not into yoga, and I have to take that into account too, like find a YMCA and take everybody swimming. That's sometimes a more appropriate choice for the group than taking them to a local yoga center.

Shubalananda: So you travel with different musicians at different times. You probably have a large group of people you call on.

Wah!: After I worked on the *Opium* CD, things opened up a little bit more. I had more contacts. We now have a lot of different musicians that travel with us. It's good. It's forced me to get my chops up to a different level. I play electric bass; I communicate with the drummer through my rhythms, melodies, and eye contact. There's a whole unspoken language that's going on. To establish it with new drummers all the time is very good training.

Shubalananda: It's a wonderful dialog.

Wah!: Yes, but on the days when the dialog is falling apart, and the drummer is just not getting it, you've got to have some chops, some musical skills, to be able to lead the rest of the band to the place where you want to go.

Shubalananda: Chuck Berry just turns his volume up and pretty soon all you can hear is him.

Wah!: (Laughter) Well, that's one way to do it.

Shubalananda: I'd like to get some general perceptions from you about what's happening in this country with kirtan. It seems like so many Westerners have adopted chanting the way they've taken to hatha yoga. It's happening all over the place. How come it's become so popular and why do people seem to enjoy it so much in the West?

Wah!: I don't think any of us really know. When I was managing Krishna Das, at first we had like thirty to forty people in the audience. By the time I left, about three years later, we had three hundred to four hundred people.

Shubalananda: That must have been an amazing experience to go through that.

Wah!: Once you reach a certain turning point, it multiplies exponentially. Touring with him was a very unique experience. Because he just stays with the practice, he sticks to a certain intention. The only reason he's doing it is to have the practice. The fact that there are people practicing with him is always a surprise.

Shubalananda: You mean he'd be doing it anyway.

Wah!: I don't know if he'd be doing it anyway, but it has helped him have a consistent practice. He often said if people didn't show up, he'd just go home and watch "The Sopranos." We anchored into the practice and it really is just about the practice. Not everybody is into it as a lifestyle. Nor should they be, but if they find something out of it they can use, that's good. If all they do is put on CDs and chant in the car, well, then there'll be a lot less road rage in the world. The boundaries have dissolved. The chanting scene has dissolved boundaries, not just between the groups that were set up in the '70s (Sivananda, Muktananda, Satchitananda, etc.), but also in what style of yoga you do, all the ways we see ourselves and identify ourselves with what we're doing.

The chanting has the ability to dissolve that and let everybody hang together.

Shubalananda: And that's good.

Wah!: I believe that's very good.

Shubalananda: Is *Opium* your first CD that is more song oriented?

Wah!: No, I did an album called *Transformation*, which was patterned partly after Jai Uttal's work. It had some English in it, and some chanting. It was eclectic; the chanting was alongside some rock and roll. The album panned. I learned then that chanting and pop have to be separated. Each album has to have a unique and uniform intention. *Opium* is all English, no chanting in it at all. We called it *Opium* because it's the refined tinctured version of the meditative energy. If you took the chanting and you boiled it down and the only thing you had left was a few drops of the energy, then I feel you'd have *Opium*.

Shubalananda: You take the music and build it up with different colors, but the paint is from the same source.

Wah!: Yes. I remember a reviewer saying "*Opium* left me in a trance-like ethereal state. . ." He got it, but he knew nothing about meditation.

Shubalananda: Did you have a specific message or vision for the CD? Was *Opium* about creating a meditative state in people who don't meditate?

Wah!: When I got together with the producer, Herb Graham, Jr., we listened to music, started finding musical styles I liked, talked about lyrics. All my training in meditation was not useful with Herb. The pop musicians were not hip to meditative traditions. They knew the pop world.

Shubalananda: Herb was your voice from that other world.

Wah!: Right, so I would say things and he would go, "Big Momma, what you sayin'?" I had to bring my writing to another level.

Shubalananda: He was asking you to make it more personal.

Wah!: Exactly. I was asked to write about my life from a very personal level. Because my life was meditatively oriented, it still had that perspective without being preachy. For me, it wasn't "Get out of this house" (Shawn Colvin), it was like "If I tell you to get out of this house, we will lose what we've worked towards." Rather than concentrating on the anger, I went to the grief; the anguish that comes when you're in a really difficult place in relationship, when you have to work it through. It's kind of talking about those life issues. Maybe from a deeper level, I don't know.

Shubalananda: What's happening now? Are you working on a new CD? Some of your kirtans are so beautiful, your Hare Krishna on *Savasana* really moves me, it's so beautiful. I would like to learn it with your permission. My last question . . . . In terms of how things are developing for you, my Swami suggests we make five-year, ten-year plans, set goals, etc. Do you look at your life in that way? Where do you see yourself in ten years?

Wah!: I don't have any plans. I'm trying to listen. I listen for what I should be doing and in what direction I should be going, I don't plan, I live day to day. Some days I get a "hit," I call them hits; it's as if my guru came up and hit me on the side of the head. Like with Krishna Das, there was no question. And even at the point where I said, "I call it quits, I don't like him anymore, "I still wasn't allowed to quit. My life is so guided that even if I make plans, they get changed. So now I don't make plans anymore, I just listen.

INTERVIEW WITH SHUBAL
by Steve Rosen in 2009

As he likes to say, "My parents called me Larry Kopp," but he is now better known as Shubalananda—kirtan singer *extraordinaire*. Starting out as a blues guitarist, more into Muddy Waters than the flowing Ganges, his life took a major turn when he met Ram Dass, of *Be Here Now* fame, who introduced him to the idea of transcendence. From that point forward he started to meet numerous Indian sadhus, almost mystically. One after another, they instilled in him a taste for the spiritual, particularly through kirtan. As he became more and more absorbed in chanting the holy names, he traveled to India and studied and practiced profusely.

His journey became more pronounced when he met the controversial South Indian desert sadhu, Sathya Sai Baba. This led to other relationships that would change his life. For example, Mr. Ravindrin and Ms. Mani Bashyam, both close associates of Sathya Sai, taught Shubalananda the intricacies of classical Indian bhajan, enhancing his practice of kirtan. Learning further from spiritual adepts, such as Sri Karunamayi, Mata Amritanandamayi, Shree Maa, Ma Chetan Jyoti, and Baba Harihar Ramji, Shubalananda continues to hone his kirtan skills, sharing his unique gift throughout the United States. One of the busiest kirtan wallahs on the spiritual New Age circuit, his voice can be heard in yoga centers and workshops on a day-to-day basis.

Steven Rosen: Okay, so the beginning is just background on you—your full legal name and date of birth, where you born and what that was like . . . if you remember. [laughter] That kind of thing.

Shubalananda: Okay, well, my parents called me Larry Kopp, and I was born in New York City in 1944. As we're doing this interview, I'm sixty-five years old. I've been practicing kirtan for about twenty-five years. My first fifteen years of life involved exposure to abusive parents. This caused a major split, a vertical personality split, which actually opened the door later in life. But at that point, I had so much self-doubt and low self-esteem that for twenty years I lived a split life of being a businessman in the daytime and a blues guitar player at night.

Steven Rosen: Aha, you sound like me.

Shubalananda: In the morning, I would hide the fact that I was a blues guitar player and then, when I went out with my blues friends, I would be discrete about my identity as a businessman. So I was leading two lives.

Steven Rosen: Let's get a little background on your life as a blues boy.

Shubalananda: When I was seven years old, I insisted my
mother buy me a ukulele for my birthday and that was
the beginning of my musical journey. Neither of my
parents were musicians, but I was drawn to the ukulele
and from that, at around twelve, I started playing guitar
and singing folk songs. In the 1960s I became immersed
in roots music, traditional American music, and as much
world music as was available in those days. But also,
because of this personality split, I ended up addicted to
cigarettes and I was smoking pot, too—just living a very
hedonistic life. It was a self-destructive life, really. I call
it "spiteful shamelessness." It was kind of like a
predictable reaction to negative treatment from parents.

Steven Rosen: Were they physically abusive?

Shubalananda: To some degree. Let's just say that it wasn't
good, not at all. I was so messed up that I got into drugs,
you know, the usual stuff. Then I started going to a
therapist. She suggested, "Well, the way to deal with
your addictions might be to start meditating." So I asked
my boss at work, whom I knew had been to India, if she
would teach me how to meditate. She said, "Well, I could,
but I think I know someone who might be able to do a
better job." That person turned out to be Ram Dass. So,
the next day, I found myself in Ram Dass' living room
and, I tell you, he has some *siddhis*, mystic powers. I
would not say that he's necessarily enlightened, but the
powers of raising the kundalini come to people before
they reach the highest stage. And he did a lot of that kind
of spiritual work.

Of course, the advice of the sages is to ignore the
siddhis—that they are just distractions from the real
goal—and focus instead on the primal achievement,
which is love of God. But sometimes siddhis occur
spontaneously, though the grace of god. The siddhi that

Ram Dass has is that he is able to facilitate people, allowing them to get a glimpse of the divine through his own higher state of consciousness. This is called Shakti Path. It occurs to create an incentive for people, a little taste of the goal in the beginning. In sitting with him for three hours in his living room, the energy rose up my spine. The vibration began in my knees, it moved up my body, and when it reached my bottom jaw, my teeth chattered like little false teeth, like something Harpo Marx would have. When it reached the top of my head, my brain felt like it was exploding. I never knew such a sensation was possible

I looked at Ram Dass while I was experiencing this and I was immediately struck by the awareness that he and I were, on a most profound level, the same person. There were two bodies, but there was one consciousness. Then as I looked around the room, I realized that everything was part of this consciousness, too. It was a feeling of one pulsating consciousness, and in that state, I realized what it truly meant to be alive. Then Ram Dass literally turned into Neem Karoli Baba, and I was able to receive his darshan twelve years after he left his body. I came to appreciate the value of the moment: "be here now with mindfulness." Be in the moment with complete awareness of your sensory experience. The truth is, all there is is now. I know that there are many teachings, but this one was "life altering" for me at the time. It turns out time exists, but only in the "now!"

Steven Rosen: What year was that?

Shubalananda: That was January 1985. I walked into his room in the early afternoon, ready to commit suicide, interested in meeting him just to find out what he was all about. I was a hippie, so I knew all about him and his work. But, I tell you, I walked out of his house a part of this amazing, wonderful, brilliant, mysterious universe that I had no idea existed. My life transformed in that hour from darkness to light. I came out of there a totally changed person. I left his house on the southern coast of Massachusetts, walked down to the beach in a January wind storm, raised my arms as the ocean spray and wind came gusting in, and sang my first kirtan, *Jai Maa!* Prior to that, I felt inside of me there was a monster, a gorilla, or maybe a yeti. In fact, I said to Ram Dass at one point, "I'm afraid to really let go because inside there is KING KONG waiting to come out and destroy both me and my son." He said, "Well, it's not quite a gorilla that I see inside of you." And then out walked Hanuman! [laughter]

Steven Rosen: So, would you say Ram Dass was your primary teacher?

Shubalananda: He was my first real spiritual teacher. He was there at the beginning and I sense he will be there at the end. Since then, for the last twenty-five years, my life has been a series of teachers appearing out of nowhere. I worked with Ram Dass for three years and at the end of those three years, on a very sad day, he said to me, "I'm only a man. There is only so much I can do." I understood that I had reached the end of my work with him. I sadly said goodbye and I didn't see him again for ten years. But within two weeks, I got a phone call from a devotee of Sathya Sai Baba who lived in Arkansas. I don't know how we connected, but we did. So I took my son and we went and visited her farm in Arkansas, which was actually a Sai Baba ashram. For seven years after that, I studied classical Indian bhajan with the Sai Baba satsang.

They, it turns out, had a huge community in Boston of about two hundred Indian families who were devotees of Sai Baba; I joined that group and they taught me bhajan. Every now and then, masters would come over from India to be with their children and they would teach me. Mr. Ravindrin and Mani Bashyam were the two teachers that I feel were the most influential in teaching me raga, taal, pronunciation, sitting properly on the cushion, all the aspects of kirtan that are, really, the hidden secrets of India. Every practice has its own secrets.

When I began to study with some great bhajan singers from India, I learned the ragas, learned to follow (even those whose leading left some musical needs unmet), learned that humility and power are not mutually exclusive, and learned my role was to support others' bhava. I learned how to pronounce Sanskrit and how to sit straight on the cushion (sort of). I learned hundreds of bhajans and kirtans.

I have personal relationships with many gurus. It is always good when a chorus responds well to a kirtan, but when a spiritual teacher says, "You put me in samadhi," as Shiva Rudra Bala Yogi told me, or as Karunamayi said, "Your voice contains the tears of god-love," or when Shivabalananda wrote, "Your kirtan is a treasure at our ashram," that is what fulfills and humbles this kirtan wallah.

Steven Rosen: I never think of Sai Baba as involved in kirtan. Frankly, there are stories . . .

Shubalananda: As Shree Maa says, "As long as you are in a body you have more to learn." At Sai's ashram there is a sign that says, "Before you speak, think, is it the truth, is it kind, and does it improve upon the silence?" Sai Baba is no different than the rest of us. If you abuse it, you lose it. In his early days, miracles happened all around him.

Mr. Ravindrin, one of my teachers, came to Sai with throat cancer, and not only was the throat cancer cured, but he developed this beautiful singing voice. When I met him, Ravindrin was eighty, and when this happened he was forty, so for the last forty years he's been singing devotional music. Make of it what you will. However, a major part of Sathya Sai Baba's practice *is* bhajan.

Steven Rosen: Hmm.

Shubalananda: Mr. Ravindrin taught me a lot about pronunciation and proper timing. You know, to sing bhajans is different than kirtan. Namasankirtan is an aspect of bhajan, but it's bhajan with the adjectives, verbs and adverbs removed; it's just the proper nouns, the Sanskrit names of God.

Steven Rosen: Well, namasankirtan, certainly. It's just the holy names, strung together in unlimited melodious ways.

Shubalananda: Oh, yes. That's what I mean. Well, it's namasankirtan that has been so popular in the United States. They say this was originally created by Jnaneshwar in fourteenth-century Maharashtra, and spread around the world by Chaitanya Mahaprabhu a hundred years later. It's just the proper nouns. But bhajan is much more complicated, with the classic ragas and the very sophisticated pronunciation of complex Sanskrit phrases. You could say kirtan is meditation on God and bhajan is prayer to God.

Steven Rosen: Well, it will mean different things in different areas, or according to the dictates of regional languages.

Shubalananda: Yes. I was thinking: bhajans can be sung in many languages, but the Sanskrit language is the most powerful. Namasankirtan is always in Sanskrit, or related languages. You have to become expert in Sanskrit pronunciation to do it right. So they taught me all that and at the end of seven years, Karunamayi, who is a wonderful saint from the Andhra Pradesh province in India, became my guide. She's very famous in the United States now because for ten years she's been coming over here and spreading dharma. For the first six years that she came, I did her promotion in Boston, which was a major stop for her. I was the one who rented the hall and did the publicity and the whole thing. So I studied with her and she also had a bhajan lineage similar to Sai Baba's, using the more complicated techniques, which I learned. At the same time I got to know Mata Amritanandamayi (Ammachi), whose kirtan has grown very sophisticated lately. In the beginning, her style was much simpler than Karunamayi or Sai Baba, and more in the mode of *namasankirtana*. Then, after some time, Shree Maa, one of India's greatest saints, came to my house and stayed with me. We did a couple of programs in Boston, and she came back the next year and stayed with me and we did some programs in Northampton. We grew to love each other and I owe her my life.

Steven Rosen: Who is she? What lineage is she from?

Shubalananda: Shree Maa is from Assam. She lives now in Napa, California. She's been here for about twenty years now. Her lineage is the tantric Ramakrishna tradition. They say that she's an incarnation of Sarada Devi, the wife of Ramakrishna. She teaches the Chandi Path, and that's part of my practice—chanting this beautiful seven-hundred-verse Sanskrit poem that tells the stories of the Divine Mother.

Steven Rosen: To Chandi, the Goddess. Do you do related pujas, the standard worship services?

Shubalananda: I do the pujas. I learned to be a pujari, a priest for the Goddess. That's part of Shree Maa's practice. She teaches everyone, men and women, how to be pujaris in their own temple or in their homes. She came and blessed my home and turned it into a temple. In a way I have become a tantric priest, as well as a wandering sadhu. I know you're more familiar with Vaishnava teachings, but this is our lineage.

Steven Rosen: So, you see yourself as one with the deity. That idea is somewhat problematic, or, let's says, I think there's more to it than that. The sacred texts of India tell us about Brahman, Paramatma, and Bhagavan realizations. This sense of oneness with the deity, that's more characteristic of Brahman, which is rudimentary. It's fundamental to the spiritual path.

Shubalananda: Actually, in my highest self I feel a oneness with all, this deity is within everything and everything is within Her. The actual knowing experience of the oneness of the universe may be called fundamental, but others might call it samadhi. There are at least three levels of samadhi, and each Hindu lineage has its own concepts overlaid on spiritual experience; the experience itself is beyond conceptual thought and you cannot discuss it or label it. I think it is good to conceptualize spirituality just like it is good to worship the formed god, as a way to true experience, but Ram Dass taught me that all paths have to self-destruct in the end.

Steven Rosen: Right. But next comes Paramatma, wherein one recognizes undeniable distinction between oneself and the deity. Here, we understand that God is in every atom and within the hearts of all souls. *But we are not Him.* We are one with Him and different from Him as well. And then there is Bhagavan, God. At this level, when we

298

realize God as a person, we can relish an intimate relationship with the sweet absolute, with the supreme entity, our source. This relationship includes both Brahman and Paramatma realization. So it's all-inclusive.

Shubalananda: I see. Well, yes, we all want intimacy with the divine. You are speaking of the way to a true vision of god through one specific system. If you read Sri Nisargadatta, a *jnani* (one on the path of knowledge), you will discover a completely different system for reaching the same goal. If you study Tulsidas, you learn about Ram; if you study Ramakrishna, you learn about form versus formless. There are some who say that it is better to love god than to be god. There are twelve gates to the city. From my lineage, ultimately this universe is composed of shakti or God, and thus, we are all shakti, stardust, divine incarnations, all of us are a unified consciousness. There are so many ideas about the way it is. Ultimately, it's that oneness we're after, even if we express it in various ways. Our traditions may be different, but we have many things in common, too. All lovers of God are, over the concepts, united in that love. And there are as many Hindu religions as there are Hindus.

Steven Rosen: Well, we certainly have kirtan in common. That's the great equalizer.

Shubalananda: Yes, and there's been this long musical thread, where I've been observing kirtan and bhajan from all these different traditions. Kirtan in yoga centers began about fifteen years ago and those threads all started coming together. I got a call from a then new yoga center in Northampton. Someone had told them that I did Sanskrit chanting and they wanted a weekly chanting event in their studio. We met and I agreed to do it. It was the beginning of kirtan's popularity and the timing was just right. It exploded into this incredible weekly event in Northampton that's been going on for some fifteen years now.

Steven Rosen: Do a lot of people show up?

Shubalananda: We get tons of people, and everyone knows the kirtans at this point. So we sing in unison and in harmony, not necessarily kirtan kosher, but this is America and the tradition is in transition. People love it. However, I have certain values around kirtan, one of which is that you can't charge for it. It's free. I mean, kirtan is grace and you can't charge for grace. It's okay to receive dakshina, that is, a small donation. Okay. That's the tradition. But I don't think it is okay to charge for kirtan, so I don't. That's just me. Krishna Das says, "My kirtan is free; they just pay me to travel." If you meet a spiritual teacher who charges for darshan, watch out! Same for kirtan, except for our national traveling kirtan wallahs, who have to charge to cover their expenses. I find that when people understand the principle of dakshina, they are very generous, and the practice remains clean from financial attachment,

The other thing is that I won't let it become a business. Right now, I'm being invited to many yoga centers on a monthly basis. So I'm doing kirtan most nights each month now, leading kirtan all over the northeast now, I do this without trying to sell myself. And that's important to me. On rare occasions, I've called someone up and said I'd like to come and do kirtan, but it's usually been the other way around. I answer the email or the phone, and my circle has grown into the thousands. My principle is to avoid making it a sales thing or a business. It is my sadhana, my practice, and therefore I keep it pure, I don't go around selling it to people. I don't mind sharing it, doing it with others. I love that.

Steven Rosen: How do you make a living, then?

Shubalananda: Donations.

Steven Rosen: Like a real Brahmin.

Shubalananda: Like a starving Brahmin, exactly. Normally, if I do kirtan at a center, there are fifteen to hundred people there, and they give donations. Just enough comes in from donations. I could get more if I charged a fee, but I won't do that. Kirtan is sacred. The principle of dakshina works like this. If you go to a spiritual program that you feel is worthwhile, you give it some green energy to get it to the next venue. In other words, the gift given last night was to everyone who joins the program tonight, and the gift given tonight will be to the community where the program moves tomorrow. That's the way it works.

Steven Rosen: You mentioned earlier that you used to be a businessman. What kind of business?

Shubalananda: I was doing marketing consulting over the phone with a couple of small businesses in Boston to pay the rent, until doing kirtan became full time. Some time ago I met another saintly person—I gravitate toward them—named Shiva Rudra Bala Yogi. When he came to Boston, he said to me, privately, "Shubalananda, you have a mission. Your mission is your gift and your gift is your kirtan. You've got to start treating your body like a temple, taking care of it, because you have this sacred mission, to help your community with kirtan."

Steven Rosen: What do you think is required in order to be a kirtan wallah?

Shubalananda: If you are going to lead kirtan you need to have 1. A pleasing singing voice. 2. Excellence on an instrument, and 3. A regular sadhana practice in bhakti yoga with a guru...an initiation. 4. EXPERIENCE! It is important to remember that this is not a business or a performance; it is sadhana. These are principles taught to me by my gurus, as well as many of the great American kirtan wallahs, like Bhagavan Das and Wah! Ma Chetan Jyoti taught me that it is better to work a day job than to charge for kirtan, that you must clean your mouth before you place God's names in it, that you must wear clean neat clothing when you lead kirtan, that you must pranam to your instrument before you start, and you must remember you are creating a holy sacred space, so all *niyamas* (duties or observances) must be firmly in place.

Steven Rosen: Very good. So kirtan is your life's mission.

Shubalananda: When I do kirtan, I become lost. It's not me—it's all the holy people I ever met; it's the divine power; it is her, it is God. When I first met Shree Maa, she said, "What do you want?" I said, "I want you to sing through me." I think that ever since that moment, it's really her. She takes over when it's time to do kirtan and she fills the room. I don't understand it and I don't tamper with it. I honor it and respect it as a divine gift. It is a wonderful thing to find your dharma during your lifetime. Your dharma is the most perfect thought, word, or deed in each moment to awaken to who you truly are. In other words, should I watch tv or meditate? I have discovered what I was made for, why I incarnated, and I know exactly how to use the rest of the time I have in a body. I am a lucky man.

Steven Rosen: Let's talk a little bit about the philosophy behind mantra and kirtan. Why do you think it works and what exactly is it? What is it about sound and singing that can bring someone to a very high spiritual level?

Shubalananda: The most basic principle of kirtan, which I say all the time, is "You can't think when you sing." I like to think back to the earliest kirtan wallahs and what being in their association would have been like. People like Jnaneshwar and Namadeva in Maharashtra. I can't imagine what this must have sounded like, with large groups of realized souls singing God's names at the top of their voices. And Chaitanya Mahaprabhu. Imagine what his kirtan must have sounded like!

Steven Rosen: I saw a quote on your website from Ramakrishna: "God is directly and expressively present through the heart of an awakened lover who sings with divine ecstasy. ... What else can you want or need? Why attempt to improve upon perfection? One does not whitewash a wall that is already inlaid with mother-of-pearl." I like that. It kind of says it all, you know?

Shubalananda: Our greatest teachers had this wonderful ability. Like Amma saying "The medicine for your illness lies in the space between your thoughts," or the Buddhist saint Mahagoshananda saying, "Enlightenment is easy, just don't compare." Ramakrishna was among the greatest of the greatest.

Steven Rosen; And what about your personal realizations? What do you say when someone asks you about the power and glory of kirtan?

Shubalananda: I refer them to the power and glory of God. I am not a spiritual teacher, I just sing her names. But kirtan is god's great gift to the human race. Music is the only art that has no form. It has no meaning conceptually, it exists only in this moment and then is gone. Kirtan is a vibration on the wind, yet music-kirtan moves us to such deep spiritual experiences, from Mozart to Ravi Shankar to a toothless blind Baul on a street corner in Benares to Murali, Krishna's intoxicating flute, music-kirtan is the doorway to the true reality. All you have to do is sing. I remember a story about Swami Shivananda. A student asked what is the power of the names of god, and he replied, "Why you moron! I cannot answer because you are too stupid to understand even simple answers, you are a moron . . . moron . . . . moron . . . . moron." The student became enraged, with veins bulging on his neck. Just as he was about to speak, Shivananda said, "Now see the power of a bad word!"

Steven Rosen: Good. I like that.

Shubalananda: So kirtan is a language in which the very syllables, the seed syllables, vibrate in the body in such a way as to activate the kundalini. This would be the tantric point of view. So, by saying "Sita Rama, Sita Rama" or "Radhe Krishna, Radhe Shyam" over and over again, those vibrations awaken our spiritual energy, long asleep. That's one aspect of kirtan.

Steven Rosen: You mention kundalini repeatedly, and, yes, that's a tantric concept. But how would you define kundalini, very briefly?

Shubalananda: Well, tantra and yoga both make use of this terminology. Mother Kundalini is the building block of the universe. It is the power of God, locked within our own mortal frame. It is Shakti, the creative awakening force. It is the essence of the Divine Mother. It resides in the base of the spine in a dormant state. To the degree that our karma, our actions, thoughts, words, and deeds vibrate this energy to move, it rises up the spine, and when it reaches the crown of the skull, it completes its journey and god-realization occurs.

Ramakrishna used to describe this god-realized state in a parable. There was once a doll made of salt. It wanted to understand the nature of the ocean, so it dove in. It dissolved. So, kirtan, in fact, is one of the things that we can do to begin to move that energy upward. The other things we could do would be: prayer to your chosen deity, Patanjali's eight-fold path, (hatha yoga, concentration, meditation, niyama, pranayama). There are actually one hundred and eight billion paths to god, as many paths as there are fingerprints; we all find our own way in our soul's journey. I am told, however, that the best sadhana for any of us to do in the materialistic age of the Kali Yuga is to chant god's names, to sing kirtan, to chant japa.

Steven Rosen: It's interesting to think of kirtan as a form of yoga, or the perfection of yoga. And, certainly, if we speak of a kundalini energy in the body, it would naturally be raised by chanting the Lord's name. Can you think of other parallels between kirtan and yoga?

Shubalananda: Kirtan is part of the practice of bhakti yoga; it has spread to most of the various forms of Hindu practice, especially around gurus. Essentially bhakti is the yoga of opening your heart to universal love with the help of a realized guru with whom you are practicing what is called *guru kripa*. Swami Shivananda once said to the women: "Bring your drunken husbands to kirtan; it will open their hearts." Then there's the whole idea of controlling the breath. When you are nervous, frightened, or agitated you breathe very quickly. Your breath is shallow and fast. When you're calm and restful and peaceful, you breathe very deeply and your breath is slow. It works the other way around, too. If you're agitated and begin breathing deeply, you can reverse the agitated state. Now, when you sing, your breath naturally comes into rhythm, into calmness . . .

Steven Rosen: Ah, so kirtan is also a form of pranayama . . .

Shubalananda: Absolutely. You can call it, Pranayama-kirtan, in fact. There's a kind of bellows between the kirtan wallah and the people who sing chorus, in that the kirtan wallah sings and the chorus responds. It's a back-and-forth exchange, like in breathing. That's a bellows-like effect, right? When the chorus is breathing IN, the kirtan wallah sings out. And then the kirtan wallah breathes in, the chorus sings out. That's a form of pranayama—using breath to attain the supreme. Pranayama means controlling your breathing in order to control your mind. So no matter what state your mind is in, as you begin to breathe, chanting or singing these mantras while breathing in and out, your thoughts slow down. They become focused on God.

Steven Rosen: Right.

Shubalananda: Then there is an instant when the kirtan stops, and there's silence. All of the people who do kirtan, at that moment, have a special experience—a great depth of silence. When the kirtan ends, that's when you can access the space between your thoughts. In other words, we've quieted our conscious thoughts down by singing kirtan, but when the kirtan is over; our mind is so calm and so relaxed that we don't even have to think anything. We just feel. We're raw; we're open to God. Otherwise, our conscious minds and our thoughts are so busy and noisy. So much so that we can't really get the information that's coming from the deeper parts of our brains, the eighty percent that scientists say we don't use. If we can quiet our minds, we can hear the voice of god.

Steven Rosen: Very nice. That's the basic fruit of kirtan, at least in the beginning stages.

Shubalananda: It's beautiful. I see people coming to kirtan who have never done it before, especially when I go to the Kripalu Center in Lenox, Massachusetts, where they have many people who want to know about yoga, so they go there as their introduction. I attend once or twice a month to lead kirtan, and I get two hundred people in the room and I say, "How many of you have never done kirtan before?" Well, three-quarters of them raise their hands. They'd never even heard of it. I look at their faces. Then, at the end of the night, if they're still there, I look at their faces again. They've changed. They got the message. It hits home every time. It's astounding. I mean, I'm so happy to see others discover the power of kirtan, because it's been my doorway in for deeper experiences, and my dharma is to share it. Shree Maa said to me, "If you could live your whole life the way you are when you lead kirtan, you'd be fine."

Steven Rosen: [laughter] Yes, my teacher used to say that kirtan is the safest place in the world.

Shubalananda: The safest place in the world is right here, you and me. but while doing sadhana one can feel the inner presence of the divine and by beginning to love yourself and then the ones closest to you, and then more and more until there is nothing left that you do not love, you begin to sing the true kirtan, which is soundless. Hazrat Anayat Khan, the enlightened Sufi teacher and master veena (Indian guitar) player, upon his enlightenment said, "Now I put down my instrument. Now I have become the instrument." Kirtan is a holy event. It's not a performance. It's not a place where you go buy your ticket and get entertained. It's a spiritual practice, a shortcut to one-pointedness, a sweet taste of the divine.

You go and open your heart to it, sing with your full heart. If you can do that, you're in.

Steven Rosen: What are your current projects?

Shubalananda: There are many. First, my guru brother Shivananda Sharma and I are supporting a free school in Rishikesh, the Ma Chetan Jyoti School of classical music, teaching Hindustani music to the poor children for free. Shivananda comes from a lineage of classical musicians; he was Mataji's accompanist for many years. When she left, I inherited Shiva. This school was started by Mataji, and several of us in the USA, Europe, and India have been funding it since Mataji left her body on Hanuman's birthday in 2008. With the help of so many, we have kept the school running for the past few years, and it continues to grow, with over sixty students. We supply everything, the instruments, the place, and Shivananda teaches the kids.

Shivaji and I are also involved in several recording projects. We have just completed an east/west Ganges delta blues CD, Two Sadhu's Blues, tabla, steel resonator guitar, Hindustani violin, and my "Hindi-accented" Jewish blues vocals. We finished Rama Rahima, our CD tribute to the oneness of all religions, and a raw live kirtan CD that really rocks. Vortex of Love is my latest record. I think it is my best kirtan work. I have taken initiation with an Aghori baba named Harihar Ramji, from Benares. Avadhut Bhagwan Ram is behind it all. He has been teaching me Aghor sadhana, and for some reason, I cannot stop changing. Mostly, though, I sit out in the woods of western Massachusetts, trying again and again to get it right . . . . madtha pidtha!

ACKNOWLEDGEMENTS

My editor asked me if I wanted to have an acknowledgment page. My first thought was that my whole book is an acknowledgment of all the great souls that have crossed my path. Then I thought about my band, and the friends and community who have supported me throughout these thirty-five years of kirtan sadhana.

My love and thanks go to Everest Howe for the big love . Much love also to Ashley Flagg, who has been such a wonderful support as my kirtan partner. I thank Anna Sobel and Richard Adams, my two great percussionists, who have traveled with me near and far. I totally love and send thanks to Kalidasa Joseph Getter, my brother. We've been playing together for almost thirty years; his bansuri and drumming have been a mainstay of my sound. Ananda Jyoti (Alisa Tanny) graces my kirtan with her wonderful singing and dancing that bring a beauty to my kirtan that I certainly lack. And then there is Bob Veronelli, my loyal bass player, who is always happy to drive.

I also want to thank Paul Risi, my producer for his support and editing skills; Jim Matus, my engineer; Horace Albaugh for his early edit help; Cheryl Bertsch for her cooking; and Durga for being there anyway. Thanks also to Swami Satyananda Saraswati for his advice and edit suggestions.

I give thanks to Parvati Markus, whose edit transformed the book from a diary to a tale of striving and enlightenment.

And love to the universe for allowing incarnation.

GLOSSARY

Abishekam –ritual bathing of deities

Advaita– a Hindu philosophy saying that only *Brahman* (universal awareness) is real, and the material world, including our egos, is a transient illusion.

Amma – mother; *Ammaji* is a term of respect for beloved mother

Ananda – bliss

Arti – song in praise of the guru

Asana – seat, posture

Bhajan– Call-and-response singing of holy names and phrases, adhering to the rag and taal of Indian classical music,

Bhakta– a *sadhak* practicing bhakti yoga

Bhakti– one of the three branches of yoga (*karma* yoga, path of action/service; *jnana* yoga, path of knowledge; and *bhakti* yoga, the path of devotion).

Bhandara– a huge meal cooked by the devotees of a group to feed everyone in the village.

Bhang– cannabis tea consumed in order to create a peaceful, stressless mind.

Bhava– spiritual emotion, Ray Charles-like soul.

Bhava samadhi – the state of being lost in love

Biksha– Literally means "begging," but commonly used to mean "gaining knowledge, or study."

Chai– Indian tea made with spices and milk.

Chandi Path– three stories of the exploits of the Divine Mother from the Upanishads.

Chakra– sensory perception organs on the higher planes. There are seven chakras along the spiritual spine. As awareness reaches up the spiritual spine and the chakras become activated by the kundalini energy, one gradually becomes more aware of true reality.

Dakshina– that which is given without effort in order to communicate the intensity of one's surrender; a token of respect that demonstrates the sincerity of one's love.

Dakshina is not an agreed-upon business transaction; it is a privilege to honor the conveyor of knowledge and to enable the recipient to do more in order to make this world a better place.

Darshan – the sight of a holy person, being in the presence of spirit

Dharma– as Swami Satyananda says, "Dharma is an ideal of perfection." One is living their dharma when they use their life to awaken to their true nature.

Dhoti– a sarong-like wrapping around the man's waist in lieu of pants.

Diksha– initiation by a spiritual master into a personal mantra that should be kept secret. As Baba Hariji has said, "First *Biksha* (study), then *Diksha* (initiation)."

Ektar– one-stringed instrument with a long neck and a gourd. The string is played and the gourd is tapped like a drum. This was the primary instrument for India before the harmonium was introduced in the nineteenth century from France.

Guru – one who removes the darkness

Guru kripa – the grace of the guru

Harikatha– a kirtan wallah who travels India singing kirtan, telling stories of his or her guru, and bringing the dakshina back to the ashram.

Homa –fire ritual

Hridaya– the spiritual heart

Japa– repetition of God's names, usually practiced with a mala. Singing God's names is also a form of japa. The sacred syllables of the Sanskrit language have their impact on our kundalini energy, forcing it upward.

Jivatma–the individual soul. The aspect of one's individual soul that remains connected to the "Great Unknown," as Bhagwan Ram calls the universal consciousness.

Jyoti– the spiritual light

Kirtan – call-and-response chanting

Kirtan wallah – leader of kirtan; kirtan *walli*, occasionally used for female kirtan leader

Kumari – young, prepubescent girl

Kumkum– sacred red powder, composed mostly of turmeric, that symbolizes the shakti of the Divine Mother.

Kundalini– the sacred energy that resides at the base of the spine, coiled like a snake. Spiritual practice awakens this snake and she begins to move upwards, animating each chakra as she passes by.

Kurta– Indian long shirt for men.

Lila – play

Lingam– an oval-shaped stone that symbolizes the seed of the universe. It sits on the *yoni*, the base. It is symbolic of the union of Shiva and Parvati, planting the seed to give birth to the material world.

Mantra– A holy phrase made of *bij* syllables. The sacred bij syllables of Sanskrit were specifically created so that the vibrations stimulate the kundalini. As one chants these syllables, one begins to awaken. There is an entire science to mantra.

Mahasamadhi– when a great soul leaves his or her body.

Mala– rosary of 108 beads used to practice japa.

Mandala– also referred to as *yantra*. It is a diagram for traveling in the higher dimensions and attaining one-pointed consciousness. Sri Yantra is one of the most powerful mandalas– the maze of triangles acts to focus the mind inward.

Mandir – a Hindu temple

Mandalis– circles of devotees

Mata – mother; *mataji*, respected mother

Mauna – the practice of silence

Mudra– a symbolic gesture usually involving the hands and fingers. These gestures influence the flow of energy throughout the body.

Muni – saint

Murti– a statue of the Hindu deity, which becomes activated through *abishekham* (a puja that includes ritual washing, dressing, and feeding the statue to initiate a spiritual connection between the power behind the deity and the practitioner).

Namasankirtan– *nama* means the names of God, *san* means a group of people, and *kirtan* means singing your brains out.

Namaste – a common greeting in Hindi-speaking India. In spiritual circles, it adds the meaning of honoring the aspect of the person that is one with God.

Nirvana– the term used by the Buddhists to refer to the enlightened state.

Nishumba– the demon from the Chandi Path whose name translates as self-deprecation.

Prana– life force, sometimes called breath.

Pranayama– one step in Patanjali's eight-fold path to enlightenment:1) *yamas*, to not do bad things, restraint; 2) *niyamas*, to do good things, observances; *asanas*, hatha yoga; 4) *pranayama*, breathing exercises; 5) *pratyahara*, withdrawal of senses; 6) *dharana*, concentration; 7) *dhyana*, meditation; and 8) *samadhi*, union with God.

Prasad– food consecrated by puja or spiritual practice and shared among the community.

Prema – divine love

Puja– a ritual practice dedicating one's acknowledgment, respect, love and friendship to one's internal God in the form of an external deity. A puja table is an altar.

Pujari– the one who practices puja.

313

Rajas– The Samkya philosophy teaches that there are three forces that make up the entire material universe, known as the three *gunas*: *rajas* is the energy of movement, activity or excitement; *tamas* is the energy of inertia or stability; and *sattva* is the perfect balance of the other two– consciousness and truth. It is said that all matter is composed of these three gunas to varying degrees, including our egos.

Ramayana– the Ramayana is one of the two great epic poems of Hindu philosophy. It tells the story of Rama and his wife Sita, who get involved in a war with Ravana, the king of the demons. Along with Hanuman and an army of monkeys and bears, Rama invaded Sri Lanka and destroyed the demons. (The version by William Buck is the most readable for Westerners.)

Rishis – Vedic sages

Rudraksha– when Brahma created the universe, he forgot how to create food for many of his creatures. When they asked him about it, he said, "Eat each other." When Shiva took a look at the mess Brahma had made of creation, he shed tears. Those tears took the form of Rudraksha seeds. Shiva thought, "What can I do to help here? I know! I will teach yoga."

Sadguru – the true teacher

Sadhak– a spiritual student

Sadhana– a spiritual practice, e.g., meditation, hatha yoga, kirtan, and many other forms.

Sadhu – mendicant holy man

Samadhi – absorption in higher consciousness; *bhava* samadhi is absorption in compassion and love; *savikalpa* samadhi is when the entire universe is your beloved; *nirvikalpa* samadhi is the final stage, when you are the beloved.

Sanatana Dharma – the "eternal path," the original name for Hinduism

Sanyas – renunciation

Sanyasi – renunciate

Satsang– spiritual community. It is said that if you took all the pleasures of the world and combined them into one giant pleasure, it would not equal the pleasure of satsang. Buddha said that *sangha* (Buddhist term for satsang) is one of the three elements required for transcendence.

Sattvic – the quality of balance, harmony, and purity

Satyam, shivam, sundaram – truth, goodness, and beauty/cleanliness

Seva– selfless service, service without the expectation of any reward.

Shakti– the basic building block of the universe, the essential feminine energy that pervades and animates all creation.

Shaktipath – an exchange of energy between a teacher and student

Shlokas – poetic forms in Sanskrit

Shumba– the other villain from the Chandi Path; his name translates as self-conceit.

Siddhi– as the kundalini moves up the spine, certain abilities or "powers" come to the practitioner, which are known as *siddhis*: reading thoughts, transforming energy into matter, bi-locating, and other seemingly miraculous behaviors. The great teachers say that these powers are distractions and should be used only to awaken others. (I have personally witnessed these siddhis.)

Soham – Vedic mantra meaning "I am That"

Swaha– usually chanted as a seal at the end of mantras or ceremonies, translated as, "so be it." Swami Satyananda translates the word as "I am one with God."

Takhat– platform on which spiritual teachers sit.

Tantra– "tan" means "to attain" and "*tra*" means "to retain"; it is a path involving initiation, mantras, meditation, yoga, and ritual.

Tantrika – one who practices the path of tantra

Tapas– extreme spiritual practice, e.g., meditating for twenty-three hours a day.

Tathastu– Goddess Durga says "I grant a boon" when pleased by one's devotion.

Upaguru– Namadeva says there is only one sadguru – the master who will carry you across; everyone and everything else is an upaguru – a teaching that points the way.

Vasana– old karmic seeds that keep showing up incarnation after incarnation.

Vibhuti– a gray ash that many gurus offer as a gift. It has no material value, but is instilled with the shakti of the teacher and therefore has great healing powers.

Vipassana – form Buddhist meditation practice involving mindfulness

Wazifa– an Islamic mantra chanted from the rooftops

Yoga – union

Yoni – the vulva, a symbol of divine procreative energy

Yuga – a very long period of time

RECOMMENDED READING

Miracle of Love, Ram Dass
The Gospel of Sri Ramakrishna, M
The Life of Ramakrishna, Romain Rolland
The Great Swan: Meetings with Ramakrishna, Lex Hixon
Play of Consciousness, Swami Muktananda
Chandi Path, Swami Satyananda Saraswati (trans)
I Am That, Sri Nisargadatta
The Janeshwari, Janeshwar
Ramayana and *Mahabarata*, William Buck
Dropping Ashes on the Buddha, Sun Sa Nim
Music of Life, Hazrat Anayat Khan
The Mysticism of Sound and Music, Hazrat Inayat Khan
The Play of God, Vanamali
Silence Speaks, Baba Hari Dass

About Of Author

Shubal has been practicing yoga for almost 40 years under the tutelage of some of India's greatest teachers. He began his musical journey at age seven with his first ukulele. He never stopped. Shubal has been playing, first in barrooms, and finally, like Johnny Appleseed, spreading the practice of namasankirtan way before it was a common phrase, in the Hindu temples and yoga communities all over the country. Over the years, he worked behind the scenes with many of the Teachers from India that we all know. His deep bhava and his gift of storytelling make this a great read.